CITIZENSHIP IN MODERN BRITAIN

CITIZENSHIP IN MODERN BRITAIN

Keith Faulks

Edinburgh University Press

Keith Faulks, 1998

Edinburgh University Press
22 George Square, Edinburgh

Typeset in Ehrhardt
by Hewer Text Composition Services, Edinburgh
and printed and bound in Great Britain
by the Cromwell Press, Melksham

A CIP record for this book is available from the British Library

ISBN 0 7486 0989 X

CONTENTS

LIST OF TABLES

ACKNOWLEDGEMENTS

In the process of researching this book I have been lucky enough to receive support from a number of colleagues and friends, and I would like to acknowledge their contribution to this project here.

Elizabeth Meehan, Laura Brace, Alex Thomson, Robert Hulme and Paul Connolly have all taken time to read and comment on various aspects of my work and have all helped me to improve the focus and text of this book. My greatest academic debt is to John Hoffman, who as a teacher and writer has proved an invaluable example to me over a long period of time. It was he who encouraged me to write this book, and for this, and his friendship, I am very grateful. Finally, I would like to thank Stevie Hallows, Colin and Steve Wood, Sue Brooks, Lewis and Jane Healey, James Hamill, Steve Wagg, Neil Faulks, and my parents, Robin and Patricia, for providing much-needed social distractions from the academic world.

The final responsibility for the arguments and errors contained in this book of course rests with me.

1

INTRODUCTION

As Geoff Mulgan has recently commented, 'citizenship is one of those words which goes in cycles . . . In some periods it lies dormant, but then at others it becomes a prism through which we think about our relationships to each other and to the state' (Mulgan, 1994a). Since the late 1980s the concept of citizenship has experienced a decided upturn in popularity in British politics after lying largely dormant as a subject of debate for over three decades. All of the major political parties and many pressure groups have evoked the concept, either to lend focus to their policies or as a goal to be struggled for.

This book aims to make a contribution to this debate by developing a critique of liberal notions of citizenship as they have been applied in modern Britain. It will be argued that liberal theories of citizenship are inherently abstract, elitist and exclusive because of their flawed assumptions concerning the relationship between individuals, the state and civil society. These flaws will be explored through a theoretical analysis of classical, social and neo-liberal concepts of citizenship and via a detailed case study of the limitations of liberal citizenship in practice, as defined by the Thatcherite governments of 1979 to 1997.

It will be argued that Thatcherism represented an assertion of neo-liberal concepts of citizenship that privileged personal responsibility and 'market rights', such as property ownership, over social and political rights. The book will attempt to show how Thatcherism failed to deliver the liberal promises of liberty, personal autonomy and security and resulted in increased social division, disorder and an impoverished conception of citizenship.

This book will also attempt to move beyond the evolutionary account of citizenship intrinsic to the liberal tradition. It will be argued that the development of citizenship in Britain has to be understood in terms of the complex relationship between the state, the economy and social change. Therefore, the book will attempt to develop a more sophisticated theory for understanding how citizenship has developed in Britain. It will be concluded that a truly inclusive and meaningful concept of citizenship must ultimately look beyond the limits of liberal theory and the liberal state.

Having introduced the main arguments of this work, this chapter has two tasks left. First, it will discuss the way that citizenship has been defined in the literature, and will develop the definition to be applied throughout the book. Second, the chapter will conclude by setting out the structure of the argument to be pursued.

DEFINING CITIZENSHIP

In the literature concerning the meaning of citizenship three main types of definition can be identified. These definitions are *legal* definitions, which define the rights and duties of citizens in relation to a particular nation-state; *philosophical* definitions, which are concerned with normative questions such as what model of citizenship can best deliver a just society; and *socio-political* definitions, which emphasise citizenship as a status denoting membership of society that involves a set of social practices. These three types of definitions often overlap, but here I will discuss each in turn.

As a legal term, citizenship is often used interchangeably with the notion of nationality (Oliver and Heater, 1994: 53) in the sense that it is an expression of who is considered to be a national of a particular country, as opposed to someone who may be merely resident, legally or illegally, in that country. The core right of citizenship in this legal sense is that of abode. If a person is a legal citizen of a country in international law that person cannot be expelled from that country, and can expect to be able to leave the country at any time in the knowledge that they can freely return. Citizenship of a particular nation-state also carries with it duties *to* that state and rights, beyond the right of abode, which the individual can claim *from* the state. A legal definition of citizenship may be expressed in the following way:

> Citizenship is a status that denotes membership of a nation-state and which carries with it certain rights and duties associated with that membership.

The modern legal definition of citizenship derives primarily from the French Revolution of 1789, which some theorists have argued is a pivotal event in the development of modern notions of the concept (Turner, 1986: 13–27; Brubaker, 1992: 35–49). As Brubaker argues, the French Revolution created the nation-state and the closely related ideas of nationalism that have shaped European understandings of citizenship

ever since. The French Revolution, for the first time, clearly differen-
tiated citizens from foreigners as residents of a nation-state defined as a
sovereign body.

In Britain, the meaning of citizenship in a legal sense is complicated by
the fact that British people are formally defined as subjects of the Crown,
and not as citizens (Benn and Hood, 1993: 14–36). However, in terms of
understanding the real nature of citizen–state relations the legal approach
to defining citizenship is limited because in practice theorists and
politicians still make use of the term citizenship, and the related ideas
of rights and duties, when discussing the relationship between the British
state and the individuals that make it up. Citizenship, therefore, can be
seen to have a greater significance in social and political discourse than
merely as a descriptive legal term (Gardner, 1994: 144–67).

To make sense of the meaning of citizenship it is necessary to turn to
philosophical and socio-political definitions because debates concerning
rights and duties inevitably reflect deep ideological, political and social
divisions.

Philosophical considerations of citizenship tend to be concerned with
such questions as: the correct role of the state in providing for citizens'
needs, what the state can reasonably expect from the individual citizen in
terms of duties, how the individual should relate to other members of the
nation, and whether rights should be absolute or dependent upon duties
rendered. In these senses citizenship is a deeply normative question, the
character of which cannot be easily separated from the central questions
of political philosophy such as, why should we obey the state, and what
should the balance be between equality and liberty?

The position of this book is that liberal theories have failed to develop
an inclusive and rounded concept of citizenship because of their abstract
and exclusive assumptions. It will be argued that future conceptions of
citizenship must have at their centre a notion of politics that stresses the
interdependence of human beings with each other and their environment,
and which emphasises compromise and the peaceful reconciliation of
conflicts of interests.

Liberalism stresses inequality in civil society, abstract individualism,
and emphasises the market rather than politics as the best provider of
human need. It also accepts the coercive state. This means that politics
has been restricted in the liberal tradition to the public sphere, which,
because of its gendered, racialised and class-based character, perpetuates
the exclusive nature of citizenship. As the case study of Thatcherism
illustrates, because of its dualistic nature, liberalism necessarily stresses
division and therefore generates the possibility of violence and suppression of those individuals who lose out in the inequality of liberal society or

who challenge its values. Whilst the main focus of this work is to present a critique of liberal citizenship, rather than advance an alternative to it, one of its aims is to develop an alternative account of how and why citizenship has developed in Britain. Therefore, we need to examine socio–political definitions of citizenship to place citizenship in its historical and social context. The sociologist Bryan Turner (1993b: 2) has defined citizenship in the following way:

> Citizenship may be defined as that set of practices (juridical, political, economic and cultural) which define a person as a competent member of society, and which as a consequence shape the flow of resources to persons and social groups.

As Turner goes on to argue, the utility of such a definition, which stresses the centrality of social practices, is that this enables us to go beyond the limited formal legal definitions or the purely normative approach associated with political philosophy. As Turner writes:

> The word 'practices' should help us to understand the dynamic social construction of citizenship which changes historically as a consequence of political struggles . . . Secondly, this definition of citizenship places the concept squarely in the debate about inequality, power differences and social class, because citizenship is inevitably and necessarily bound up with the problem of the unequal distribution of resources in society. (Turner, 1993b: 2)

In terms of understanding how citizenship in Britain has developed, socio–political definitions offer the best starting point. Citizenship in any society has to be understood in the context of the power relationships that exist in that society and the political, economic and cultural changes that affect that society. Therefore, to clearly bring out of the significance of these processes, I would to like to advance the following definition of citizenship:

> Citizenship is a status that mediates the relationship between an individual and a political community. It is characterised by a set of reciprocal rights, the extent and nature of which are defined through a complex set of social and political processes including: the struggle between opposing social forces, political compromise, and historical and economic circumstance.

This definition avoids the limits of the legal approach which expresses citizenship as a neutral status enjoyed by all citizens *equally* in any given nation-state, and also places the normative questions raised by philosophical definitions in their proper social context. In the modern era, the progress of citizenship cannot be understood outside of the nation-state and its relationship to society and the economic system on which the state depends for its income. However, I have deliberately avoided defining citizenship purely in terms of the nation-state because historically citizenship has also denoted status in a number of political communities other than the modern state, such as the polis in ancient Greece or the Italian city-states in the Middle Ages (Oldfield, 1990; Heater, 1990: 2–37). The advantage of defining citizenship in such a way is that it allows room for a consideration of citizenship beyond the nation-state. With the development of a more interdependent world economy and international organisations such as the United Nations and the European Union it may be, as Part III of this work argues, that future considerations of the nature of citizenship will have to look increasingly beyond the boundaries of the state (Held, 1995).

THE STRUCTURE OF THE ARGUMENT

Part I of this book is concerned with the development of the concept of citizenship in liberal theory. In Chapter 2 the main tenets of classical liberalism and its conception of citizenship will be analysed. The main purpose of this chapter is to set out the problems that all liberal theories face in terms of the methodological assumptions they make concerning the nature of citizenship. Liberalism's dualistic nature, and its flawed assumptions about the relationship between individuals and society and the nature of social power, will be explored and criticised via other important theoretical traditions which have examined the nature of citizenship; namely, republicanism, conservatism, Marxism and feminism. A unified critique of liberal theories of citizenship will be developed from these perspectives.

Chapters 3 and 4 will explore two versions of liberal thought, which will be interpreted as attempts to rethink classical liberal theories of citizenship in the context of the development of industrial society. However, it will be argued that both social liberalism and neo-liberalism fail to overcome the dualistic nature of classical liberalism and indeed they reject its more radical elements. Unlike classical liberalism, both social liberalism and neo-liberalism take as given the institution of the state that has been the basis of the exclusive nature of liberal citizenship in practice. Neo-liberalism also rejects the egalitarian potential of classical liberal theory.

The abstract, elitist and exclusive nature of liberal citizenship is illustrated in Part II of the book through an analysis of the practice of citizenship in modern Britain. Chapter 5 argues that Thatcherism represented an approach to the relationship between the state and citizen which was neo-liberal. It is contended that Thatcherite conceptions of citizenship were a logical outcome of the dualistic nature of liberalism. Chapters 6, 7 and 8 explore these dualisms in some detail.

In Chapter 6 the abstract approach of liberalism to the historical development of citizenship in Britain will be rejected and an alternative model developed. This chapter will set the context of Thatcherism by explaining the evolution of citizenship in terms of its relationship to the state, the economy and social change. The elitist aspect of liberal citizenship in practice will be the focus of Chapter 7, which will show how government policies such as the Citizen's Charter were based upon an abstracted view of the notion of the active citizen that rested in reality upon the unequal distribution of the resources necessary to the practice of citizenship. Chapter 8 will analyse the antithesis of active citizens, that is (in Thatcherite terms), the passive citizens who through the failure of government policy saw their citizenship rights increasingly narrowed in the 1980s and 1990s.

The final part of the book will consider the failure of the liberal tradition to produce an inclusive citizenship, and it will argue that if citizenship is to be rendered inclusive it will have to rest upon a more secure foundation than the liberal state. Chapter 9 includes an analysis of recent social changes that have presented important challenges to liberal conceptions of citizenship, and its concluding section will assess the prospects for a post-liberal citizenship under the Labour government of Tony Blair.

PART I

CITIZENSHIP IN LIBERAL THEORY

2

CITIZENSHIP IN
CLASSICAL LIBERAL THEORY

There can be little doubt that liberalism, of all the modern ideologies, has had the most influence upon the theory and practice of citizenship in Britain. Therefore in order to understand how citizenship has come to be defined in modern Britain, it is necessary to analyse the concept of citizenship in the liberal tradition. It is not the intention of this book to present an overall critique of the huge body of liberal thought. Rather, the aim of the first part of this work is to identify the main assumptions of some of the most important liberal theories of citizenship, and the way that these theories relate to the practice of citizenship in modern Britain.

Since the second part of this book focuses upon the development of citizenship in the second half of the twentieth century, Chapters 3 and 4 will explore those liberal theories that have had the most impact on the practice of citizenship since 1945. However, both social liberalism (which became influential particularly in the mid twentieth century) and neo-liberalism (which has been the dominant liberal paradigm in the 1980s and 1990s) can only be understood in relation to the general assumptions of liberalism, which were developed well before the twentieth century. Indeed, both social and neo-liberalism can be perceived as attempted solutions to the problems which arise out of classical liberal theories of citizenship.

Although the term liberalism was not in common usage until the nineteenth century, it is generally accepted that many of the themes of liberalism were well developed long before then. In this book I will use the term classical liberalism to refer to those pre-nineteenth-century thinkers, such as John Locke, who laid the foundations for future liberal theories of citizenship. Social liberalism will be used to denote those thinkers such as T. H. Marshall, who, by the twentieth century, represented a distinctive strain of liberal theory and an influential vision of citizenship. The final stage of liberalism I wish to consider is neo-liberalism. This version of liberalism is associated with thinkers like Frederick Hayek, who, in the late twentieth century, has been extremely influential in the way citizenship was defined by the Thatcherite governments.

These three stages of liberal thought are outlined in Table 2.1. Obviously this table cannot express the complexities of the development of liberalism, nor does it aim to do so. What the table attempts to do is to illustrate those stages of liberal development that have been most influential in practical terms on the government of Britain. Each of the stages relates to a particular form of the British state. These three stages in the development of liberalism will be analysed in the first three substantive chapters of the book.

Table 2.1 Stages in the development of liberalism

Stage of liberalism	Date	Thinkers	Political form
Classical liberalism	Pre-19th century	Locke, Paine	Constitutional state
Social liberalism	Late 19th, early to mid-20th century	T. H. Green, T. H. Marshall	Social democratic state
Neo-liberalism	Late 20th century	Hayek, Nozick	Thatcherite state

This chapter will be concerned with identifying some of the flaws in the classical liberal tradition of citizenship by drawing upon other ideological traditions which have been critical of liberal notions of citizenship. It will be concluded that classical liberalism can be best understood in terms of its essentially dualistic nature, which has resulted in a theory of citizenship that is abstract, elitist and exclusive. It is this dualistic nature which presented future liberal theories of citizenship with a series of irresolvable problems which have meant that, in practice, liberal citizenship in Britain has failed to deliver upon classical liberalism's optimist vision of a society that enhances security, liberty and autonomy for all citizens.

ELEMENTS OF A LIBERAL
THEORY OF CITIZENSHIP

Although there are important variations within liberal thought, as Eccleshall (1984a: 37–79), Frazer and Lacy (1993: 41–53) and Gray (1995: 3–45) argue, liberalism has a coherence which allows for a generalised treatment of its theoretical assumptions. As Gray writes:

> Common to all variants of the liberal tradition is a definite conception, distinctively modern, of man and society. What are the main elements of this conception? It is individualist, in that it asserts the moral primacy of the person against the claims of any social collectivity: egalitarian, in as much as it confers on all men the same moral status and denies the relevance to legal or political order of differences in moral worth among human beings; universalist, affirming the moral unity of the

human species and according a secondary importance to specific historic associa-tions and cultural forms; and meliorist in its affirmation of the corrigibility and improvability of all social institutions and political arrangements. It is this conception of man and society which gives liberalism a definite identity which transcends its vast internal variety and complexity. (Gray, 1995: xii)

Gray neglects to include two other crucial elements of liberal thought; that is the common commitment to private property and to the free market. However, when we add these important factors to Gray's definition we get somewhere close to an understanding of the assump-tions that underpin liberal theories of citizenship. We shall now consider some of these assumptions in detail.

As Gray argues, liberalism is a distinctly 'modern' body of thought. Liberalism is an ideology bound up with the social, economic and political changes associated with the development of modernity from the mid sixteenth century onwards (Nisbet, 1967: 3–47). Processes of rationalisa-tion, bureaucratisation, industrialisation and urbanisation underpinned the development of the modern nation-state, which culminated in the French Revolution of 1789. The gradual evolution of secularisation and the rationalisation of legal and political systems also helped to create the conditions for the development of liberal thought, which saw progress, rather than providence, as the key to the future of humanity. As Lyon writes, 'modernity started out to conquer the world in the name of reason; certainty and social order would be founded on new bases' (Lyon, 1994: 21).

The processes of social change associated with modern society helped to shape the thought of early liberal thinkers who firmly believed in the ability of rational thought to solve human problems by constituting systems of authority based on logic, rather than on tradition or super-stition. This view of the possibility for rational authority is based on a particular view of human nature which defines humans as ego-centric, autonomous individuals. The normative judgement that follows from this view of human nature is that any political community should be based on the principle of securing the maximum possible levels of personal autonomy and individual liberty.

The principal figures in the development of individualism as a basis for political theory are normally taken to be Thomas Hobbes and John Locke (MacPherson, 1962). Historically, individualism can be seen in part as a by-product of the move from pre-modern to modern society. Crucial to this transformation was the collapse of feudalism in which personal identity was gained through one's position in a rigidly defined social hierarchy that allowed for little individual advancement or change.

However, the fragmentary nature of authority in the feudal period allowed for the emergence of relatively autonomous city states which facilitated the growth of a new merchant class, whose increasing success in trade and commerce created a money economy and laid the seeds for capitalism to emerge (King, 1986: Ch. 2).

The gradual growth of a market-based society encouraged fluid and mobile social relations and greatly weakened old ties and feudal loyalties. This process encouraged individualism, as people became less bound by a particular location or community. Ironically, the absolutist states which were created by aristocrats eager to preserve the feudal order from around 1500 onwards facilitated this process by increasingly centralising and rationalising forms of social control, such as the legal system (Giddens, 1985: 83–115; Held, 1987: 38–41).

The emergence of state sovereignty during the sixteenth and seventeenth centuries provided the framework for a modern concept of citizenship to emerge. The growth of the absolutist states also undermined alternative sources of loyalty such as the Catholic church, which was further weakened by the Protestant reformation in the sixteenth century, led by such figures as Martin Luther.

Luther saw the relationship between the individual and God, rather than the relationship between the church and its flock, as crucial; thus emphasising the autonomy of the individual and laying the foundations for the social contract theory of Hobbes and Locke (Skinner, 1978: 12–19). By the time that Hobbes and Locke were examining the nature of 'man' and the political community in the seventeenth century, the central doctrines of feudalism, such as loyalty of peasants to Lords, and Lords to the Monarch, were being challenged economically with the development of a market society, and politically by the struggle for constitutionalism.

The primary question for Hobbes and Locke was, given the imminent collapse of the old absolutist order, on what grounds could political authority be based. Both Hobbes and Locke start their construction of a political order with the assumption that humans are autonomous, rational and individual who are equal in terms of their relationship to the political community. In *Leviathan*, Hobbes writes that 'nature hath made men so equal in the faculties of body and mind' (Hobbes, 1973: 63), while Locke states that men are 'by nature all free, equal, and independent' (Locke, 1924: 164). Though, as we shall see, this equality is largely an abstract concept divorced from social realities, the acknowledgement of equality by classical liberals was central to the future meaning of citizenship. If, as Hobbes and Locke argue, political communities should be constructed on rational grounds and have as their ends security, liberty and equality, then citizenship as a status denoting membership of that community must necessarily be an inclusive and equal status. Any political community can then be reasonably judged on how well it performs the function of maintaining liberty, security and autonomy for *all* citizens. This raises the question of what kind of political community should individuals consent to.

Hobbes contends that the natural egotism of individuals needs to be constrained by a powerful sovereign body. The basis of society would be a contract between equal individuals where the sovereign is the individual writ large. The sovereign power ensures order, for the citizens of a community give up whatever freedom (except the right to self-preservation) that is necessary for that order to be maintained. No developed concept of citizenship emerges in Hobbes's theory since he is concerned primarily with issues of security. As such, liberty and autonomy are reduced in significance in Hobbes's theory. The only right that individuals hold within this order is the right to self-preservation and this right is an exercise of the will to survive, which no sovereign could deprive citizens of (Hobbes, 1973: 165).

For Locke, Hobbes's solution to the problem of authority does not provide enough protection for the individual rights of citizens. Locke is therefore concerned to build upon Hobbes's defence of the natural right of self-preservation and he asserts the importance of individual liberty and autonomy, as well as security, as important elements of citizenship. Like Hobbes, Locke uses the concept of a state of nature to speculate upon life outside of the state. Unlike Hobbes, however, he does not think that the state of nature was characterised by constant conflict. Even prior to the formation of the state all men possess rights to life, liberty and property, which are God-given and permanent (Locke, 1924: 179–80). What the creation of a political community means for Locke is greater stability and protection for freedoms that already exist.

In his classic work *Two Treatises of Government* Locke is concerned with constructing a political community which would allow each individual to thrive in the market place, free from arbitrary rule by a government which did not have the consent of its citizens. Like Hobbes, Locke sees the basis for a desirable political community to be the social contract where the absolutist concept of the divine right of kings was replaced with the idea of consent. Locke rejects the natural hierarchies of the feudal order, arguing that God created all 'men' as equals and therefore the political institutions of any system of rule should reflect that fact. If any sovereign fails to maintain popular support, and does not pursue policies conducive to the fulfilment of the citizens' potential, then that sovereign could legitimately be replaced by another.

Both through his defence of natural rights and, in certain circumstances, the overturning of a sovereign by force, Locke avoids the potential absolutism inherent in Hobbes's theory. Although both thinkers base their social contract on the idea of consent, only Locke's theory allows for the possibility of citizenship. It is only with Locke's notion of individual rights and the idea that the state is responsible to its citizens that a reciprocal relationship between citizens and the state can exist. However, although Locke's theory may appear to acknowledge the social character of humanity, in fact his theory is centred upon an abstract individualism. It is not through social interdependence that the social contract and rights emerge. In Locke's theory natural rights derive from God, that is they are rights given to each individual by God without reference to society. As Hoffman states, 'it is this abstract individualism which allows Locke to present the state as the product of a contract freely entered into' (Hoffman, 1995: 103).

Central to Locke's account of the relationship between the individual and the state is the argument that though the state may be useful as an institution to maintain order, its functions should be strictly limited: Locke's defence of private property as a natural right necessarily entails a division between the public and private spheres of social life. Indeed, for Locke private property is a necessary pre-condition for citizenship. As Gray notes, 'the claim that civil society demands the widespread diffusion of personal property becomes a staple theme of liberal writing, and it is this insight which embodies Locke's greatest contribution to liberalism' (Gray, 1995: 14). The defence of civil society based on the free market and private property has been at the centre of liberal theories ever since.

Locke assumed that all hard-working people (he thought these individuals would be in a minority) could acquire private property and could therefore develop a stake in society. A key assumption in classical liberal thought was that in a pre-industrial society land was freely available in the new world, if not in the old. There could therefore be no excuse for failing to acquire property, which, for Locke, was the basis of freedom.

Those who did not own property were to be excluded from decision making, partly because their lack of wealth meant they had no stake in society, and partly because their need to work undermined their capacity to develop their rationality (MacPherson, 1962: 209–29). By tying citizenship so closely to property the possibility of a division between active and passive citizens in inherent in Locke's theory.

Locke's assumptions about the fecklessness of ordinary people meant that although he argued for limited government, he was not adverse to strong government. As Heineman writes:

Locke was not opposed to absolute governmental power, he was concerned about arbitrary absolute governmental power. But as long as proper procedures were observed, Locke seemed satisfied that a government based on the participation of the propertied could be trusted to provide just leadership for the nation. (Heineman, 1994: 46)

In theory, then, Locke acknowledges the right to equal citizenship, but in practice political rights are dependent upon property ownership. By privileging property in this way Locke asserts the maintenance of economic inequality, rather than the achievement of political equality, as the key organising principle of the state.

However, in the eighteenth century, Locke's theory of natural rights and contract ironically had a great influence upon the two great liberal revolutions in America and France, which both aimed at popular sovereignty. It was in the writings of the English revolutionary Tom Paine that the egalitarian logic of Locke's assumptions was emphasised.

Paine was perhaps the most optimistic of the early liberal thinkers. He firmly believed that the rational nature of 'man' could create a society which was both free and harmonious. Like Locke, he defends a political community founded upon the defence of natural rights and sees private property as an important source of freedom. Because of his faith in the individual's ability to direct his or her own affairs Paine is a strong advocate of the free market. He contends that it is not the job of government to interfere with the workings of the economy, which is best left to regulate itself. Moreover, Paine argues that the market would unite people through the process of trade. As he states in his *Rights of Man*, 'I have been a great advocate for commerce, because I am a friend to its effects. It is a pacific system, operating to cordialize mankind, by rendering nations as well as individuals, useful to each other' (Paine, 1995: 265).

The main difference between Locke and Paine is in the area of representative government. Throughout his political life Paine argued for universal (male) suffrage as a barrier to arbitrary and aristocratic government. However, it is clear that a main concern of Paine's is to ensure that the public sphere of government does not interfere with the operation of civil society, and in particular the market. For instance, Paine considers one of the key aims of revolution to be the freeing of the market from excessive taxation: 'revolutions, then have for their object, a change in the moral conditions of governments, and with this change the burden of public taxes will lessen, and civilisation will be left to the enjoyment of that abundance, of which it is now deprived' (Paine, 1995: 265).

Paine defends the right of 'men' to be equal in the public sphere and unequal in civil society. He writes that 'wherever I use the words freedoms or rights, I desire to be understood to mean a perfect equality of them', but he goes on to say, 'let the rich man enjoy his riches, and the poor man comfort himself in his poverty. But the floor of freedom is as level as water' (cited in Philp, 1989: 34). What emerges from Paine's theory is an abstract and negative view of equality and freedom which is more consistent than Locke's, because of its emphasis on universal male suffrage, but nonetheless shares the same assumptions about limited government, the sanctity of private property and the priority of individual freedom narrowly conceived.

Although Paine's version of citizenship focuses primarily upon the defence of civil and political rights, he does see the possible need for some form of welfare or social rights, not because of the failure of the economic system, but because of political mismanagement (Paine, 1995: 217). However, he asserts that ultimately, with the creation of limited and representative government and the freedom of the market, the problems of poverty and deprivation could be overcome.

Classical liberal theory, as outlined by Locke and Paine, is the starting point for all liberal theories of citizenship. It can be summarised in the following ways:

- For classical liberals the rational autonomous egoist forms the basis of any political community. Individuals exist in a state of nature prior to the development of society and have qualities inherent to them as individuals. All individuals possess natural rights to life, liberty and property, which they take with them into any political arrangement.
- Given their assumptions concerning the prior nature of individuals, liberals argue that any political community that is formed should exist only to protect the rights of citizens. The best form of political community is created when citizens give up a degree of liberty in order to enjoy the protection of the state. The social contract based on consent is an expression of this: governments exist to serve the interests of the people and may be replaced if they fail in this duty.
- Liberals argue that there should exist a clear division between the public and private realms of social life. In the private realm individual citizens should be free to buy and sell their land or labour, and to live as they choose without interference from the state. Through representation citizens supposedly control the public realm and ensure that the state is based on the principle of consent. However, citizens are not expected to participate if they

do not wish to. They remain free to enjoy a passive citizenship if they choose.

- In classical liberal thought the state is a necessary evil, or a useful convenience: it is not an expression of communal citizenship, rather it is a means to an end. It is argued that the state protects the development of a good life, where that good life is the freedom to exercise one's will and to act as one chooses, provided others' rights are not infringed by any such action.

- Underpinning the liberal vision of the political community is a belief in free exchange in the market place. Capitalist systems of production are the best source of wealth creation and the state should not limit the accumulation of wealth and property, provided they are gained legally. The accumulation of wealth by the most talented will help to create prosperity for all since the elite will invest their money, and jobs and economic success will be created, benefiting everyone in society. The market, rather than the state, is a more effective provider for individuals' needs.

- Citizenship in classical liberal thought is an expression of a contractual relationship between equal individuals. It involves the balance between the liberty enjoyed by autonomous individuals, including rights they hold to protect that liberty, and the authority of the state, including duties it can demand from citizens to ensure its survival. The vision of the citizen in liberal theory is of an individual concerned with self-advancement within the context of a limited state which exists to protect that individual from others' self-interest. There is no sense of duty to others other than to respect the fact that all humans will act in a similarly self-interested way and their right to do so should be respected.

CRITICISMS

Classical liberalism, with its limited conception of citizenship, has been criticised from a variety of sources, all of which aim at a more rounded and deeper theory of citizenship. This section will summarise the critique of liberal citizenship from the republican–communitarian, conservative, Marxist and feminist perspectives. These criticisms will then be unified into a general critique of the limits of citizenship in the classical liberal tradition.

THE REPUBLICAN CRITIQUE

It is not my intention here to provide a detailed account or critique of civic republicanism (see Oldfield, 1990). Rather I wish to highlight those areas where the theories of civic republicanism are critical of liberal conceptions of citizenship. Historically the concept of civic republicanism can be traced to the ancient Greek polis and in particular the political ideas of Aristotle (Aristotle, 1962). The concept was revived in the fifteenth century during the Renaissance by figures such as Machiavelli, and again two centuries later by Rousseau. More recently the concept has been the theoretical starting point of the communitarian critique of liberal individualism associated with such people as MacIntyre (1981).

The civic republican model of citizenship shares with liberalism the wish for a rational and consensual state to underpin citizenship. Citizenship has little meaning in a system governed by tyranny. Therefore, they stress the need for a republic as the best source of political authority. However, in most aspects concerning the nature of citizenship, those thinkers who advocate a civic republican model have something very different in mind from their liberal counterparts.

Unlike liberalism, the republican tradition starts with the assumption that human beings are indivisible from community; that is, they are only truly human in a social context. The idea that the individual can be abstracted from the collective is anathema to civic republicans. Citizenship is not a means to an end, but an end in itself. The only path to the good life is through communal political life. Individualism, in the abstract liberal sense, tends to develop only when, for some reason, communities break down (Glaser, 1995: 27).

Aristotle argues that it is not merely enough to be resident in a community and tacitly consent to its formulations and decisions. All citizens have a duty to participate actively and therefore any sense of passive citizenship is excluded. Participation in the state is a mark of humanity and civilisation. In a famous passage in *The Politics*, Aristotle states, 'the man who is isolated, who is unable to share in the benefits of political association, or has no need to share because he is already self-sufficient is no part of the polis and must be either a beast or a God' (cited in Clarke, 1994: 45). For Aristotle, 'man' is by his very nature a political animal. If the liberal state is a machine made to serve autonomous rational individuals, the state envisaged in civic republicanism is a living organism where the members of the polis are its limbs and organs who have no meaningful existence outside its boundaries.

Because of the relationship to the state that citizens have, the republican model places a great stress upon civic virtue. Whilst the liberal citizen seeks protection from the state, the republican citizen seeks to serve it. Whilst the liberal citizen asks, 'what can the state do for me?', the virtuous citizen asks, 'what can I do for the state?' In short, the interests of the state and citizen are seen as one and the same in the civic republican model. Through political participation citizens fulfil both their own needs and the needs of the common good. Indeed the very meaning of the word good referred originally, not to an internal moral condition (the Christian sense of good), but to noble actions carried out for the good of the community. Republicans seek an individualism that is rooted firmly in a social context.

In an ingenious but flawed attempt to reconcile the liberal concept of contract with the republican desire for a political community under-pinned by a radical and virtuous citizenship, Rousseau, in his *Social Contract*, highlights many of the weaknesses of the classical liberal version of citizenship. Although Rousseau's own theory contains many liberal elements, such as an abstract individualism, his stress upon community and civic virtue means that he has often been interpreted as a successor to the republican tradition of Aristotle (Oldfield, 1990).

A key problem in liberal formulations, argues Rousseau, is the inevitable division between the community and the citizen. For Rous-seau, 'man was born free and is everywhere in chains' (Rousseau, 1968: 49) because the institutions that 'man' has constructed have accentuated social divisions. The problem of the social contract theory of Locke is that it fails to show how individuals can be reconciled with their political communities through active citizenship. Rousseau endeavours to recon-cile liberty with authority, and to develop a deep sense of citizenship which goes beyond a mere contractual relationship of rights and duties. Rousseau attempts to unite the citizen with the state with his concept of the 'general will', that is the 'true' will of all, which has as its goal the common good, and not just particular interests.

For Rousseau, the state is a corporate body that enshrines the general will. Like Aristotle he argues that all citizens *must* participate: representa-tion is a source of individuals' alienation from their true selves as communal, participatory, beings. Classical liberal theories of citizenship are, for Rousseau, a corruption of true citizenship because they encourage selfishness and discourage duty to others.

Despite the flaws of Rousseau's own arguments (Hoffman, 1995: 110–112; Ball, 1995: 108–112) he nonetheless makes an important contribution to the republican critique, which highlights several weaknesses in liberal conceptions of citizenship. The republican critique can be summarised in the following ways:

- Republican theorists reject, on methodological grounds, the notion that the individual can be understood as existing outside of the social, economic and political conditions in which they exist. For civic republicans and communitarians, individuals are not prior to the community. As MacIntyre (1981) argues, individuals' lives are best understood as biographies that overlap and develop alongside other individuals' biographies in a communal context.

- Following from the notion of the interconnection between individuals' identities, it follows that any given community, like any individual, will have a particular story which is always contingent. Given this, there can be no universal principles which apply to all communities for all time.

- Civic republicans stress the social nature of human beings. The good life is more than a collection of self-interests. It involves moral obligations to others, which are an expression of our social natures. The theory points towards a possibility of a citizenship beyond a mere contract of convenience.

- The political community is a positive good, not a necessary evil. The state must be normative in the sense that it provides a moral framework for the citizen body. The political community should involve all citizens in the process of ruling and being ruled. Meaningful citizenship cannot develop in a purely representative political system, but must flow through and condition all social and political institutions so that the community constantly reasserts itself and its collective identity.

- The division between a public realm and private realm in liberal theory is a source of fragmentation. It encourages the separation of one's interests from the interests of the community as a whole. It encourages apathy in political matters and it also presupposes inequality through the operation of market relations, thus undermining notions of equality associated with citizenship. In liberalism liberty becomes a negative concept, rather than a positive good, where one is both able and willing to participate in the wider community unrestrained by material need.

- Rights are shown to entail duties, where such duties are not merely contractual exchanges but moral actions. The problem with liberal citizenship is that is generates a weak sense of obligation towards the political community and other individuals.

THE CONSERVATIVE CRITIQUE

The connection between conservative political thought and liberal notions of citizenship is a direct one, since it was as a reaction to the French Revolution of 1789 (a key event in the development of liberal notions of citizenship) that led to the emergence of modern conservatism through the writings of Burke.

In his *Reflections on the Revolution in France*, Burke (1968) rejects the French Declaration of the Rights of Man and of Citizens (Clarke, 1994: 115–17), which was the foundation stone of a new constitutional citizenship in France. Much of Burke's concern in his book is to debunk the whole concept of natural rights as the basis for a political community.

For Burke, rights can only make sense in a prescriptive form. That is, rights only have substance and meaning when they develop historically, as a result of tradition. Rights, Burke argues, are always contingent upon a complex set of social and political arrangement which cannot be wilfully or rationally constructed as liberals would maintain. In Britain, for example, the evolution of civil freedoms is associated with a long historical process, signposted by events like Magna Carta in 1215, the English civil war, which signalled the end of unfettered monarchical power, and the development of Habeas Corpus. Civil rights in Britain were the 'offspring of convention'. Revolutionary proclamations such as those contained in the Declaration of the Rights of Man are mere slogans and ahistorical assertions.

Burke is a strong advocate of small-scale civic associations precisely because voluntary and spontaneous actions are the best way to guarantee the true rights of individuals held in the historical fabric of the nation that is itself a product of these small-scale communities. He rejects the notion that social institutions should be constantly subjected to rational appraisal in an effort to 'perfect' them. It is this kind of corrosive analysis which for conservatives such as Burke lies at the heart of liberal theory. As Ryan argues, for conservatives like Burke, 'it is the liberal reformer, the person who wants to keep on examining the roots of the organic growth that constitutes society, who is the real menace' (Ryan, 1986: 25).

Burke stresses the mysterious nature of the political community which cannot be reduced to rationalist statements and proclamations as contained in the Declaration of the Rights of Man. Burke feared that revolutions, which destroy old noble orders as happened in France, could only end in disaster for the people of that state. He feared that the citizenship rights asserted by the French Revolution would disrupt the natural order of things. The danger with such claims to natural rights is that they are claims to rights which are said to exist outside of political community, and are therefore a source of unrealistic expectations that allow individuals to set themselves above the very community which makes their individuality possible. In displaying such scepticism towards abstract liberal individualism, Burke demonstrates a striking similarity to the civic republican tradition examined above.

The community, argues Burke, is more important than the individual and is necessary to maintain a civilised existence. For Burke the state is a permanent body composed of transient parts. It cannot be allowed to be disrupted by abstract claims to natural rights, which cannot be shown to have any meaning outside of the minds of those individuals who construct them. The abstract individualism and ambiguity of the state in liberal theory mean that the community will be destabilised by natural rights. Therefore, for Burke, rights cannot be concerned only with individual liberty because 'the restraints on men, as well as their liberties, are to be reckoned among their rights' (Burke, in Waldron, 1987: 105).

The main contribution of the conservative critique of liberal theories of citizenship is that it helps to expose the tensions in liberalism between the abstract claims of natural rights and political community. It also shows how liberalism fails to present a convincing historical account of how and why citizenship develops. Like the republican thinkers Burke points to the contingent nature of citizens' rights.

THE MARXIST CRITIQUE

The most important Marxist critique of liberal citizenship is contained in Marx's 1843 essay, 'On the Jewish Question'. Although the essay (Marx, 1994) appears to be concerned with the problem of religion, and in particular the place of Jews in German society, it is in fact a profound critique of both the bases of rights in a liberal society and the failure of those rights to undermine the inequalities endemic to the market society.

For Marx, God is an expression of alienation. Religion and notions of God have no external existence outside of the meaning that humanity bestows upon them. The real question that Marx is concerned with is what the social and economic conditions are that create the need for comforting illusions like religion.

The background and context of these issues was the consideration by Bruno Bauer of the state of Jews in Germany, who since the Middle Ages had been subject to repression (Maguire, 1972: 15–31). Despite reforms in the eighteenth century, Jews were still second-class citizens in Germany. According to Marx's interpretation of Bauer's essay, Bauer suggests the cure to the problem of the Jews is not that they should struggle for the extension of rights as a sectional interest, but rather that both Jews and Christians should cast off their religious prejudices, as it is these belief systems which are the source of division between Christians and Jews. The state should become secular and not bound up with any religion. Only by both groups giving up their beliefs could civil and political emancipation for all citizens be created. Thus, according to Marx, Bauer saw religious emancipation as the key to the development of political citizenship by creating the conditions for a universal set of rights and duties based on rational grounds, rather than religious prejudice.

However, Marx argues that religion is the product of a deep sense of alienation, which would not disappear if the state became secular. This is because the source of alienation is the liberal division between the state and civil society: as long as this division remains, political citizenship will be highly limited. Classical liberal notions of political citizenship declare all men to be free and equal, but in people's day-to-day existence those rights do not undermine the real inequalities of wealth, income, conditions of work, access to good diet and health care. Marx correctly argues that the assumption of abstract individualism as the basis for citizenship does not fit the reality of social conditions. The liberty championed by liberal theory is for the powerful, property-owning classes, who exploit those who have no such stake in society. The equality of all in liberal theory is an empty facade, which may have meaning in an abstract legal sense, but does not reflect the reality of the vast material and cultural inequality.

Marx recognises that the development of political rights is a step forward, and the extension of the franchise should be welcomed, but the idea that getting rid of property qualifications for political rights would render material inequalities as irrelevant to politics is, for Marx, a nonsense. Politics cannot be perceived as a part of life divorced from the private sphere of social relations. Only when rights and notions of equality are extended into the private sphere can true human (as opposed to mere political) emancipation be won.

Marx's recognition of the limits of the public sphere marks a critical break with the work of Hegel. For Hegel, the public sphere, represented by the state, is an arena whereby conflicts in civil society could be reconciled. For Marx, the public sphere is ultimately an abstraction which legitimises divisions within civil society. The division between a public sphere and a private sphere is contrary to humanity's nature as social beings. The split between the two spheres, inherent in liberal notions of citizenship, results in a pathological 'schizoid' identity for individuals in the liberal state. As Marx argues, individuals live simultaneously in the political community, where they are regarded as communal beings, and in civil society, where they are competitive and egoistical (Marx, 1994: 36–7).

In the modern era, the state secularises God as the supposed reconciler of the intrinsic conflicts of liberal society. In liberal theory the compact that one makes with God is transformed into an abstract social contract that one makes with the state, but instead of securing real freedom this contract ensures that freedom is limited by the rights afforded to others. A human's identity as an abstract citizen will not render them truly free, hence the need for religion and other comforting illusions. As Marx contends, human emancipation can only be realised when 'the actual man absorbs the abstract citizen of the state into himself and has become in his empirical life, in his individual labour, a specious-being' (Marx, 1994: 50). Marx's argument is that the individual must transcend the false dichotomy of liberalism, which sets community against individuality. The individual cannot be abstracted from the social conditions which allow him or her to flourish and shapes the nature of relations between individuals.

Liberal conceptions of natural rights can, contends Marx, be seen as an ideological defence of capitalism. On the one hand liberals offer the promise of universalism in the public sphere, but on the other defend property rights, which enshrine inequality and destroy a sense of shared citizenship. Marx's writes that 'the right of property leads every man to see in other men, not the realisation, but rather the limitation of his own liberty' (Marx, in Waldron, 1987: 146). Rights, like those defended by Locke, effectively constitute the alienation of 'man' from 'man'. Only through the overcoming of the divide between civil society and the state can human emancipation take place. Rights in a liberal society can, asserts Marx, only be bourgeois rights ultimately serving the interests of the powerful.

Having established the limits of bourgeois rights in his early writings Marx saw no need to develop a more elaborate theory of citizenship. Rather, his concern in such works as *The Communist Manifesto* (1975) was to develop his theories of the inherent contradictions of capitalism, and the pivotal role of the working class in transforming society.

Marx was not overtly interested in detailing the nature of a future society, but rather in understanding and transforming the present state of things. He therefore did not outline a detailed picture of the nature of citizenship in a communist society. It is clear, however, that contrary to the contentions of his critics, Marx did not wish to suppress individuality or subsume it into a collectivist community. His main goal in understanding the limitations of capitalist society was to liberate the individual from the chains constructed by poverty and alienation, which were themselves a product of the market society so cherished by liberal thought. Indeed, because of such goals, one recent commentator has referred to Marx, not as an anti-liberal thinker, but rather a post-liberal thinker (Hoffman, 1995: 132). In 'On the Jewish Question' Marx makes a powerful contribution to our understanding as to why classical liberalism failed to deliver its promises of security and liberty enshrined in an inclusive citizenship status. In order for these liberal goals to be achieved liberalism itself must be transcended.

THE FEMINIST CRITIQUE

In recent years feminist theorists have made a considerable contribution to our understanding of the limitations of liberal notions of citizenship. Writers like Walby (1994) have pointed to the different way citizenship has evolved for women in Britain and I will consider this analysis in the next chapter. However, feminists like Frazer and Lacy (1993), Pateman (1979, 1988, 1989) and Coole (1993) have also thrown light upon the underlying gendered assumptions of classical liberals' treatment of categories like the state, the citizen and the social contract. These insights have augmented the Marxist, republican and conservative critiques, which are themselves prone to sexist assumptions.

Throughout their discussions of citizenship, classical liberals like Locke take for granted the fact that citizens, and indeed 'individuals', are men. By abstracting the individual from the communities that shape and constrain their actions, liberals fail to see the essentially exclusive nature of citizenship in liberal societies in practice. The key problem is that liberal theory has an agency-based approach to understanding social behaviour and social relationships. That is, people are conceived of as separate actors who are responsible for their actions, and whose relationships with other individuals are best understood in terms of voluntary contracts. The lack of acknowledgement of the nature of social power leads liberals into naive and optimistic assumptions about the possibility of a just and harmonious society. This naiveté is well illustrated in terms of liberal approaches to gender relations. This issue is almost totally absent from the work of many of the most important contributors to liberalism such as Hayek, T. H. Marshall and T. H. Green. Though such social divisions are often not acknowledged, they are implicit in liberalism. Locke summarises the abstract liberal position on gender relations:

> Conjugal society is made by a voluntary compact between man and woman, and though it consist chiefly in such a communion and right in one another's bodies as is necessary to its chief end, procreation, yet it draws with it mutual support and assistance, and a communion of interests too, as necessary not only to unite their care and affection, but also necessary to their common offspring, who have the right to be nourished and maintained by them till they are able to provide for themselves. (Locke, 1924: 155)

On the surface, then, personal relations between men and women represent the coming together of two equals in a voluntary contract to jointly raise a family. However, in practice such relationships are far from unproblematic, involving male violence, inequalities of family responsibilities and vast differences in levels of social power. In fact Locke soon abandons his apparent 'gender neutral' approach as he goes on to discuss the relationship between the 'master of a family' and his subordinates. These 'subordinates' include his 'wife, children, servants and slaves' (Locke, 1924: 158). This perspective displays the patriarchal assumptions behind Locke's notion of a 'voluntary compact'. The vast difference between theory and practice applies equally to relationships of class and 'race'. Such social divisions are either ignored or taken as given by liberal theorists, and therefore the way citizenship has been defined historically, in ways which reflect these basic cleavages, is largely overlooked in liberal theories. A feminist analysis of classical liberalism gives us the important insight that deeply structured inequalities both lie behind, and are reinforced by, the apparent neutrality of liberal definitions of citizenship.

As Frazer and Lacey (1993: 54) argue, liberalism's assumption of abstract individualism is itself a gendered one. The idea that we can understand our social selves by transcending the limitations of both social relations and bodily constraints is a very male approach to individuality. Women, because of their traditional role as carers and child rearers, have defined their identities much more in terms of the body and social relations. The social contract of abstract individuals consenting to come together to form a political community is also therefore based on gendered assumptions. Pateman (1988) argues that the social contract presupposes an existing 'sexual contract' which involves the dominance of men over women. When women become the 'possessions' of men, an important area of potential conflict between men, that is the struggle for sexual satisfaction, is removed. It is assumed before the social contract is made that women will be subordinate to men, will serve their needs, and take prime responsibility for domestic matters. As Pateman argues, 'neither in his discussion of the state of nature, nor civil society, does Locke indicate that women are included among "naturally" free and equal "individuals". In Locke's theory, "individuals" are men' (Pateman, 1979: 75).

The inherent division between public and private spheres in liberalism is also highlighted by feminists. Although this distinction derives partly from the desire of liberals to promote an unregulated market free from the political constraints of the public realm (Rendall, 1987: 44–78), it also reflects the assumed division between men and women's roles. In liberalism citizenship and the practice of politics are confined to the male–dominated public sphere. The private sphere is supposedly apoli-tical, but in practice is defined by massive power differentials between men and women. Liberals' commitment to negative freedom in the private sphere means that women's oppression is de-politicised (Frazer and Lacy, 1993: 61).

Underpinning the classical liberal view of citizenship is the assumption that it is only men who are fit to be citizens. For example, Paine argues that 'the only form of natural inequality is that between the sexes' (cited in Philp, 1989: 75). The classical liberal view is that women are generally irrational and therefore incapable of sensible political decision making. As Kennedy and Mendus (1987: 10) argue, 'the public–private distinction is also construed as a distinction between the rational and the emotional; the universal and the particular; the reflective and the intuitional, women being associated with the latter elements and men with the former'.

Feminist critiques add weight to the view that classical liberalism's promise of an equal and inclusive citizenship is unattainable, given the assumptions they make concerning the nature of human communities. In particular, feminists show how such liberal promises as security, equality and autonomy are based upon female insecurity in a private sphere that is often characterised by male violence, and a sexual contract that pre-supposes that women are not autonomous from, or equal to, men.

TOWARDS A UNIFIED CRITIQUE OF LIBERAL THEORIES OF CITIZENSHIP

It is noticeable that the four critiques of the concept of citizenship in classical liberal thought discussed in the previous section share many similarities. Therefore in the final section of this chapter I will develop a unified critique of liberalism by drawing together elements of the republican, Marxist, conservative and feminist perspectives. I wish to suggest that a useful way of understanding the flaws of liberal theories of citizenship is to explore the inherently dualistic nature of liberal assumptions.

Table 2.2 The dualistic nature of liberal theory

Individual	Society
Agency	Structure
Private sphere	Public sphere
Civil society	State
Freedom (markets)	Equality (politics)
Citizenship rights	Citizenship duties
Market rights	Social rights

All four critiques examined in this chapter implicitly discuss classical liberalism in terms of its dualistic nature. As Layder states, 'philosophical dualism concerns the idea that there are two fundamental elements in existence in the world' (Layder, 1994: 1). The idea that liberalism, because of its methodological assumptions, is divided into a set of opposed entities is a fruitful one for understanding the tensions and contradictions of theories of citizenship in the liberal tradition. The dualistic nature of classical liberalism is expressed in Table 2.2.

The dualisms expressed in Table 2.2 can be logically derived from the assumption of the essentially atomised nature of the individual in liberal theory. All these dualisms are in a dialectical, contradictory relationship with one another and permeate all liberal theory. It should be stressed that in certain liberal variations some of these entities are perceived as being less polarised than in others, but because of the shared assumptions that all liberal theories make, dualism is an ever-present feature of them all.

As we have seen in classical liberal theory, individuals are opposed to the society in which they reside. Relationships between people are best understood as rational, autonomous contracts between individuals, whether that be a marriage contract or a business contract (MacPherson, 1962: 2). Both the republican and conservative critiques show how this assumption is essentially ahistorical, while the feminist critique shows how the very concept of the abstract individual is a male construct.

Because of the assumption that individuals can be understood outside of, and prior to, the formation of political community, liberals largely ignore the constraints that social structures, such as class, gender and 'race' place on individual agents. Liberalism is an agency-based approach because it stresses the importance of individual action and freedom of choice as explanations of social change. It therefore fails to explain adequately inequalities of social power and the distribution of resources necessary to the practice of citizenship. Because of this flawed assumption the failure of individuals to make use of their citizenship in liberal society is often blamed upon individual weaknesses, rather than structural inequality. As this book will show, in a sense liberalism has a latent moralistic tone to it which has often come to the surface in both the theory and practice of liberal citizenship.

Classical liberals also stress the actions of individuals in extending the rights of citizenship by asserting their equality as human beings in the public sphere. In the case of Locke and Paine, political community, and therefore citizenship, results from the actions of individuals forming a consensual contract and this abstract approach means that liberalism does not generate a convincing account of how and why citizenship has developed in Britain.

The divide between the public sphere and the private sphere is also an important dualism in liberal theory. As we have seen this division has been highlighted particularly by feminist critics of liberalism since the 1970s, but its implications also form an important part of the Marxist critique. The division between a political realm and a private realm arises out of the methodological assumptions concerning the relationship of the individual to society. The public–private dichotomy is also closely related to two other dualisms which emerge out of liberal thought, namely the division between the state and civil society and the division between equality and freedom.

For liberals, the state is a problematic institution since on the one hand they assert that the state is unnatural, and yet, on the other hand, they argue that naturally free, autonomous individuals are obliged to surrender to its coercive power. The state, it is contended, is a necessary evil and one which cannot be allowed to dominate civil society. Liberals are therefore concerned to protect civil society from unnecessary interference by the state. They hope to control the apparatus of the state through representative institutions, which are based on the idea of formal equality. In civil society it is market forces which dominate, and this is a field of social action characterised by inequality of outcomes in the material sense, which, according to liberals, is both inevitable and desirable. It reflects the natural inequalities of abilities and efforts, and stimulates and rewards incentive and creativity. Politics is limited to the public sphere, whilst civil society is controlled by the economic mechanisms of the market place. The feminist and Marxist critiques show how, by limiting the realm of politics to the public sphere and assuming that the market is the best provider of human need, liberal society in practice marginalises those disadvantaged groups who do not have the necessary resources to assert their rights.

This last point brings us to the final two dualisms of liberal theory outlined in Table 2.2. These two dualisms relate directly to citizenship and follow logically from the liberal assumptions discussed above. By assuming the prior nature of individual rights and the problematic relationship between the state and civil society, liberalism necessarily creates a tension between citizenship rights and obligations. As the republican critique illustrates, in societies where rights are rooted in society and individuals are indivisible from the political community, no such division between rights and obligations occur. The problem of the 'free rider' is a real one for liberal societies since there exists a tension in liberal theory between defending the rights and freedom of the individual from the state and the practical need for citizens to pursue some duties for the maintenance of the state, which classical liberals recognise only as a necessary evil.

There also exists in classical liberalism the potential for tension between different kinds of rights. I would argue that limited civil rights, or as I wish to call them *market rights*, are essential to liberal market society favoured by Locke and Paine. I define these as market rights because, as we shall see in Chapter 6, these rights were limited in early industrial society to a small male economic elite. They existed to serve the interest of the market and capitalist society. Many civil rights, such as freedom of assembly, were ruthlessly suppressed by the state. For Locke, these market rights were, given his optimistic assumptions concerning the progressive impact of the market and private property, the only rights that were needed to promote security and prosperity. Paine, unlike Locke, recognised that individuals may sometimes require economic help, but ultimately he, too, believed that 'the market could provide normally for all' (cited in Claeys, 1989: 101).

As we shall see, the problem of social rights in a liberal society was to become important with the development of social liberalism in the twentieth century. Social rights are in tension with market rights because they make claims on the state, which in turn increases the functions of the state and impinges upon market rights, such as private property, low taxation and negative liberty. As Arblaster notes, even in Paine's work there appears the beginnings of a 'contradiction between anti-interventionist theory and an increasingly interventionist practice' (Arblaster, 1984: 230).

With the development of urbanisation and rapid industrialisation in Britain in the nineteenth century, many of these problems were increasingly exposed and the limits of classical liberal citizenship highlighted. The need for a more extensive and rounded concept of citizenship that began with the classical liberal assumption of equality was a key aim of the social liberals, and therefore in the next chapter we shall look at their attempt to rescue liberal conceptions of citizenship from the criticisms outlined in this chapter.

3

T. H. MARSHALL, SOCIAL LIBERALISM AND CITIZENSHIP

Any examination of the development of citizenship in modern Britain must place the work of T. H. Marshall at, or close to, its centre. There are several important reasons for this. First, through his analysis of citizenship Marshall has to be acknowledged as coming up with that rare thing, namely a truly original theoretical standpoint from which to understand a social phenomenon (Mann, 1987: 339–40). Second, few British social scientists other than Marshall (1963) have directly considered the concept of citizenship and made it a central focus of their work. It has therefore been Marshall's contribution that has been taken by recent commentators as a starting point for their own research into the subject of citizenship rights (Turner, 1986; Barbalet, 1988). Third, as Roche (1992: 16–17) has pointed out, Marshall's writings are the central texts of what Roche has called the 'dominant paradigm' in citizenship theory in Britain: Marshall's work lies at the heart of the social liberal consensus of the post-war period up to the 1970s when all major political parties in Britain seemed to share similar views on the desired nature of citizen–state relations (Kavanagh and Morris, 1989). Finally, Marshall's work represents the culmination of the development of social liberalism as a variant of classical liberal thought.

Social liberalism can be understood chronologically as standing in the middle of a time line tracing the development of liberal theories of citizenship, which begins with classical liberalism and ends with the more recent ideas of neo-liberalism (see Table 2.1). This chapter will begin with a critique of some of Marshall's social liberal predecessors. The rest of the chapter will focus upon Marshall's contribution to the citizenship debate, and particularly on whether Marshall's theory of citizenship manages to overcome the problems of liberal theory identified in the previous chapter. It will be argued that Marshall fails, like his social liberal predecessors, to solve the problems of classical liberal conceptions of citizenship and indeed shares many of the assumptions of classical liberals which render his theory highly problematic.

MARSHALL'S PREDECESSORS:
THE DEVELOPMENT OF SOCIAL LIBERALISM

The development of social liberalism, from the end of the nineteenth century onwards, cannot be separated from the dramatic social changes which were reshaping Britain's economy and society. As Bellamy (1992: 5) remarks, 'changes in British society, not least the rise of organised labour, made it increasingly difficult for liberals to portray their own values as transcending class and defining the common good.' A key argument of this book is that liberalism, because of its abstract approach, fails to generate a convincing account of the evolution of citizenship in Britain, and the historical context for the growth of social liberalism will be dealt with in Chapter 6. However, in this section I wish to outline how writers in the social liberal tradition attempted to update liberal theories of citizenship in the light of the changing nature of British society. My concern will be to outline how writers prior to Marshall laid the foundations for his theory of citizenship, rather than a detailed account of such theorists' work. Two examples of the rethinking of the classic liberal position can be found in the work of J. S. Mill and T. H. Green.

Mill has often been cited as representing a break with the traditions of classical liberalism. Gray argues that Mill 'created a system of thought which legitimated the interventionist and statist tendencies which grew even stronger throughout the latter half of the nineteenth century' (Gray, 1995: 30).

For Mill, the problem with the doctrine of natural rights is the lack of motivation they provide for duty to others. If the community and other human beings are merely means to an end how can individuals be encouraged to act in a way that will help others and the wider community? The crucial question for Mill, therefore, is how can the good life for all be constituted while at the same time allowing for individuality to flourish? In considering this problem Mill begins to place individuals in their social context and hence, argues Gray, makes an important break with the abstract individualism of liberals like Locke.

Mill argues that important freedoms such as those of conscience, speech and worship can only develop in the context of society. Mill therefore rejects the reductionist logic of the individual who exists with rights prior to society. Neither does Mill think that liberty can be reduced merely to the quest for pleasure and the avoidance of pain, as utilitarians like Bentham suggest. In his most famous work *On Liberty* Mill (1974) argues that through the promotion of liberty, human potential can be developed, not only to benefit the particular individual, but also society as a whole. Mill appears then to embrace and extend the logic of equality which is inherent in the classical liberal tradition. Citizenship as an equal status cannot be achieved by negative conceptions of liberty but must involve a deeper and more inclusive vision of liberty which is more positive in nature.

The work of T. H. Green, and of the British idealists generally (Nicholson, 1990), can be interpreted as an attempt to build upon Mill's vision of a community of individuals who enjoy freedom, but nonetheless are capable of acting for the good of the community as a whole. In terms of citizenship, this involves an attempt to dissolve the dualistic division between rights and duties, which, as we saw in Chapter 2, is inherent in classical liberalism.

Green, like Mill, rejects the doctrine of natural rights as a basis for citizenship on several grounds. First, individuals cannot be assumed to hold rights outside of, or prior to, the community in which they reside. Second, given that rights are made possible only by society, it is absurd to make claims for individual rights held against that society. Third, by asserting natural rights liberals like Locke separate rights from duties, which are crucial to a harmonious community. For Green, individuals can only attain their ends through co-operation with others and therefore 'a right against society, in distinction from a right to be treated as a member of society, is a contradiction in terms' (cited in Freeden, 1991: 21). Green's theory allows space for a more interventionist state than was envisaged by the classical liberals. For Green, the state should be concerned with actively promoting the good of all rather than purely defending individual rights.

Green's work, like Mill's, marks a step away from negative liberty; that is, the freedom from interference by the state or others in an individual's affairs, to a vision of positive liberty whereby the state would play an enabling role in its promotion. Individuals should be encouraged to participate actively in the community by a state which ensures that economic and other important inequalities, such as educational achievement, are not so great as to prevent such participation. Through such arguments Green laid the theoretical foundations for the social liberalism of people such as L. T. Hobhouse, Lloyd George, W. Beveridge and T. H. Marshall. These new social liberals accepted that there existed the potential for conflict between capitalism, with its emphasis on inequality, and citizenship, which stresses equality.

However, before we turn to an analysis of how Marshall built upon the work of his predecessors it is necessary to examine critically the extent to which the liberalism of Mill and Green can be seen to have overcome the dualisms identified in classical liberal thought. Indeed, some writers have argued that the social liberalism of Mill and Green marked a 'regressive desire to preserve the liberal ideal from much of the incoherence which the modern industrial order had revealed it to contain', rather than a progression towards a more inclusive notion of citizenship (Bellamy, 1992: 16).

The key to understanding the flaws of social liberalism can again be found in the dualistic nature of its assumptions. Although at first sight Mill and Green embrace a more socially grounded notion of individualism, in fact their theories retain a highly abstracted individualism. In particular their theories are still agency-based. Neither Mill nor Green considers adequately how inequalities of social power, rooted in deep structural divisions, prevent *all* citizens from developing their individuality. This means that although they talk about individuals in society, their notions of society, community and the state are divorced from their structural context. For example, in Green's *Lectures on Political Obligation* he reifies and mystifies notions of community and the state. For Green, the state is an 'act of will' which acts in the interests of the common good, rather than a coercive institution (Green, 1986: 64).

Green and Mill take as given the existence of the state and the distinction between public and private spheres of society. They do not seriously question the fact that the state may act in the interests of a particular class, gender or social group. In this sense their liberalism does represent a regressive step away from radical elements of classical liberalism found, particularly in the work of Paine, with its emphasis upon the problematic nature of the state.

Given the assumptions of Mill and Green, it is not surprising to find that their theories make many of the same mistakes as classical liberalism. Particularly significant in their work is the implicit division between active and passive citizens. This division derives from their flawed assumptions about individual agency. Mill and Green's concern with rethinking liberalism was to promote a certain kind of individuality or 'character' which had at its centre self-improvement and self-restraint (Bellamy, 1992: 20). Their view of the *good* citizen resembled a particularistic view of individuality which was essentially a mirror image of their own identities. That is, the 'ideal' citizen would be male, middle-class and intellectual. This view allowed both thinkers to condemn those individuals who did not conform to this image. Thus, Mill supported the harsh measures of the poor law on the grounds that it would help to mould people into his image of the good citizen (Bellamy, 1992: 30). Green spoke of the 'dangerous classes' who 'if they have the opportunity of saving, they do not use it, and keep bringing children into the world at a rate which perpetuates the evil' (Green, 1986: 176).

Green's abstract notion of the individual also blinded him to the unequal relationships between men and women. Although the idea of community lies at the heart of many of Green's discussions, he does not question the gendered basis for that community, but instead takes as given the 'natural' roles of men and women. For example, Green argues that 'if the sense of family responsibility is to have free play, the man must have due control over his family' (Green, 1986: 173). It is ignorance of social structures that underpins such a view.

It is a lack of understanding of the relationship between structure and agency that also make liberals like Mill so ambivalent about transforming the logic of equality, which he accepted theoretically, into practice. In his *Considerations on Representative Government* Mill devises a complex formula of voting to reflect the relative 'sophistication' of the voter. Those who resembled his image of the good citizen should be given greater rights to political citizenship than other, less deserving citizens. Also, it is ironic that in a book concerned with the equality of all individuals to enjoy liberty, Mill's *On Liberty* was largely motivated by a fear of political reform which would extend voting rights to the masses, who, Mill felt, were ill-equipped to make use of those rights.

One of Mill's greatest fears of a truly egalitarian citizenship was that it would bring with it the threat of a 'tyranny of the majority'. Individuals would be subjected to a democracy of the lowest common denominator, where mediocrity reigned supreme. Mill's solution to this dilemma was to put off the fateful day when citizenship would be granted to all people equally. Citizenship could only be extended when the masses had been through various character-building exercises. Thus Mill called for the setting-up of national institutions of education calculated to invigorate the individual character. Social liberalism, as advocated by Mill and Green, has potentially coercive and paternalistic implications because it assumes that the masses need to be 'instructed' in the ways of active citizenship by a coercive state. Mill and Green's commitment to the free market also made them nervous about extending political citizenship, which may in turn be used to undermine the freedom of the market in civil society. For instance, Green consistently argued against the notion that the market was at the root of injustice and inequality in society. He thought that the accumulation of wealth was a good thing and argued that it led to a sense of responsibility in society (Green, 1986: 173). He also denied the coercive nature of the market. Writing on the capitalist contract between capital and labour, Green argued that all individuals could become capitalists. He writes, 'there is nothing in the fact that their labour is hired in great masses by great capitalists to prevent them from being on a small scale capitalists themselves' (Green, 1986: 175). The only justification in the social liberalism of Mill and Green for controlling the free market was when the state was acting in a paternalistic way, to enhance 'moral character'.

It is clear, then, that the insights of social liberals into the contradictions between a citizenship based on equality and a market society based on inequality are, at best, only partial. Social liberals fail to escape from the dualistic nature of classical liberalism. Although Mill and Green talk much about community, they do not transcend the abstract individualism of classical liberalism, but merely introduce an equally abstract notion of society alongside it. In fact, by abandoning a critical approach to the state they emerge as less radical than their classical liberal predecessors. Because they fail to comprehend the inequality of social power, which restricts access to the resources necessary for the practice of citizenship, they implicitly assume that individual agents are responsible for their success or failure. In a theory which takes the existence of the state as given, and champions the free market, the possibility for the state to become increasingly coercive is created. As Bellamy argues, social liberals fail to question the foundations of liberal society:

> The salient weakness of British liberalism sprang from a tendency to equate individual with social morality . . . The basic structure of British society was interpreted as the natural product of human development. In consequence, it became increasingly difficult for British liberals to question the practices of the liberal order itself. (Bellamy, 1992: 57)

The conception of citizenship which emerges from the thought of Mill and Green is one which fails to overcome the abstract, elitist and exclusive assumptions of classical liberalism. It is based upon a particularistic and moralistic conception of who constitutes a citizen. Its continued support for the free market, when taken together with its agency-based approach and statist assumptions, means that social liberalism conceives of a citizenship emanating from a state which is both paternalistic and coercive. The failure to transcend the dualism of classical liberalism was also to undermine the more developed social liberalism of Marshall, which aimed at reconciling the apparently contradictory concepts of capitalism and citizenship.

THE CITIZENSHIP THEORY OF T. H. MARSHALL

It is in his essay 'Citizenship and Social Class' that Marshall makes his most important contribution to citizenship theory. In this essay Marshall begins with an appraisal of the work of his namesake, the economist Alfred Marshall. In his paper of 1873, 'The Future of the Working

Classes', Alfred Marshall argued that modern industrial progress was gradually creating a society which was more 'civilised', because increasingly excessive, heavy and backbreaking work was being eliminated, owing to technological advances.

Alfred Marshall's thesis is classically liberal in its optimistic vision of the triumph of progress driven by reason and industrial development. Throughout his essay, T. H. Marshall largely shares his namesake's optimism, but unlike Alfred Marshall he argues that it was the development of rights, and in particular social rights in the twentieth century, that has allowed for a 'civilising' process to occur. This process, for Marshall, benefits not only the working class, it also undermines the sources of conflict inherent in capitalist society. Marshall's main concern in his essay is with attempting to solve one of the problems which troubled Mill and Green; that is, how are citizenship and capitalism to be reconciled? Marshall has four major aims in his essay related to this central question.

First, he wishes to examine whether citizenship is compatible with class in the setting of a modern capitalist society; namely Britain. As we have seen, his answer is a cautious yes. Second, he argues that full citizenship cannot be achieved in Britain without altering the operations of the market. Marshall's third consideration is the effect of the shift to rights and away from duties as the most important aspect of citizenship in modern Britain. Finally, Marshall attempts to ascertain the limits of social equality and determine just how far the struggle for social justice could realistically go.

Marshall attempts to analyse these four concerns by taking a historical approach to the development of rights. For Marshall, citizenship can be defined as 'full membership of a community' (Marshall, 1963: 72). In its modern form, that is post 1945, it includes three kinds of rights, civil, political and social. Civil rights developed in Britain largely in the eighteenth century and include 'the rights necessary for individual freedom − liberty of the person, freedom of speech, thought and faith, the right to own property and to conclude valid contracts, and the right to justice' (Marshall, 1963: 74).

Political rights followed in the nineteenth century, and they include the right to vote and stand for political office. The third element of citizenship is social rights, which developed primarily in the post-war period and are defined by Marshall in the following way:

> By the social element I mean the whole range from the right to a modicum of economic welfare and security to the right to share to the full in the social heritage and to live the life of a civilised being according to the standards prevailing in the society. (Marshall, 1963: 74)

Each of these three kinds of right corresponds to a particular set of institutions. Civil rights are protected by the court system, political rights correspond to the institutions of local government and parliament, and social rights are associated with the welfare state and public education system. Marshall speaks of these three types of rights, the civil, political and social, as developing along separate paths, but each kind of right provided a foundation on which another type could build.

According to Marshall, in feudal times these three elements of citizenship were as 'three strands wound into a single thread' (Marshall, 1963: 74). In general, feudal Britain was characterised by a hierarchical status system based upon personal loyalty, rather than a specified collection of rights and duties. Limited notions of citizenship were confined to some medieval cities. The evolution of a modern conception of citizenship rights in Britain can be explained according to Marshall by a dual process of fusion in terms of geography, and separation in terms of function. That is, the form of citizenship in Britain became common to the whole country, whilst its nature became separated into the three distinct types of rights outlined above.

From the seventeenth century onwards Marshall points to the development of such institutions as the Royal Justice, which, by bringing together various fragmented common laws, helped to establish a coherent set of civil rights. These rights were protected by national law courts, which acted to protect the rights of citizens against possible abuse by other citizens. The development of civil freedoms was a crucial step in the dismantling of the hierarchical feudal society and helped to create the necessary conditions for a capitalist society. Civil rights were necessary for a market-based economy since they freed individuals to engage in economic struggle, unfettered by feudal restraints of status or duty to one's social superiors. Civil freedoms were also a necessary foundation for the later development of the second type of rights noted by Marshall, namely political rights. As Giddens has argued, 'only if the individual is recognised as an autonomous agent does it become reasonable to regard that individual as politically responsible' (cited in Held and Thompson, 1989: 165).

Political rights are chiefly associated with local government and parliament, and through the Reform Acts of the nineteenth century the rights to the exercise and influence of power in these institutions were gradually extended. The Act of 1918 severed the link that had previously existed between economic wealth and voting rights, and by 1928 universal political citizenship was recognised when men and women were given equal voting rights.

Social rights, Marshall argues, had a more complex history. Whilst civil and political rights had evolved in a more or less linear fashion, social rights had existed, to some extent, in certain medieval towns through the operation of the guild system. However, these social rights were eventually to be undermined by the economic changes associated with capitalist modes of production.

The poor law, which evolved with this new system, was different in nature from these medieval rights because it was not seen as part of a citizenship package. In its early manifestations the poor law was more akin to charity than citizenship. Indeed, Marshall argues that the poor law's main aims were suppressing vagrancy and relieving acute destitution. It was only with the development of the so-called Speenhamland system of poor relief, with its provisions for minimum wages, family allowance and the right to work, that social rights began to be problematic to the capitalist order because Speenhamland marked the point where social rights clashed with civil rights.

The new bourgeois class had championed civil rights because it was essential that contracts were made safe by the guarantee of the state, which could use its authority to assert property rights. However, social rights, even in a limited form, were a threat to the market system since they were collectivist by nature and involved increased public expenditure, and therefore higher tax burdens and reduced profits. Under pressure from the propertied classes the Poor Law Act of 1834 reasserted the market in determining wage levels, and the poor law again became detached from a notion of citizenship. As Marshall points out, the poor law became a refuge for the non-citizen, rather than a social right which citizens could claim from the state (Marshall, 1963: 83).

Such reforms as the Factory Acts protected women and children not because they were citizens, but precisely because they were not considered to be citizens. It was only in the twentieth century that genuine social rights developed. It is here that Marshall's argument is focused, since it is with the development of the third stage of citizenship that capitalism and citizenship became potentially opposed.

As Marshall argues, developments such as the beginnings of compulsory public education, which had begun in the nineteenth century and can be classed as a social right, did not present a challenge to the capitalist system. In fact it could be argued that such educational developments were not only compatible with civil rights, but they equipped citizens with the necessary intellectual skills to best utilise those civil freedoms.

The kinds of social rights which developed in the twentieth century with the evolution of the welfare state, however, were of a different character from early reforms of a social nature. The tension between citizenship and capitalism arises out of the fact that citizenship stresses equality, whilst capitalist presupposes inequality. This basic problem leads Marshall to argue that 'in the twentieth century citizenship and the capitalist class system have been at war' (Marshall, 1963: 87).

Marshall does not, however, see outright victory for either force, but rather envisages a workable, if uneasy, peace between the two. Marshall sees citizenship, and in particular social rights, institutionalised within the framework of the welfare state, modifying capitalism to the extent that it allows for the worst excesses of the market to be overcome. Marshall develops this notion in later works, through the concept of the 'hyphenated society'. The hyphenated society is democratic-welfare-capitalism, where each part of the system is crucial to the legitimacy and longevity of the other: 'the parts are meaningless except in their relationship with one another. That is the model of "hyphenation" against which I suggest that we should view our post-war social system' (Marshall, 1981: 128).

Citizenship, as it had developed according to Marshall's theory, finally promised to deliver the meritocracy championed by classical liberalism. Although Marshall (1963: 73) writes that 'our modern system is frankly a socialist system', it is not socialism which Marshall hopes for, but a capitalist system with a citizen's face. In a crucial sentence Marshall summarises his hopes for citizenship as a force for social good: 'citizenship has itself become, in certain respects, the architect of legitimate social inequality' (Marshall, 1963: 73).

Marshall's main argument in 'Citizenship and Social Class' is that with the post-war construction of the welfare state the progress of citizenship, as a rounded and meaningful status, was complete. Social rights had legitimised liberal society by ensuring that although inequality still existed, its impact was increasingly confined to the relatively unimportant area of consumption. For Marshall, social rights rendered citizenship compatible with capitalism by 'civilising' the impact of the market. Marshall points to the rise of money incomes, the growth of savings and the success of mass production as enabling society to redistribute wealth and social power, not only through progressive systems of tax, but also in other important areas of social life such as legal aid. Through such developments the influence of class has been reduced and social rights have 'infected' the market place with the language of social justice. It was with the development of social rights that the harmonious society, which was sought by earlier social liberals like T. H. Green, could be achieved.

In the concluding paragraphs of his essay Marshall attempts to answer his four original questions. He argues that when taken together the compression of the scale of income distribution and the extension of common culture and common experience has led to an enriched and full sense of citizenship. The market has been civilised, and therefore saved from those who would overturn it in favour of common ownership and equality of outcome. As he makes clear in his 1981 collection, *The Right to Welfare and Other Essays*, Marshall sees the pre-eminence of the market as crucial to the health of society (Marshall, 1981: 135). What the hyphenated society offers is a citizenship that provides equal opportunity for citizens to compete in the market system. Marshall asserts that there are limits as to how far the movement to social equality can or should go but with more and more provision being made for people through welfare systems, additional earned income will be increasingly insignificant as a provider of people's basic needs.

What is required from citizens in terms of duties is that they work hard and refrain from abusing their rights. This particularly applies to trade unions who should refrain from unofficial strikes in return for the rights that liberal society has granted to them. Implicitly Marshall argues that in an increasingly just and civilised society, citizens will be willing to display more sociable behaviour as the grounds for social conflict are reduced.

Marshall's work can be seen as an attempt to extend the implicit logic of previous social liberals. The solution to the contradictions inherent in liberalism appears, argues Marshall, to be a full and rounded concept of citizenship, which includes social as well as civil and political rights. In subsequent discussion of his work many authors have had cause to question Marshall's basic assumptions. It is to these critiques that I will now turn.

CRITICISMS OF MARSHALL'S THEORY

Whilst most recent theorists have sought to criticise and, to some extent, transcend the limitations of Marshall's work, there is a general acknowledgement that his contribution to citizenship theory is a profound and enduring one. Although one of the criticisms made by social theorists is that Marshall's account is 'anglocentric' and therefore not universally applicable, Mann concludes that in relation to Britain 'Marshall's view of citizenship is essentially true' (Mann, 1987: 340).

However, I would argue that Marshall's theory is vulnerable in several ways and these criticisms can be divided into four types. First, there is the general question about the nature and categories of rights which Marshall employs. Second, the foundations on which Marshall rests his concept of citizenship can be questioned. Third, his theory, because of its assumptions, is exclusive. Finally, commentators have pointed to the problem of explaining how citizenship has changed over time in relation to other social institutions and processes. In this section I will deal primarily with the first three types of criticism as the fourth set of criticisms will be explored in detail in Chapter 6, which aims to develop an alternative understanding of the development of citizenship in Britain.

MARSHALL'S TREATMENT OF RIGHTS

We have seen how Marshall breaks citizenship down into three types of rights: civil, political and social. Taken together Marshall assumes that these rights form a complementary set of entitlements. Whilst accepting that a certain tension may exist between civil rights as a necessary foundation for capitalist society, and social rights as entitlements which may sometimes mean 'the subordination of market price to social justice' (Marshall, 1963: 115), Marshall believes that they can coexist in liberal society. Recent commentators such as Barbalet (1988: 15–28) and Hay (1996: 78–9) have argued that the problem with this optimistic assumption is that in a capitalist society civil rights and social rights are inherently contradictory. This therefore makes social rights vulnerable in times of economic recession:

> During periods of economic decline there may arise a contradiction between the need for the maintenance of the institutional basis of social rights through taxation and the requirements of capital accumulation. At such times a pressure against social rights may take the form of a reassertion of civil rights. (Barbalet, 1988: 20)

However, whilst correctly observing the potential conflict between different rights, Barbalet and Hay both make the mistake of accepting Marshall's definition of civil rights. As was argued in Chapter 2, the rights that Marshall describes as developing in the eighteenth century would be better termed market rights, as this term more clearly reflects the fact that these rights worked in the interests of a small economic elite. These market rights included the right to accumulate property and the right to forge contracts, and as such were essential to the development of a capitalist economy. The rights which served the interests of the market were accepted while other civil rights, such as the right to free speech, assembly and protest, were suppressed by the state in the interests of capitalist accumulation. For example, trade unions were banned in Britain until the mid-1820s under the Combination Laws (Saville, 1994: 14–30). Therefore the concept of market rights more clearly reflects the ideological construction of citizenship in capitalist societies like Britain (see Chapter 6).

Marshall argues that there was no conflict between the development of a capitalist economy and market rights. In fact just the opposite was the case because the former required the latter to free the entrepreneurial spirit. Once the developing bourgeois class of the eighteenth and nineteenth centuries had secured market freedoms, political rights were inevitable. It was not enough to rely on the state to protect their interests. The capitalist class needed to control the organs of the state through the parliamentary system. Therefore, voting rights and the development of liberal politics followed naturally from the needs of the new mercantile classes and reflected their economic power. At this point, around the time of the first Reform Acts, a limited notion of citizenship fitted very well with the needs of capitalism. Market rights greatly aided the development of market society. Political rights, granted to those with property, ensured that the market place would remain largely unregulated.

Marshall contends that it was only with the development of social rights in the twentieth century that capitalism began to be seriously modified by citizenship. This brings us to Marshall's optimistic assumptions about the longevity and stability of these rights. Marshall argues that these rights are firmly embedded in British society. However, Marshall does not adequately explore the tensions inherent in capitalist society, which necessarily make social rights vulnerable.

CITIZENSHIP, THE STATE AND SOCIAL CLASS

Although one recent commentator (Halsey, 1996) has tried to claim Marshall as an ethical socialist, in his assumptions of the neutrality of the state in capitalist society Marshall is clearly a liberal (Rees, 1995). Nowhere in his work does Marshall question the motives of the state, or its relationship to capitalism. Marshall assumes that the state supports a rounded concept of citizenship, as opposed to a purely market-based system of individual producers and consumers enjoying minimal protection from the state. Marshall does not explore the possibility that the state may work in the interests of a class or group of elites. Though Marshall does not make clear his theory of the state, he is implicitly a classic pluralist because he assumes that the state works as a neutral referee, which, with the development of political citizenship, favours the interests of the majority.

For example, in his discussion of the gradual development of trade union rights, and the use of such rights to develop social citizenship, Marshall assumes that once such rights had been won they would be irreversible. Trade unions would no longer have to campaign for social rights such as a 'living wage' because the state recognised this claim as just and would therefore not reverse it. In a typically optimistic passage, Marshall states that 'to have to bargain for a living wage in a society which accepts the living wage as a social right is as absurd as to have to haggle for a vote in a society which accepts the vote as a political right' (Marshall,

1963: 116). Such an observation was naive even in the context of 1950s Britain, let alone in the 1990s when over two million people are unemployed and many more live at, or below, levels of income support (Oppenheim and Harker, 1996: 23–46).

The problem is that Marshall's conception of citizenship is essentially abstract. Although his analysis is historical, he does not attempt anything like a sophisticated examination of the relationship between the state and capitalism. As Turner (1993b: 8) argues, it is not clear in Marshall's account whether citizenship ultimately supports or contradicts capitalism. Marshall appears to assume that by the 1950s capitalism had stabilised and would always be willing and able to support universal social rights.

Marshall's discussion of social class is also superficial and divorced from social reality. When Marshall argues that with the development of social citizenship class inequalities have become less significant, his analysis is focused upon income. Other aspects of class division such as market situation, conditions of control and safety at work, and job security are ignored. The development of citizenship has not radically altered the nature of capitalism because social rights have had little impact on wealth differentials (Scott, 1991: 63–92). As Hindess (1987: 33–61) argues, it is the concentrated ownership of wealth, rather than income, that is the key to understanding class division. Citizenship has had little impact on the control of the means of production. This means of course that citizenship, and in particular social citizenship, is dependent upon the imperatives of capitalism.

Marshall also underestimates the extent to which class differences in terms of culture are engrained in British society. Marshall is particularly optimistic about the extension of mass education as a root to the creation of equal opportunity and a civilised society. He argues that 'the status acquired by education is carried out into the world bearing the stamp of legitimacy, because it has been conferred by an institution designed to give the citizen his just rights' (Marshall, 1963: 115).

However, Marshall's optimism underestimates the extent to which class division is reflected in the unequal distribution of what Bourdieu has called cultural capital (Bourdieu and Passeron, 1977). That is, the possession of the cultural resources necessary to make effective use of citizenship rights. The problem is that because of the lack of cultural capital, many working-class children are unable to utilise fully the opportunity offered to them by education.

In his account of citizenship and social class, Marshall fails to see how institutions that he regards as having emancipatory potential are in fact deeply structured along class lines. Rather than providing a way to transcend class barriers and create a developed sense of citizenship, the educational system has helped structure and legitimise those barriers through the reproduction of very different patterns of aspiration. While educational establishments may aim at the promotion of a sense of shared equal citizenship and national culture, they also aim to sift and select people through a process of examination in order to allocate them to various occupations according to the needs of the capitalist division of labour. The education system is also geared to serving the capitalist system in more subtle ways. As Bowles and Gintis argue, the education system in a capitalist society has at its heart a 'hidden curriculum' whereby people learn the rules of the capitalist way of life. Children are taught to get used to a routine life of discipline and authority in preparation for the world of work (Bowles and Gintis, 1976).

Marshall also illustrates his pluralist assumptions in his uncritical appraisal of the nature of welfare delivery. Any large-scale welfare system is highly bureaucratic and therefore receivers of welfare rely upon welfare providers, such as social security officers, teachers, lecturers, National Health Service doctors and administrators to regulate the provision of any given service. Recipients are also subjected to administrative and normative scrutiny, which may have almost constantly shifting criteria. As Hindess (1993: 26) argues, welfare providers have power over decision making that renders social citizenship largely arbitrary in nature, or it is undermined by criteria based on prejudice of one kind or another.

Some writers have concluded that the welfare state has been of more benefit to white middle-class males than to the working class, women or ethnic minorities, partly because of the unequal distribution of cultural capital necessary to make full use of its services (Titmus, 1963; Williams, 1989; Le Grand, 1982). The failure of the welfare state to eradicate poverty, a fact increasingly established from the 1950s onwards (Townsend, 1979), was to expose it to criticisms in the 1970s by those neo-liberal thinkers who wished to discredit the values upon which it was supposedly constructed.

To summarise, class is a more profound and deeply structured division than Marshall allows. Indeed implicit in Marshall's account of citizenship is an agency-based approach to social change. Marshall underestimates the structural constraints of class, 'race' and gender in preventing individual agents from making use of their rights (Layder, 1994: 207–24; Willis, 1977).

CITIZENSHIP, WOMEN AND MINORITIES

Although Marshall's thesis assumes that the extension of citizenship applies to all groups in society equally, clearly this has not been the case.

The welfare state, on which Marshall pinned most of his hopes in terms of social rights, was, from its creation, based upon a set of assumptions that discriminated against women. Feminist critics of welfare and citizenship have shown that the assumption of the British welfare state has been that the public realm of work and politics is the preserve of men, and the private world of the home and family is women's 'natural' domain. Much of the debate surrounding Marshall's contribution and legacy has ignored the fundamental issue of gender. There are two main issues here. First, citizenship rights have not developed in the same way, and in the same sequence, for women. Second, women have separate needs from men, which must be protected through different kinds of rights.

Walby (1994) has shown that by taking each of Marshall's categories of rights in turn, it is possible to show the limitations of these developments for women. In terms of civil rights, women have experienced severe curtailments of the control they have had over their own bodies. Legislation for what might be termed reproductive rights has been recent and piecemeal. Questions of abortion and contraception, decisions about which are made by male-dominated institutions such as parliament and the law courts, are also crucial to women's freedom.

Marshall argues that most civil rights were in place by the nineteenth century, but until the end of that century women lacked the right to own property and to conclude valid contracts. Only in recent years have married women been assessed for taxation as individuals, rather than as wives of a male breadwinner. Women's freedom is also severely limited by male violence; this takes many forms such as rape, domestic assault and sexual harassment. Male violence is a great restriction upon women's civil liberties as many women are prevented from travelling freely when, and where, they choose. Official statistics are not a good guide to the levels of abuse and violence women suffer, since many women feel that male-dominated institutions such as the police and the courts system will not ensure justice (Hanmer and Saunders, 1984). For example, male judges have continually shown themselves to be unsympathetic to women who wish to assert their right to act and dress as they please without inviting unwanted sexual advances. Although of course protected in law, in practice many women have found to their cost the limits of formal rights, when these rights are 'enforced' by male police officers and judges.

Women's civil rights have also been restricted in the area of work, both in the form of the marriage bar to many white-collar occupations or apprenticeships, and through lack of access to the skills necessary for certain kinds of work (Sharp, 1994).

A good example of the limits of formal rights expressed in law relates to the issue of equal pay. Despite the implementation of the Equal Pay Act in the 1970s, women in Britain still experience much lower wage levels. In 1994 the gross weekly pay of women was 72 per cent of men's (Oppenheim and Harker, 1996: 95). At the time when Marshall was writing his essay the situation was even more unequal (Glennerster, 1995: 149–51).

Even more damaging to women's opportunities to work and pursue a career has been the impact that the structuring of the division of labour has had upon the distribution of income in society. Historically women have been largely confined to the private sphere of the family, where their role as carers of children, the sick or disabled, the elderly and men has remained unpaid and undervalued. Women are concentrated in part-time work, largely because of this domestic burden. When women are employed they suffer from vertical and horizontal segregation, that is, women tend to be employed in a more narrow field of jobs than men and are normally located in the lower scales of any given job. The numbers of women in work that reach the top of their chosen career is proportionally very low (Abercrombie and Warde, 1994: 219–23).

Political rights have also developed differently for women, finally achieving parity with men only in 1928. Contrary to Marshall's arguments it would appear that for women, political citizenship was achieved prior to the development of civil rights, which as we have seen are still severely limited. As Walby contends, 'for British women, political and civil citizenship were won as part of the same wave of political action, with at least as many aspects of civil citizenship being won after political citizenship as before. This contradicts Marshall's thesis that civil citizenship is won before political' (Walby, 1994: 385).

Social citizenship in Britain is still largely structured around paid work, which discriminates against women and creates dependence upon men. Marshall makes no acknowledgement of the patriarchal nature of welfare and the structural limitations upon women, even though the constraints on women were more severe in the 1940s and 1950s (Lowe, 1993: 33–5).

Access to housing and social security benefit are to some extent dependent upon gender differences. For example, access to housing is dependent largely upon income. Women's lack of equality in this area puts women at an immediate disadvantage in the housing market. In terms of social security, higher levels of benefit are only available to those who have contributed to national insurance, penalising women who, because of their role as carers, are more dependent on benefit than men. Britain, then, is undoubtedly a patriarchal society: that is, a society where men dominate and oppress women in whole areas of political, social and economic life. Marshall's analysis makes no reference to this fact and makes unfounded assumptions about the power of formal citizenship to transcend gender divisions.

Feminist critics of liberal citizenship have also stressed the inherent problems of applying a universal concept of citizenship, such as Marshall's, to a highly plural and diverse society. Phillips (1993) argues that liberal citizenship as a political concept stresses the public realm not the private realm. It also encourages us to see a commonalty of rights and responsibilities that transcend social differences such as gender. However, a key question for feminist theory is the extent to which formal citizenship is a useful goal for women to pursue, given its apparent denial of the politics of difference.

Some feminists (Mary Dietz has called them 'maternalists') have argued that women should attempt to feminise liberal citizenship by stressing the rights and needs women have which make them distinct from men (Dietz, 1993). Jean Bethke Elshtain (1982) has argued that women's role as mothers place them in a unique position of selflessness, because their primary concern is with the welfare of their children. Women could therefore play a key role in developing a more caring, collectivist notion of citizenship. By replacing the liberal, egoistical individual as the focal point for rights theory with a politics informed by the female-dominated private realm, maternalists attempt to resurrect the idea of citizenship. Other feminists, such as Dietz, have rejected such notions as a capitulation to the public–private divide that favours men and maintains women's position as second-class citizens. Citizenship is a political concept and can only be understood with reference to the public domain. For Dietz, the challenge is to construct a vision of politics which is concerned not just with state–citizen relationships but which also permeates more local arenas such as the city, the neighbourhood and the family.

Despite the difficulties and limitations of the development of citizenship for women, writers like Phillips, Walby and Dietz argue that the concept can be useful on a political level, in promoting equality of the sexes. Walby argues that 'political citizenship has been central in the transformation of gender relations over the last century' (Walby, 1994: 390). However, despite the limited progress women have made through the extension of political rights, the danger of emphasising the universal nature of citizenship remains. As Young (1990) has pointed out, the seemingly progressive point that citizenship should extend to all regards of age, sex, and 'race' can become easily mutated into an assertion that sectional interests are unimportant and everyone, regardless of his or her different needs, should be treated the same. This is a central problem with Marshall's theory. His abstract treatment of the category of rights leads him to neglect the complex problems of reconciling conflicts of interest, where these interests are shaped by social structures.

The notion that one can speak of one unified citizenship is also called into question by issues of 'race', religion, age and disability. For instance, citizenship's link to national identity is ignored by Marshall. He takes as read state neutrality in applying citizenship as a status of residence and identity in a just way. British concepts of citizenship have, however, been complicated, first by the lack of a codified notion of citizenship and second by the extension of the rights of residency to all members of countries under British sovereignty. Once Britain began to lose its empire, both Conservative and Labour governments introduced a series of immigration controls in an attempt to resolve the problem of exactly who qualifies for citizenship status in Britain.

The 1948 Nationality Act divided those with claims to citizenship into five distinct groups: British citizen, British dependent territories citizen, British overseas citizen, British subject and British protected person. Only the first of these categories was allowed the right of residency. Further legislation has complicated the picture. The 1962 Immigration Act placed controls on commonwealth citizens based on a voucher system linked to the likelihood of a person gaining employment, illustrating the relationship between economic factors and the status of citizenship in liberal society.

Under the Acts of 1968 and 1971, controls were extended to British passport holders, having the effect of restricting immigration from the British commonwealth. The 1971 Act introduced a work permit system for most immigrants; the notion of patriality (the right to be resident in Britain if a person has a parent or grandparent who was born, adopted, naturalised, or registered in the United Kingdom) meant that this legislation discriminated against black people, as most overseas patrials were to be found in Canada and Australia rather than countries with large black populations. The Nationality Act of 1981 brought citizenship legislation into line with immigration control. Full citizenship applied only to those with patrial status, or those already qualifying for settlement, together with any of their children born after 1980 (see Mason, 1995: Ch. 3; Layton Henry, 1992).

This brief discussion of immigration law shows that Marshall's implicit assumption about the inclusive nature of citizenship has to be questioned, since the definition of who has the right to citizenship is dependent upon political, social and economic change. Immigration controls tend to tighten up during periods of economic recession and high unemployment. However, as we have seen in the above discussion of gender, even those with formal rights of citizenship are by no means guaranteed substantive rights in practice.

Attempts at formal guarantees, such as the Race Relations Acts of 1965,

1968 and 1976, have done little in substantive terms to extend full citizenship to ethnic minorities. In the same way that women have found male-dominated institutions incapable of protecting their rights in law, ethnic minorities have discovered the limits of formal rights in a racist society (Mason, 1995: 107–28).

In terms of civil liberties, many blacks have found that they are subject to harassment by the police and inconsistent sentencing by the courts. This, despite the fact that according to some statistics black people are actually more likely to be victims of crime than white people (Central Statistical Office, 1994a: 155). Political rights have been limited by racism within most major political parties, political movements and trade unions. This has meant very low levels of participation by certain sections of the black communities, both in terms of voting and standing for office (Saggar, 1992: 136–69). Social rights, such as the rights to work or to education, are restricted by negative images promoted by the media of, for example, Afro-Caribbeans as workshy, lazy and aggressive (Hall et al., 1978: Ch. 10). These cultural stereotypes have greatly restricted opportunities for ethnic minorities in employment and education.

In the area of employment, ethnic minority workers have tended to be concentrated in low-wage, low-security jobs: unemployment rates for ethnic minorities in 1996 were well over double those of white workers (Department for Education and Employment, 1997: 6). In education there is marked differences in educational achievement amongst different ethnic groups. For example, in 1988–90 68 per cent of the white population had some form of academic qualification, compared to only 40 per cent of the Pakistani community (Jones, 1993: 15–20). The resulting economic and social effects of ethnic difference in modern Britain cannot be easily cured through claims to legal equality of citizenship. Marshall's analysis is again found wanting when the social realities of Britain are examined.

In terms of region and religious minorities, Marshall's thesis again needs substantial qualification. If we take Northern Ireland as an example, it is clear that the kind of citizenship Marshall describes was not universally applicable across all social categories in 1950. Through the deliberate gerrymandering of electoral boundaries, Catholics in Northern Ireland had been greatly restricted in their political rights (Purdie, 1990: 100–2). In addition, since 1922 the Special Powers Act had given the British state extensive powers to arrest people in Northern Ireland on suspicion, and to detain them in custody for as long as government saw fit. The ability of the state to infringe fundamental citizenship rights of many British citizens in Northern Ireland is ignored by Marshall (Purdie, 1990).

The civil rights movement of the 1960s, which culminated in violence and the sending in of British troops by the Labour government in 1969, illustrated the strength of feeling amongst Catholics, whose civil freedoms were greatly restricted on the basis of religion. Social rights, such as access to education and work, also varied greatly between Catholic and Protestant areas.

The limits of formal citizenship are also evident in the lack of effective access to basic rights for the young (Jones and Wallace, 1992: 117–57), the elderly (Carnegie Trust, 1993) and the disabled (Scope, 1995). For example, in the case of disabled citizens, it has been estimated that a disabled woman earns 88 per cent of an 'able-bodied' female worker (Graham et al., 1990: 83). The exercise of political rights is also problematic for the disabled, and a report by the Spastics Society (1992: 1) on the 1992 general election concluded that 'in the 1992 election many disabled people were faced with further proof that this society has yet to afford them equal citizenship'. During the 1992 election only 12 per cent of polling stations were fully accessible to the disabled, and though £22 per person was spent by the government on publicising the right of citizens abroad to vote, less than 2 pence per person was spent on informing the disabled of alternative forms of voting.

Although Marshall does argue that citizenship requires a social dimension to make it meaningful for most individuals, ultimately because of his statist assumptions, the social rights he advocates are paternalistic and dependent upon the condition of the market economy. Marshall reproduces the dualisms of classical liberalism in his notion that citizenship can be divided into separate types of rights and in his conception of the hyphenated society. He does not see that meaningful citizenship demands active participation by citizens who possess the necessary resources to facilitate that participation. By failing to transcend the agency-based approach to citizenship, Marshall does not consider the structural constraints which the market and coercive state place upon the distribution of the resources necessary for citizenship.

CITIZENSHIP AND SOCIAL CHANGE

Anthony Giddens (1985: 205) and Michael Mann (1987) have pointed out that Marshall's thesis has a strong evolutionary element to it. According to such critics Marshall appears to assume that the three stages of citizenship he describes, progress in an inevitable fashion, and that Marshall provides little or no explanation as to why these rights developed as they did.

According to Giddens, Marshall writes as if citizenship grows according to some inevitable inner logic of modernity; class struggle is hinted at by Marshall, but not really developed as a theory of social change (Marshall, 1963: 116–17). He does not consider why capitalism was willing to accept the inevitable cost of social rights. Neither does Marshall explore the role of the state in this reconciliation between citizenship and capitalism.

Marshall's failure to see the limits of the kind of social rights that have developed in liberal capitalist societies like Britain is related to his unsatisfactory account of the evolution of those rights. He assumes that the development of such rights is mainly of benefit to the working class, and therefore he fails to see how the development of citizenship can be understood as functional to the capitalist system. He overestimates the impact of social rights on social inequality and assumes they are firmly and permanently embedded in capitalist society. Therefore, Marshall's theory of citizenship fails to acknowledge the contingent nature of rights. As the definition of citizenship advanced in this book implies, citizenship is never static but is dependent upon complex processes of social and economic change.

Clearly the assumptions Marshall makes about the effectiveness of citizenship rights in restricting social division in capitalist society have to be questioned. The limitations of citizenship prior to the late 1970s allowed those opposed to universal social rights to argue that it was these rights, rather than the flaws of liberal capitalism, that had failed to deliver prosperity and social harmony. Therefore, in the next chapter we shall consider neo-liberal theories of citizenship, which reject many of Marshall's assumptions concerning the desirability and effects of social rights.

4

NEO-LIBERALISM
AND CITIZENSHIP

From the mid-1970s onwards, the ideas of the so called New Right have become crucial to governments in the United States and Europe (Green, 1987; Barry, 1987). The term New Right has tended to be used as a convenient shorthand for a diverse group of thinkers from the political right, embracing not only neo-liberalism, but also neo-conservative thinkers such as Lawrence Mead (1986), monetarist economists such as Milton Friedman (1962), and public choice theorists such as James Buchanan (1962).

The term New Right is, then, a very imprecise one because the range of opinions contained under such an umbrella term are often opposed and contradictory. However, all such thinkers are united, not so much by what they believe in, but by what they reject. All the thinkers of the New Right oppose the social liberal consensus established in the post-war period, all are highly wary of socialism and welfare statism, all support the market as the best creator of wealth and guarantee of personal freedom. In the context of this present work, and its concern with liberal theories of citizenship, the focus in this chapter will be on the neo-liberal elements of the New Right.

In Britain neo-liberal social and political philosophy represented the dominant ideology of the last four Conservative governments. The Thatcherite governments of Margaret Thatcher and John Major drew much of their inspiration from neo-liberal thinkers, particularly with regard to our main concern here, namely the relationship between the state and the individual (see Chapter 5).

What is in no doubt is that since the election of Margaret Thatcher in 1979 there has occurred a break with the post-war period which had seen a large degree of consensus on many social and economic issues concerning the relationship between state and citizen. In particular, a large question mark was raised by the Conservative government as to whether the state should continue to provide the same social rights for its citizens through welfare provision, which had been established after the second world war by the Labour governments of Attlee. In effect, the Conservative Party sought to redefine citizenship by reducing the significance of social rights and by reasserting market rights. Neo-liberal thinkers provided the Conservative Party with the theoretical ammunition to redefine citizenship. Two of the best known and influential advocates of these neo-liberal ideas are Frederick Hayek (1944, 1955, 1960) and Robert Nozick (1974).

It may appear at first sight that an analysis of neo-liberal conceptions of citizenship is redundant because neither Hayek nor Nozick make any direct reference to the concept of citizenship. Indeed one recent commentator has argued that 'from the point of view of an interest in the theory and practice of citizenship, radical New Right views [neo-liberal views] are of limited relevance since these views seem to have no use for and little understanding of the idea of citizenship' (Roche, 1992: 72). This view, however, underestimates the impact of neo-liberalism upon right-wing thinking and politics, in particular in Britain and America, concerning the correct relationship between the state and the individual. If we return to the definition of citizenship outlined in Chapter 1, the relevance of neo-liberalism becomes more evident.

It is obvious that neo-liberals such as Hayek and Nozick have important things to say concerning the extent of citizenship, the centrality of the individual, the character of the political community, and the most desirable balance between the various social, political and economic forces present within any given society. Indeed we shall see in subsequent chapters the profound influence the neo-liberal perspective has had upon these debates, and upon the practice of citizenship in modern Britain. In addition to its influence on the right of politics it is important to note the impact of neo-liberal thought on the revival of citizenship on the left of British politics since the 1980s. Neo-liberalism put on the agenda several issues directly related to the theory and practice of citizenship, which writers from the left have had to critically reassess, such as:

- The importance of considering individual agents as autonomous beings whose actions can influence social structures (this issue has particularly influenced commentators with a Marxist perspective).
- The place of rights in protecting the individual from the state and other individuals.
- The limitations of statist solutions to problems of poverty, gender and 'race' inequalities.

To complete our analysis of liberal conceptions of citizenship it therefore becomes essential to examine the neo-liberal variant.

INDIVIDUALISM VERSUS COLLECTIVISM

We shall begin with how neo-liberals conceive of the relationship between the individual and society. Both Hayek and Nozick privilege the individual, and in particular individual liberty, as the basis for any political arrangement. Liberty is seen as the most important value to be obtained and protected, not as means to some other social goal, but as the end in itself. One of the central concerns of both writers is the fear that in the post-war period, the freedom of the individual has been undermined by various forms of socialism which have sought to manipulate individuals in the attempt to achieve some form of equality in society.

Hayek argues that it is dangerous to put the needs of society, which is a vague and ill-defined concept, above those of any one individual. The concept of society, so celebrated by socialists, is dismissed because it reifies something which cannot have an identity or will outside of, or separate from, the individuals that make it up. The starting position for Hayek and Nozick's social and political theory is captured by Hayek when he states:

> Individuals should be allowed, within defined limits, to follow their own values and preferences rather than somebody else's, that within these spheres the individual's system of ends should be supreme and not subject to any dictation by others. It is this recognition of the individual as the ultimate judge of his ends, the belief that as far as possible his views ought to govern his actions, that forms the essence of the individualist position. (Hayek, 1944: 44)

Nozick and Hayek share with the classical liberals examined in Chapter 2 the strong desire to preserve the sovereignty of the individual against the threat of collectivist theories, which, it is argued, seek to submerge the individual in some artificial form of community. Hayek contends that the extreme ideologies of communism and fascism had their roots in a collectivist and socialist philosophy. Both are opposed to the freedom of the individual and liberalism in general. Both aim to create a kind of artificial universal community based on, in the former case, a fraternity of workers or as in the case of the National Socialists in Germany, an Aryan super race. Social liberalism is almost as threatening as these radical ideologies because the social rights Marshall advocates necessarily undermine individual liberty. As early as 1944, Hayek detected how 'our attitude towards society has changed . . . The change amounts to a complete reversal of the trend we have sketched [the movement towards collectivism], an entire abandonment of the individualist tradition which has created Western civilisation' (Hayek, 1944: 15).

THE IMPORTANCE OF UNEQUAL AGENTS

In terms of the relationship between structure and agency, Hayek and Nozick differ little in their position from classical liberals like Locke. In fact neo-liberals are more militantly abstract than the classical liberals. However, and this is crucial to their conception of citizenship, writers like Hayek and Nozick reject the egalitarian aspects of Locke and Paine's theories.

Neo-liberals assert the inevitability and the desirability of inequality between agents, which is explained in terms of natural ability, effort and personal incentive, rather than in terms of structured inequalities based on social cleavages such as class. The importance of inequality in neo-liberalism marks an important break with classical liberalism and the social liberalism of Marshall. The optimistic vision of a society moving, all be it slowly, towards social justice, is abandoned in favour of a vision of highly unequal individuals competing for scarce resources.

The apparent failure of the post-war social liberal consensus to solve problems such as poverty and cultural deprivation strengthened the opposition of neo-liberals like Nozick and Hayek to any future society that had as its aim the eradication of inequality. The weaknesses of social liberalism, identified in Chapter 3, allowed for a critique of writers like Marshall from within a liberal framework.

As Gray (1984: 95–103) points out, Hayek, though in many ways an admirer of J. S. Mill, was highly critical of the direction that Mill took classical liberalism, and the influence this had on 'revisionist' liberals such as T. H. Green, Hobhouse and Marshall (Gray, 1995: 31–2). As we have seen, these thinkers argued for a more positive view of liberty than Hayek or Nozick would support, and thereby laid the theoretical foundations for the development of the welfare state so criticised by neo-liberals.

Hayek and Nozick argue that any attempt to create an equal society would be bound to fail (because people are naturally unequal), would infringe upon individual liberty (because policies of redistribution reduce individual choice), and would undermine wealth creation, which is best created by unequal individuals struggling for unequal rewards. Both thinkers strongly advocate the protection of the private sphere from the interference of the public sphere.

Nozick argues that the best way to ensure the protection of the private sphere is through the device of natural rights. Thus his defence of individual freedom and the private sphere has, Nozick argues, its origins in Locke's defence of natural rights. These are rights that individuals possess regardless of whether a state exists or not. They consist of the right to life, liberty and property; the last of these being justified largely in terms of the first two, in the sense that ownership of property is deemed necessary to protect life and liberty. These rights should not be violated by individuals or institutions. However, it is important to make clear that the rights that Nozick defends are negative rights and do not involve a corresponding duty by someone else to act in a certain way which will fulfil that right (Wolff, 1991: 19).

The right to property is particularly important to Nozick, and the right to the accumulation of property and wealth, protected by natural rights, lies at the centre of his theory of justice. Because of inequality of ability the amount of property one person may own may well be vast. This, however, is defensible as long as property is acquired justly. In Nozick's theory, meaningful citizenship is linked strongly to the acquisition of property.

Hayek, though sharing Nozick's desire to secure the private realm from interference from the public sphere, is less clear about the role of rights. In this context Norman Barry distinguishes between Hayek and Nozick in terms of the moral arguments they employ to defend the individual. Hayek is defined as a utilitarian liberal because, Barry argues, he does not make a specific moral argument to establish his guiding principles of prosperity and liberty. Barry says, when discussing (amongst others) Hayek, 'objections to intervention are not primarily focused on the rights-violating nature of such intervention'. Nozick's liberalism, on the other hand, 'is based entirely on the argument that there are moral side-constraints on action which limit what men may do (as individuals or through the state) to each other' (Barry, 1987: 28). However, contrary to Barry's argument, Hayek does discuss the importance of recognising the rights of 'man' as a basis for the Rule of Law:

> Whether, as in some countries, the main applications of the Rule of Law are laid down in a Bill of Rights or a constitutional code, or whether the principle is merely a firmly established tradition, matters comparatively little. But it will readily be seen that whatever form it takes, any such recognised limitations of the powers of legislation imply the recognition of the *inalienable right of the individual*, the *inviolable rights of man*. (Hayek, 1944: 63, emphasis added)

Hayek goes on to discuss the contradictions of socialist thinkers, like H. G. Wells, who defend socialist planning, but yet advocate the 'rights of man'. In his discussion of Wells (Hayek, 1944: 63–5), Hayek makes clear his support for individual rights and argues against the socialist notion of 'rational' societies having individual duties as opposed to individual rights, which are perceived by socialists to be a 'bourgeois sham'. Hayek quotes *The Economist*, which stated (a few years before Hayek was writing) that:

> Democratic government no less than dictatorship must always have plenary powers in *posse*, without sacrificing their democratic and representative character. There is no restrictive penumbra of individual rights that can never be touched by government in administrative matters whatever the circumstances. There is no limit to the power of ruling which can and should be taken by a government freely chosen by the people and can be fully and openly criticised by an opposition. (*The Economist*, cited in Hayek, 1944: 64)

Hayek implies his support for some form of individual rights when, in analysing the above statement, he contends that:

> This may be inevitable in wartime when, of course, even free and open criticism is necessarily restricted. But the 'always' in the statement quoted does not suggest that *The Economist* regards it as a regrettable wartime necessity. Yet as a permanent institution this view is certainly incompatible with the Rule of Law. (Hayek, 1944: 64)

Hayek and Nozick clearly share a strong desire to preserve the autonomy of the individual, and both thinkers assert the importance of inequality. Indeed it could be said that both Hayek and Nozick defend a vision of citizenship which has as its foundations the right of inequality, the right to choose and the right to fail. Their view of the relationship between civil society and the institution of the state marks an important break with social liberalism because given such a view of citizenship, which strongly defends the individual's freedoms, the state cannot be allowed to encroach upon these liberties and must be limited in its welfare functions.

THE ROLE OF THE STATE

The neo-liberal perspective on the role of the state is that it should allow safe contracts to be made without fear of violence, theft or fraud. The state should guarantee such basic rights as liberty and the right to property. It should prevent conflict in society by enforcing these rights and contracts. Neo-liberals normally claim as their inspiration on matters of the state the work of Adam Smith. However, it should be noted that Smith's work is often oversimplified in the neo-liberals' anxiety to claim that his work lends weight to their arguments. In fact, Smith acknowledged that the state was bound to reflect class division (Hoffman, 1988: 40), he embraced a relative view of poverty (Gilmour, 1992: 135) and doubted that 'capitalists made good citizens' (Jordon, 1989: 75).

However, it is the vision of the state that Adam Smith (1976) argued for in his *Wealth of Nations* that is still the model that many neo-liberals would consider more or less ideal. In Smith's view, the state should operate only to protect its citizens either from internal breakdowns in law and order, or from external threats such as invasion by a hostile neighbour. Smith also allowed the state to undertake certain tasks relating to the infrastructure of society which would not be profitable for private companies to invest in, for example roads. Smith's perspective is summarised by him in the following passage:

> Little else is requisite to carry a state to the highest degree of opulence from the lowest barbarism, but peace, easy taxes, and a tolerable administration of justice; all the rest being brought about by the natural course of things. All governments which thwart this natural course, which force things into another channel . . . are unnatural, and to support themselves are obliged to be oppressive and tyrannical. (cited in Stewart, 1858: 68)

Neo-liberal thinkers skate over Smith's acknowledgement of the problem of class, and argue that his theory supports their notion that the individual is a self-interested actor who is generally best left alone to satisfy his or her own personal needs with the minimum of state intervention.

Hayek's view of the state–civil society relationship begins with this militant individualistic perspective. Hayek suggests that even mild forms of state planning are almost equally as dangerous as extreme manifestations of collectivism such as fascism and communism, since any plans that a state may have will always involve outcomes which cannot be foreseen by the planners. Thus, when the plan is carried out in practice, the individual is violated in some way. The problem with state planning for Hayek is not so much the aims (welfare for the poverty stricken for example), but the methods used to achieve those aims. The vast bureaucracies needed to operate state welfare systems are by their nature inefficient and tend towards totalitarianism.

Hayek's concern over state planning was increased during the war of 1939–45 when state management was enforced in Europe either on ideological or practical grounds. In *The Road to Serfdom*, and the work that followed, he attempts a restatement of the ideal of liberty, which he sees as the cornerstone of the West's development.

According to Hayek, liberty consists of the absence of coercion, where coercion is a personal attribute. In order for someone to be coerced it must involve intention on the part of one or more human beings. Thus it cannot be said that one's liberty is affected by the workings of the market, because the market carries no moral priorities: it does not discriminate in a normative sense. It is up to individuals to succeed or fail according to their abilities to manipulate, to their own advantage, the laws of supply and demand. A society which maximises liberty and minimises state interference is one where citizens can best prosper. Freedom, argues Hayek, is not to be confused with equality in terms of material wealth or power. If the two are linked, this leads to welfare statism and serfdom, where true liberty is lost. Freedom then is a negative concept, which should be protected by the state through a system of law.

States which aim to pursue planning or social engineering, to offset natural inequalities in civil society, are attempting the impossible since vague concepts like a 'common purpose' or the 'common good' can never fulfil the needs of a diverse population, but will instead inevitably attempt to coerce individuals to fit the needs of the plan because, 'in our society there is neither occasion nor reason why people should develop common views about what should be done in such situations' (Hayek, 1944: 42–3).

In *The Constitution of Liberty* Hayek expands his scepticism about the ability of states successfully to plan or manage civil society. One of the key reasons for his doubts about the utility of state planning is because of the way in which knowledge about society is generated over time. On the question of knowledge Hayek is heavily influenced by the work of Karl Popper (1957) (an ardent defender of individual liberty against any philosopher or political scientist who has advocated collectivist solutions to societal problems). For Hayek, following Popper, knowledge progresses in a confused and haphazard way and we can never be sure that any single plan or theory is the definitive answer to a problem. There are limits to human beings' expertise and abilities since knowledge tends to be distributed across a society. It follows from this observation that government should not centralise power but allow it to be dispersed down to a local or individual level. If a government allows this to happen, Hayek argues a 'spontaneous order' would naturally develop where prosperity and individual liberty would be best served. The concept of a spontaneous order is a similar one to Smith's own idea of the so-called 'invisible hand' whereby the iron laws of supply and demand would ensure that human needs would be met. Hayek rejects state planning precisely because it attempts to interfere with this process by trying to create an artificial order that complies with a certain set of ideological preconceptions about how society should be constructed.

Order is maintained because people observe certain social norms which have developed through time. Interestingly, Hayek's social theory displays a strong element of conservatism. Indeed, Gray has argued that this is what makes Hayek's contribution so powerful:

> We find in Hayek a restatement of classical liberalism in which it is purified of errors – specifically, the errors of abstract individualism and uncritical rationalism – which inform the work of even the greatest of the classical liberals and which Hayek has been able to correct by absorbing some of the deepest insights of conservative philosophy. (Gray, 1984: viii)

I will argue later that Gray is wrong to assert that Hayek has overcome or abandoned abstract individualism. Indeed as Chapter 2 argued, abstract individualism and rationalism are central to classical liberalism and cannot be dispensed with without disrupting the logic of liberalism itself (Forsyth, 1988: 237). It is true to say that in his discussions of the importance of tradition and the inability for a single individual or group of individuals to know the truth and to apply it universally through the power of the state, Hayek does sound more like a conservative than a liberal. Thus in his work *Law, Legislation and Liberty* he argues that traditional institutions should not be tampered with unless one is sure that the alternative is better. It is the integration between individuals, guided by tradition and self-interest, under the negative regulation of a strictly limited state which maintains stability in society:

> Particular aspects of a culture can be critically examined only within the context of that culture. We can never reduce a system of rules or all values as a whole to a purpose construction, but must always stop with our criticism of something that has no better grounds for existence than it is the accepted basis of the particular culture. (Hayek, 1976: 25)

Hayek's conservatism is also evident in his uncritical approach to the state, which I will discuss below. Nozick displays no such conservatism in his view of the state–civil society relationship. However, he shares with Hayek the desire for a strictly limited state and a high degree of autonomy for civil society. Unlike Hayek, Nozick does question the validity of the state and his book *Anarchy, State and Utopia* begins by taking seriously anarchist arguments concerning the need to get rid of the state in its entirety. Nozick concludes, however, that through a process of market exchange a minimal state would be created because of the need for protection and policing, which would be best conducted in a monopolistic way. The state does not occur as the result of a social contract based on consent, but arises out of the operations of the market.

According to Nozick the role of the state should merely be to act as a 'night-watchman' ensuring peace and security and protecting, but not positively guaranteeing, natural rights. Nozick rejects the notion that the state should attempt a redistribution of wealth. The very idea that the state could achieve equality in society is absurd because the unequal nature of human beings will disrupt any artificially constructed equality. The state would have to become totalitarian in an effort to control closely the actions of individuals, thereby undermining or even preventing charity and private deals. Economic exchange under such a system would rest on compulsion rather than voluntary action (which, argue liberals, is the best source of freedom and of wealth creation).

The superiority of market forces over state planning in terms of creating a wealthy and prosperous society is something on which Nozick and Hayek concur. This leads us to consider the fifth dualism which arises from classical liberal theory outlined in Table 2.2; that is, the relationship between markets (which are the best guarantee of personal freedom) and politics, where citizens are perceived by classical liberals as being formally equal in terms of political rights, and therefore in their ability to check the power of the state.

THE LIMITS OF POLITICAL CITIZENSHIP

Because of his strong defence of individual autonomy, free choice, voluntary action and market forces, Nozick's discussion of politics is limited as to how government can best be controlled and kept to a minimum. Clearly in Nozick's ideal utopia, many areas of life that would traditionally be seen within the realm of politics and political decisions would become redundant. The key value to be defended is liberty and this is best provided by the market. Therefore, politics is limited to the protection of the state from outside threat and the need to make and enforce laws to protect natural rights. People in such a society succeed or fail on their own merits and therefore there is little for parliaments or assemblies to decide or legislate upon. It is not the role of political institutions to distribute wealth and resources because Nozick rejects 'end result' types of distribution as they will always violate the individual's natural rights.

He argues against John Rawls's (1972) proposition that if everyone in society could be removed from their position in society, and were asked to choose a just system of distribution without prior knowledge of their future social position, they would allow for the state to guarantee a reasonable level of income for everyone. Nozick says that individuals would be just as likely to choose a totally free market and rely on their skill to succeed in it. Nozick contends that it is only the laissez-faire system of economic exchange which can work effectively because it uses as its motor human beings' natural inequality and self-interest.

It follows that the individual should not be forced to pay for a system of social justice, for example a welfare state, through a progressive tax system. Taxes should only be levied for the costs of constructing a minimal state as outlined by Nozick. Nozick is clear that the state should have no role in the moral life of its citizens or in their ethical behaviour. Neither should the state attempt to compel people to help others. Nor should it pursue policies which aim to make citizens act for their own good. These matters should be left solely to voluntary action. As Nozick puts it, the state 'may not use its coercive apparatus for the purpose of getting some citizens to aid others or in order to prohibit activities to people for their own good or protection' (cited in Wolff, 1991: 11).

Nozick, like Hayek, starts always with the individual as the basic unit of society, and his primary concern is to protect that individual against state power because it is desirable in terms of efficiency, as well as in terms of morality (that is, in terms of maximising individual freedom). It is Nozick's utopia which will provide the basis for mutual respect, voluntary action and ethical behaviour and will abolish the need for paternalist political institutions: 'the minimal state treats us as inviolate individuals, who may not be used in certain ways by others as a means or tools or instruments or resources; it treats us as persons having individual rights with the dignity this constitutes . . . How dare any state or group of individuals do more. Or less' (Nozick, 1974: 333–4).

Hayek shares Nozick's suspicion of political institutions which attempt to redistribute resources, or interfere with the market, in an effort to render society more equal. Hayek argues against the notion that the state can create social justice by intervening in the economy. Hayek states that the use of the term justice when referring to material wealth is misplaced, since justice implies a social actor should have, or should not have, performed some action according to some set of predetermined rules setting out what is and what is not desirable (Hayek, 1976: 33).

Because the market does not operate in a way which allows for actors to predict or know all the consequences of their actions within the market place, questions of justice have no place in relation to the accumulation or distribution of wealth. The idea of limiting the accumulation of material wealth is, says Hayek, an attack on the freedom of the individual. Since the operation of the market cannot coerce anyone it cannot be argued that it affects their freedom and therefore cannot be called unjust.

Hayek, unlike Nozick, does write at some length concerning political institutions. In particular, Hayek discusses the place of democratic institutions in relation to the market. Given Hayek's commitment to market mechanisms that for Hayek are the dynamic behind the success of Western nations, it is not surprising that he is sceptical of the value of democracy. As argued in Chapters 2 and 3, an ambivalent attitude to democracy can be found in the work of many earlier liberals including Locke and J. S. Mill, but this scepticism is even more developed in the work of Hayek because of the stress he puts on the importance of inequality in civil society. In this sense neo-liberalism can be seen to be less committed to egalitarianism than classical liberalism, with its emphasis on formal equality in the public sphere and the defence of the constitutional state.

Hayek believes that in the modern era we have 'made a fetish of democracy', and that 'our generation talks and thinks too much of democracy and too little of the values it serves'. We must, according to Hayek, realise that democracy is a means to the end of liberty and as such should be seen as 'a utilitarian device for safe-guarding internal peace and individual freedom. As such it is by no means infallible or certain', and in certain circumstances 'a democracy may set up the most complete despotism imaginable' (Hayek, 1944: 52). Four main fears of democracy can be identified in Hayek's work:

- That the will of the majority may be used as a justification for interference with the market, thus reducing freedom and wealth throughout society.
- That democratic institutions will increase people's expectations but fail to deliver these expectations, thereby de-stabilising society.
- That because of the difficulty of agreeing on the implementation and detail of policy, decisions may be handed over to unelected bureaucrats or experts.
- That the masses are naturally unable to govern effectively.

First, then, Hayek is keen to maintain a large gap between economic and political spheres. He argues that political solutions to problems tend towards the centralisation of power. Therefore, a socialist system, in an effort to rid society of inequalities of power, would in fact take more and more power into central control, whereas market systems disperse power much more widely throughout society. Because of his view of the limits of human knowledge Hayek is keen to avoid the 'tyranny of the majority' where the economy is interfered with by a misinformed mob, thus reducing individual freedom. As Hayek writes:

What is called economic power, while it can be an instrument of coercion, is in the hands of private individuals never exclusive or complete power, never power over the whole life of a person. But centralised as an instrument of political power it creates a degree of dependence scarcely distinguishable from slavery. (Hayek, 1944: 108)

An alleged fundamental danger to freedom in modern liberal democracies that Hayek identifies is the idea that because democracy claims to represent the majority opinion, it makes the claim that it is justified in having unlimited control over society. The representatives or agents of the people can, according to this argument, intervene to achieve aims which would be better served by the market. The temptation is to attempt to create an order rather than let one develop spontaneously. Hayek is wary of the operations of modern democracy because it increases the number of decisions taken politically and therefore reduces the autonomy of the market. Since modern society is so complex, the will of the majority cannot be trusted as a guide as to how it should be constructed. Once again Hayek points to the limits of human knowledge and the fallacy of building up the power of the state based on the attempted achievement of an overriding social goal or plan that in practice is bound to limit freedom.

Second, Hayek asserts that the danger of raising expectations such as the achievement of social justice is that the masses will be disillusioned if the state is seen to fail to deliver on its promises. In this way democracy will be undermined. It is interesting that variations of this argument were employed in Britain during the 1960s and 1970s when some commentators began to talk about the ungovernability of Britain or state overload (Hay, 1996: Ch. 5).

Third, even if one could achieve a unanimous vote on a comprehensive plan for economic restructuring based, for example, on some misguided notion of social justice, the weakness of a planned economy will mean that the government will be tempted to hand the problem to 'experts'. Thus social problems will be dealt with by neither the market nor democratic institutions but by a self-interested, unelected bureaucracy: 'parliaments become regarded as ineffective "talking shops", unable or incompetent to carry out the tasks for which they have been chosen. The conviction grows that if efficient planning is to be done, the direction must be "taken out of politics" and placed in the hands of experts, permanent officials or independent autonomous bodies' (Hayek, 1944: 46).

The difficulty of achieving agreement on social ends in a democratic fashion makes it more likely that state bureaucracy will increasingly take decisions which centralise power, and in turn make those areas of society not directly controlled by the state nevertheless dependent upon the state in an indirect way. Hayek argues that though an overall plan may be agreed upon by society as a whole, the sub-plans and implementation of actual policy will not be decided, nor could be decided, in a democratic way. This fact again encourages the development of the government by 'experts' and unelected bureaucrats.

Democracy can only work when its realm of activity is strictly limited.

Hayek argues that the great advantage of the liberal creed is that it does not require a lot of agreement by people concerning the desirable ends of their lives, or what may constitute the 'good life'. In a liberal system all men and women can decide their version of the good life and pursue it in the market place.

The fourth main reservation displayed by Hayek towards democracy concerns his essentially elitist approach to the capability of average men and women to govern their own lives through democratic institutions. Hayek is no doubt that where democracy should be allowed to hold sway (and this should be in strictly limited areas of life), it should not be confused with collectivism in any way. Hayek sees democracy as 'an essentially individualist institution stood in an irreconcilable conflict with socialism' (Hayek, 1944: 18). However, the question is *which* individuals are in reality able to effectively involve themselves in democracy? Hayek abandons the, at least theoretical, classical liberal commitment to the notion of equality in the public sphere when he argues that in a democratic system 'it will be those who form the "mass" in the derogatory sense of the term, the least original and independent, who will be able to put the weight of their numbers behind their particular ideals' (Hayek, 1944: 102–3). Hayek is in little doubt that the masses are incapable of self-government and would therefore be open to manipulation. He argues that 'probably it is true enough that the great majority are rarely capable of thinking independently . . . In any society freedom of thought will probably be of direct significance only for a small minority' (Hayek, 1944: 122). Such a perspective on the limits of political citizenship suggests that there is a case for seeing Hayek's theory of democracy as being closer to that of the elite theorists, such as Pareto and Mosca, than to the liberal constitutionalism of earlier liberal thinkers like Locke and Paine.

NEO-LIBERALISM, CITIZENSHIP RIGHTS AND DUTIES

With Nozick's defence of natural rights, and Hayek's insistence on the importance of upholding the rule of law, both thinkers clearly recognise the need for the protection of individuals from state interference. Thus the ideal type of citizenship that emerges from their social and political thought is one in which the state serves the individual and protects their freedoms in civil society. Whilst Nozick is much clearer than Hayek on the importance of civil rights, that is he sees them as inviolable, both theorists are clear that the state should not impose duties on citizens to ensure the positive delivery of rights to all its citizens. Therefore, all citizens have the right to freedom in the negative sense, but have no right to be helped by the state or other individuals to achieve an equal ability to exercise their freedom. In a sense citizens have rights to inequality, a right to exercise their natural abilities, and to rise and fall in a market place which does not discriminate on moral or personal grounds (which according to neo-liberals makes its outcomes acceptable) but which merely provides an avenue for natural inequalities to emerge. Given these assumptions neo liberals are particularly opposed to the concept of social rights as advocated by social liberals like Marshall. Neo-liberals argue that social rights are flawed in a number of ways:

- They fail to achieve equality because it is a social fact that people are unequal and therefore inequality will quickly reassert itself no matter how extensive social rights may be.
- The temptation for states committed to social rights is to increase spending and thereby to undermine further the wealth-creating private sector and civil freedoms.
- Because they can never succeed, they have the effect of rising expectations amongst the poor, and when these expectations are not fulfilled the state can be de-stabilised and suffer from a crisis of legitimacy.
- In enforcing social rights the state will increasingly take on more centralised power and thereby, once again, undermine individual freedom, particularly through the 'black hole' of taxation. Legislation to enforce social rights would also disrupt the natural inequality that the spontaneous order, which neo-liberals seek, rests upon.
- Citizens will become increasingly reliant upon the state for their material well-being. Therefore individual innovation, invention, and personal responsibility will be undermined.

The antipathy towards social rights amongst neo-liberal thinkers is clear. According to neo-liberals the social liberalism of writers like Marshall is opposed to the classic liberal values of individual freedom because the implication of social rights is a stronger role for the state in intervening and regulating the private sphere: the very thing that neo-liberals oppose so strongly. However, by so strongly opposing social rights neo-liberals raise some interesting questions about the extent and effects of political rights as defined by Marshall. These are the right to vote and the right to hold office, as well as the general right of participation.

In neo-liberalism there exists an inherent tension between a defence of political rights that, it is argued, ensure society is governed in the interests of a 'free' society, and the possibility that the extension of political rights gives to disadvantaged groups to use them to argue for social rights. This dilemma explains why Nozick and Hayek argue so vehemently for a limit to decisions in society being taken politically, as opposed to being decided by the market. This problem also partly explains why both thinkers oppose the idea that citizens have duties to others to ensure that all citizens have the ability to exercise their freedom in practice. Any attempt to impose or enforce duties will be counter productive and reduce people's reliance on themselves, and therefore their ability to be useful and responsible citizens.

For neo-liberals the right to economic freedom 'inevitably also carries the risk and the responsibility of that right' (Hayek, 1944: 75). Socialism cannot provide the correct balance between rights and responsibilities because 'a movement whose main promise is the relief from responsibility cannot but be anti-moral in its effect however lofty the ideals to which it owes its birth' (Hayek, 1944: 157).

Hayek, then, is in no doubt that collectivism, including the striving for social rights, has undermined good citizenship by weakening personal responsibility and civic virtue. For neo-liberals the only way to engender good citizenship is to see as its basis the individual freely choosing to act in a responsible way.

AN ASSESSMENT OF NEO-LIBERAL THEORIES OF CITIZENSHIP

One way of analysing the neo-liberal perspective is to return again to the outline of dualisms arising from the classical liberal position that are set out in Table 2.2. We have seen how in many ways neo-liberals wish to defend the entities on the left of the table, namely the individual, the private sphere and market rights from interference from those phenomena identified in the column on the right of the table, such as society, the state and social rights. The dualisms of classical liberal theory are even more polarised in neo-liberalism, and therefore the criticisms of classical liberalism outlined in Chapter 2 can be applied even more strongly to neo-liberalism.

Social liberals, as we have seen, attempt to reconcile the theoretical equality of classical liberalism with the inequalities of civil society by arguing for a positive, rather than negative, view of freedom. Writers like Marshall argue for the need of social rights, guaranteed by the state, to increase the chances of all citizens to benefit from the advantages of a liberal society, namely opportunity, choice, autonomy and wealth. Neo-liberals reject this theory as a form of collectivism.

The neo-liberal answer to the problems identified by social liberals like Marshall is to argue strongly in defence of negative liberty and the inevitability of inequality. However, this argument leaves neo-liberals open to the criticisms that their perspective takes as the basic unit of society the self-interested individual, ignores the structural constraints upon individuals in enjoying any meaningful degree of liberty, and therefore fails to create real autonomy for many citizens. In neo-liberalism the individual is artificially removed from the cultural and social factors which in reality shape, and are in turn shaped by the individual. However, neo-liberals reject the radical potential of classical liberalism because they have no state of nature thesis. Their brand of individualism is more abstract, and less consistent, than the classical liberals because they abandon the anti-statist logic of Locke and Paine's theories. Also, their individualism is not only theoretically illogical, it is also ahistorical.

Historically human beings are social beings, not egoistical loners. The natural unit has been the community not the individual, and therefore all human societies have required the need for rules, regulations and government, which are by their nature collective acts: a fact well established by archaeology and anthropology (Gledhill, 1994: Ch. 1; Hoffman 1995: 38–9). Culture is above all a learnt experience and a shared experience, presupposing some form of collective organisation (Kluckhohn, 1951; Linton, 1945). Nozick, in particular, rests his arguments on an ahistorical vision of the individual, who in fact responds to the expectations, needs and fears of society, rather than being determined purely by his or her own will as Nozick suggests.

Hayek is also confused in his view of the individual. This is because he recognises the importance of history and tradition in shaping culture, but does not see the contradiction between that observation and his defence of an abstract individual and a free market, which some traditional conservatives argue are distinctly disruptive to tradition and convention (Gilmour, 1992).

The fact that wealth creation is itself a collective act is particularly damaging to the neo-liberal view of human nature. Human beings not only live in communities, they also make associations and form companies. The idea of the individual producer would not only be unproductive, it would be impossible without reference and help from other individuals. As Marx observes, from simple hunter-gatherer societies to complex industrial societies, production is a social activity (Appelbaum, 1988: 70–5). Neo-liberals are convinced that the individual is the best unit for a progressive wealth-creating society, but in any large-scale production some form of association will be needed. It is only by recognising the interdependence of individuals, and the environment that surrounds them, that the development of individual potential and autonomy is possible (Twine, 1994). The influence of such easily identifiable social realities such as class, gender and 'race' means that the individual's chances of joining a successful association will not be equal, regardless of the abilities that an individual might possess. Therefore a spontaneous order based on natural inequalities of skill cannot exist in reality.

In fact, a logical extension of the idea that individuals should be free from restraint to develop their talents would be to undermine those unjust barriers which prevent the 'best specimens' from succeeding. Nozick himself is forced to recognise this problem when he talks about allowing for a temporary state which would have a much greater role than his ideal night-watchman state would have. This state would try to rectify past injustices, based on such structural inequalities as 'race', which he acknowledges has impaired the development of the 'natural' order. Nozick argues that 'past injustices might be so great as to make necessary in the short run a more extensive state in order to rectify them' (Nozick, 1974: 231).

The fact that Nozick is forced to accept that previous injustices will require a more developed state when he actually looks at a real society (in this case he was observing his native America) undermines his theory. Nozick may be right in his view that to attempt to create equality of outcome by state intervention would be impossible, but surely just as economic inequality would reassert itself so would inequality based on prejudice, class, and so on. It is therefore hard to see how this 'temporarily' increased role for the state could be reduced unless more extensive action could be taken to isolate individuals' life chances to ensure that only the most able succeed. Thus legislation would have to be taken to remove property that was unfairly acquired (by force or legal tricks), and such laws would have to forbid, or at least limit, inherited wealth since this would seem to be just as damaging to the 'natural order' as the welfare state since it makes the family more important than the individual. Also any privileges based on class (for example aristocratic privilege) would have to be removed if wealth and power are to bear a close relationship to skill and talent.

When examined in a social and historical context, it seems that the idea of a spontaneous order or a society ordered by an 'invisible hand' is spurious. In human society powerful individuals and groups have invariably institutionalised their influence and thus sectional interest develops which limits individuals' chances to fulfil their potential. Again neo-liberals, like their classical and social liberal predecessors, demonstrate a superficial understanding of the operation of power in society.

Hayek's negative view of freedom also seems to be weak when examined in the light of social reality. Hayek states that freedom cannot be limited by the action of market forces because the outcomes of these cannot be foreseen and do not intend harm to individuals. However, the very fact that Hayek advocates a market system as the best guarantee of freedom implies some knowledge of its results and outcomes. Therefore, Hayek's argument that markets cannot coerce because they do not intend to coerce is contradictory. Clearly in a modern industrial nation, where macro-economic policy is carefully monitored, governments and other bodies do have access to a large body of knowledge that allows for predictions of the general outcome of policies, or at least the effects can be noted after a policy has been implemented. Hayek argues against the ability of the social sciences to tell us anything about the outcome of market relations, such as unemployment and higher inflation. As with the concept of the individual, he makes an abstraction of the market without reference to real historical instances. In short, neo-liberals, critical of the reification of society by 'collectivist' thinkers, are themselves guilty of mystifying the market, which, because of the interdependence of producers, the institutionalisation of inequality and the need for government, can never be, and never has been, 'free' in the pure form suggested by neo-liberals.

Neo-liberalism is also highly problematic in its considerations of democracy and the operation of politics. The problem of political obligation is a particularly difficult one for neo-liberals since there seems to be little basis in their theoretical position for loyalty to the state. In Nozick's theory the state emerges as nothing more than, in the words of John Kingdom, 'a kind of monopolistic protection and punishment agency, forcing its clients to pay for its services through the tax system' (Kingdom, 1992: 83). Such an institution has little basis for legitimacy and would likely be challenged, avoided or by-passed by its citizens.

As we observed in our discussion of democracy, Hayek's ideal relationship between the state and the individual is also one where it is difficult to see how citizens could have anything other than an instrumental approach to politics. Under Hayek's vision political institutions would have little to do of any significance, and, as was suggested, he is, in any case, highly sceptical of the extension of political rights to the unthinking masses, who may clamber for positive rights and thereby undermine the triumph of the 'natural elites' who will prosper in the market place. With Hayek's theory the paradox of liberalism's commitment to formal equality on the one hand, and to an unequal civil society on the other hand, relegates the role of democracy to a point where his version of liberalism is difficult to distinguish from authoritarian conservatism (see Chapter 5).

Hayek and Nozick not only argue that their concept of a limited state, a restricted democracy and the absence of social rights is best for the development of individual freedom, they also contend that such a system would create the most prosperity for all. The workings of an unfettered market, based on the defence of private property, would provide society's needs and stability would result: 'what our generation has forgotten is that the system of private property is the most guarantee of freedom, not only for those who own property, but scarcely less for those who do not' (Hayek, 1944: 78).

It is highly questionable whether a society of competitive individuals struggling for resources, with little basis for loyalty to the state or indeed to each other, would merely accept the outcome of market forces and the inequality of the ownership of property as readily as Hayek and Nozick imagine. It is probable that the state would struggle to fulfil its limited role of defence and the maintenance of law and order. For example, in terms of the protection of the right to property, the state would likely be under massive pressure because of the divisive nature of vast, visible inequalities. In such a system large-scale social disorder would almost certainly be the result. Individuals or groups who failed in the market would not have the option of turning to the state for help and would instead have to seek alternative means to provide for themselves and their loved ones. Also a society which put so much importance upon individual fulfilment through the market would make the acceptance of failure even harder to swallow.

If one examines an actual society, for example modern America (where public policy strongly resembles the neo-liberal model), indicators of social conflict are higher than in most European countries where greater social welfare exists. Instances of crime, drug addiction and public disorder for instance are much higher in America. Many commentators, for example Robert Merton (1968), have linked this to the nature of American society, in which a state of *anomie* has been reached. He argues that there exists an imbalance between expectations, which are fuelled by the mass media and education, and opportunities, which are blocked for many groups and individuals for a number of social reasons, such as racial prejudice. In a society that places its emphasis on material wealth, the discontentment of those who cannot obtain these goals will, argues Merton, be a major problem. In America this has manifested itself in large-scale marginalisation of inner-city areas and high levels of organised crime. In many cases the citizen has become almost totally estranged from the state.

In a society which fulfils Nozick's vision of utopia, it is highly likely that the money the individual saves from paying tax on welfare for the poor, will be taken up instead in vast expenditure on the maintenance of law and order. In parts of America in the 1990s (and in other countries which have vast material inequalities between citizens, such as Brazil) wealthy citizens are increasingly taking extreme measures to cut themselves off from the rest of society deemed to be unsafe and violent. Wealthy people in such places are increasingly turning to barbed-wire-protected 'citadels' policed by private security firms which demand written passes for visitors, and 'outsiders' are systematically excluded. In the neo-liberal utopia it is likely that a small 'overclass' will lead increasingly wealthy but isolated lives, unavailable to venture out into the world of crumbling infrastructures, disorder and violent crime which most other 'citizens' will inhabit. In a such a world the liberal promise of liberty, autonomy and security for all citizens would be no more than a fiction.

Because of its emphasis upon inequality, its acceptance of the state and its superficial account of the agency–structure relationship, neo-liberalism emphasises the inherent weaknesses of classical liberalism, whilst rejecting its strengths. In neo-liberalism the dualistic nature of liberalism is particularly evident and because of these flaws, the liberal promises of security, autonomy and liberty for *all* citizens would be an impossibility in a society governed by neo-liberal principles.

In neo-liberal conceptions citizenship becomes a status divorced from notions of equality, fraternity and positive liberty. It carries with it no duties to others, but entails rights to be unequal and to assert that inequality, whilst being protected by a minimal, but coercive, state.

Having established in Part I that there are inherent problems with liberal theories of citizenship, this book will now analyse how Thatcherism drew upon neo-liberalism in an attempt to redefine citizenship in modern Britain and thereby overcome these liberal dilemmas.

PART II

LIBERAL CITIZENSHIP
IN PRACTICE

5

THATCHERISM, NEO-LIBERALISM AND CITIZENSHIP

In Part II of this book we turn from a purely theoretical discussion of liberal theories of citizenship to an examination of citizenship in practice in modern Britain. The focus of this part of the book will be upon liberal citizenship and its application and dysfunctions during the Thatcherite era, which will be the term used throughout the remainder of the book to refer to the period of Conservative government between 1979–90 and 1990–7, under the leadership of Margaret Thatcher and John Major respectively.

A central argument of this work is that the Thatcherite governments drew upon neo-liberalism to redefine citizenship in modern Britain. The rights of citizenship, in particular social rights, were reduced or challenged, and the government emphasised personal responsibility and a defence of market rights as the best guarantee of wealth and liberty. The rolling back of the frontiers of citizenship rights and the assertion of duty and self-reliance were seen by the government as a necessary response to the following factors:

- The legitimacy crisis of the social liberal consensus prior to the election of Margaret Thatcher in 1979: such a crisis was identified by both writers on the left, such as Habermas (1976), and commentators from the right, such as Beer (1982). According to such theorists as Habermas, in attempting to reconcile the diverse interests of capitalist society, the state under the social liberal consensus had reached a state of crisis where it could no longer deliver on its promises of social welfare and increased profitability of private enterprise.
- The increasingly global nature of the world economy meant that many of the rights of citizenship associated with the social liberal consensus were, argued the Thatcherites, unnecessary and unaffordable.
- The decline of active citizenship associated with the values of self-reliance, it was argued, led to the increasing dependency of many

members of society on the welfare state and the subsequent creation of a dangerous underclass.

It will be argued that the Thatcherite governments asserted a conception of citizenship that was elitist and exclusive, and which increased the sense of insecurity and powerlessness felt by many citizens in Britain. The Thatcherite project emphasised the incoherent nature of citizenship in the liberal tradition by making explicit the division between active and passive citizens.

In Chapter 6 the pre-conditions for the development of Thatcherism will be explored in the light of economic, political and ideological circumstances in modern Britain. Chapters 7 and 8 explore in detail how Thatcherite policies resulted in an increasing divide between active and passive citizens. However, it is necessary, given the argument of this book, first to clearly define Thatcherism. In particular, it is essential to explore the relationship between Thatcherism and the liberal theories of citizenship analysed in Part I of this book.

This chapter will therefore be concerned with two main questions. First, to what extent was Thatcherism an essentially neo-liberal strategy to redefine the relationship between the state and the citizen? Second, did the fall from office of the key architect of Thatcherism, namely Margaret Thatcher in 1990, signal the end of the Thatcherite project?

THATCHERISM AND NEO-LIBERALISM

The connection between neo-liberalism and the Thatcher governments, and how Thatcherism should best be defined, has been a topic for debate amongst politicians and academics, even before the actual term was coined (by Stuart Hall in the late 1970s). As Jessop et al. state in their study of Thatcherism, 'Thatcherism sometimes seems to have acquired almost as many meanings as there are people who mention it' (Jessop et al., 1988: 5).

It will be argued here that liberalism (specifically its neo-liberal variant) formed the foundation of Thatcherism and informed its conceptions of citizenship in Britain. Thatcherism aimed to transform the relationship between the state, as a provider of social citizenship, and the individual whose freedom (it was argued) had been undermined by social rights. Speaking in 1983 Thatcher made clear her guiding principle towards citizenship when she commented that 'we offered a complete change in direction. I think we have altered the balance between the person and the state in a favourable way' (cited in Gilmour, 1992: 108).

THATCHER FOR HAYEK

The main figure, seen by many commentators as the connection between Thatcherism and liberalism, has been Frederick Hayek. Key actors in the construction of Thatcherism, as an alternative paradigm to the social liberal consensus, such as Keith Joseph, various prominent figures in several right-wing think-tanks, and indeed Thatcher herself, have made clear the importance of Hayek's work in shaping their beliefs. As Lord Thomas observed in the 1980s, 'I would guess that Hayek's *Constitution of Liberty* and the three volumes of *Law, Legislation and Liberty* have been the most influential books behind the present leadership' (cited in Loney, 1986: 5).

Thatcher confirmed the centrality of Hayek in the two volumes of her memoirs, *The Downing Street Years* (1993), and *The Path to Power* (1995). Thatcher saw Hayek's work as a powerful attack on collectivism that reinforced her instinctive support for individual freedom and the power of market forces. Interestingly, Thatcher identifies collectivism as a force affecting her own Tory Party prior to her reassertion of its 'true essence' beginning with her election as party leader in 1975. The social liberal consensus was seen by Thatcher as the result of an unholy conspiracy between socialists in all political parties. Tellingly, in *The Downing Street Years*, she discusses socialism and 'High Toryism' in the same breath, implying that they come from the same collectivist origins.

Commenting on the superficial appeal of collectivism and equality to those privileged intellectual socialists or wealthy and aristocratic Tories she says, 'seen from below, however, it looked very different. Fair shares somehow always turn out to be small shares' (Thatcher, 1993: 12–13). Thatcher's rejection of paternalistic conservatism, and her view of the correct relationship between citizen and state clearly shows Hayek's influence:

> Our inspiration was less Rab Butler's *Industrial Charter* than books like Colin Brogan's anti-socialist satire *Our New Masters* . . . and Hayek's powerful *The Road to Serfdom*, dedicated to 'the socialists of all parties' . . . It left a permanent mark on my own political character, making me a long term optimist for free enterprise and liberty. (Thatcher, 1993: 12–13)

Thatcher defined her aim as leader to restore to the Conservative Party the policies and principles that had been abandoned by the 'traitors' of the consensus era. She argued strongly that Edward Heath's abandonment of neo-liberal policies in 1972 resulted in 'the most radical form of socialism ever contemplated by an elected British Government' (Thatcher, 1993: 7).

Following her election as leader of the Conservative Party she sought to construct, along with her allies such as Keith Joseph, a counter revolution against collectivism within her own party and indeed in the country as a whole. In the process Thatcher wished to redefine the Conservative Party in terms of the neo-liberalism of Hayek: 'I was again asking the Conservative Party to put its faith in freedom and free markets, limited government, and a strong defence' (Thatcher, 1993: 15). However, according to Thatcher these principles were not alien to the party. She argued that liberalism had always been a central part of traditional Conservative Party thinking, and that it had been betrayed by the paternalistic and aristocratic Tories who dominated the party prior to her election as leader. She argued that 'the traditional economic liberalism which constituted so important a part of my political make up, and which Edmund Burke himself embraced, was often alien to conservatives from a more elevated social background' (Thatcher, 1995: 50–1).

Thatcher was particularly concerned to counter, and reverse, the development of social citizenship which had developed in Britain since 1945 and which had been a cornerstone of the post-war consensus. Hayek's brand of neo-liberalism was particularly appealing to Thatcher because it did not question the importance of the state and accorded with Thatcher's view that 'it was the job of government to establish a framework of stability' (Thatcher, 1993: 14). In *The Path to Power* Thatcher states that as early as her undergraduate days at Oxford she was pondering Hayek's work and returned to it again in the mid-1970s when Hayek's works 'were right at the top of the reading list' given to her by Keith Joseph (Thatcher, 1995: 50–1).

Thatcher, then, was clearly a leader who regarded intellectual ideas and theories as crucial to developing a strategy which would alter the relationship between the state and citizen by increasing personal freedom in the market place. Some commentators have dismissed the notion of Thatcher spending time studying Hayek as an attempt to give Thatcherism intellectual creditability (Keegan, 1984: 81–2). However, close associates of Thatcher have noted the importance of neo-liberal ideas to the development of Thatcherism.

In his biography of Thatcher, H. Young comments that 'of all post-war Prime Ministers, she both used intellectuals and exhibited a studied interest in political ideas to a greater extent than any other' (Young, 1991: 405). In discussing the specific impact of Hayek on Thatcherism and its exponents, Young states that 'behind them all lurked the contentious but revered figure of Hayek, who while always insisting he was a liberal not a conservative, had such a formative part in shaping the Thatcherite vision' (Young, 1991: 407). It is clear from many of

Thatcher's speeches in opposition that Hayek had a tremendous influence upon her thought, for example in 1977 she gave a speech to the Zurich Economic Society which at times read like passages from *The Road to Serfdom*:

> The economic success of the Western world is a product of its moral philosophy and practice; the economic results are better because the moral philosophy is superior. It is superior because it starts with the individual, with his uniqueness, his responsibility, his capacity to choose. (Thatcher, 1977: 51)

Thatcher was not the only prominent Conservative to be influenced by Hayek in the 1970s. As Thatcher herself commented, a key figure in the development of Thatcherism was Keith Joseph, who more than any other individual shifted the Conservative Party to neo-liberal doctrines. Thatcher argued, 'I could not have become leader of the opposition nor achieved what I did as Prime Minister without Keith' (Thatcher, 1995: 251). The influence of Hayek and neo-liberalism upon Joseph is clear from his many speeches and publications while the Conservatives were in opposition between 1974 and 1979.

In his Upminster speech of 22 June 1974, he attacked 'thirty years of socialistic fashions', and argued that the public sector was 'draining away the wealth created by the private sector' (cited in Thatcher, 1995: 251–4). Joseph, like Hayek, was concerned that citizenship was being undermined by an overbearing state and a misplaced search for equality through the development of social rights guaranteed by the state. Joseph echoes Hayek in his book *Equality* when he opens by stating that 'the object of this book is to challenge one of the central prejudices of modern British politics, the belief that it is a proper function of the state to influence the distribution of wealth for its own sake' (Joseph and Sumption, 1979: 1). Joseph and Thatcher joined together in the mid-1970s to form the neo-liberal think-tank the Centre for Policy Studies, and from that point on were committed to redefining the balance between the state and the rights citizens could expect to receive. Friends and opponents of the Thatcherite takeover of the Conservative Party were in little doubt that neo-liberalism lay at the core of Thatcherism. For example, Gamble argues that Thatcherism 'favoured a return to the principles of classical liberalism; free markets and limited government. Limited government, however, does not mean weak government. The state has to be strong to police the market order' (Gamble, 1994: 5–6; see also Keegan, 1984: 15; Cockett, 1994).

This view was echoed by right-wingers as well as commentators on the left. Famously, the economic liberal Milton Friedman stated that

'Margaret Thatcher was not in terms of beliefs a Tory. She is a nineteenth-century liberal' (*The Observer*, 26 September 1982). A member of her first cabinet in 1979, John Nott, agreed that people like himself and Margaret Thatcher were essentially liberals. Another cabinet minister in Thatcher's first government, Ian Gilmour, has argued that 'Thatcherism largely consisted of nineteenth-century individualism dressed up in twentieth-century clothes. As with the Manchester liberalism of the last century, economic dogma was at its core' (Gilmour, 1992: 9).

The connections, then, between Thatcherism and neo-liberalism are very clear. Several questions arise, however, as to whether Thatcherism was a complete break with past Conservative governments, and what was the relationship between more traditional conservative thought and Thatcherism.

CONSERVATISM AND LIBERALISM

The first problem in comparing liberalism with conservatism is that it is very difficult to establish what conservatism as a theoretical approach entails. Many commentators of conservatism have tended to define it in terms of a pragmatic and undogmatic approach to government, rather than a distinct ideology (White, 1964). Honderich (1990) has stressed conservatism's emphasis upon self and selfishness, rather than any coherent beliefs about society and government, as its key characteristic. Gilmour (1992) has argued that conservatism should avoid ideological dogma and respond in a commonsense way to the real needs of an evolving society. Disraeli has summarised a similar perspective on the correct approach for a Conservative government to take:

> In a progressive country change is constant; and the great question is not whether you should resist change which is inevitable, but whether that change should be carried out in deference to the manners, the customs, the laws, and the traditions of the people, or whether it should be carried out in deference to abstract principles, and arbitrary and general doctrines. (cited in Gamble, 1994: 139)

Such a vague notion of what conservatism is has led Hayek to argue that he is not a conservative because conservatives are 'opportunists in their political practice and lacked a principled commitment to the maintenance of the conditions for a free society' (Hayek, 1960: postscript). This stance, however, reflects Hayek's highly abstract approach to social problems more than it reinforces the point that Conservative politicians can never be driven by ideology. In practice, any politician will be faced with the problem of gaining and maintaining office, and this of course has faced politicians of all political persuasions from Gladstone to Lenin. The fact that politicians have to be politically expedient to some extent does not mean that in essence a politician, from any party, cannot still be an ideologue. As Gilmour points out, 'the ideological consistency cannot be maintained in the council chamber or the corridors of power' (Gilmour, 1992: 270). Thatcher clearly rejected notions of compromise and slow, evolutionary change. Whilst obviously constrained by events, she committed herself (more than any other recent Prime Minister) to a clear political programme based on ideology.

Some commentators have denied that the ideology that Thatcherism asserted was anything other than conservatism. Letwin (1992) and Willetts (1992) deny that Thatcherism was a form of liberalism. For Letwin, Thatcherism was essentially a conservative project concerned with regenerating the morals of the national community. Willetts asserts that writers who argue that Thatcherism was a rejection of traditional conservatism are 'quite simply wrong' (Willetts, 1992: 52). The rest of this section will be concerned with refuting the claims of writers like Letwin and Willetts.

Willetts particularly emphasises the point that support for the free market is a traditional part of conservatism. However, his argument, rather than refuting the point that Thatcherism was essentially neo-liberal in its ideological approach, lends weight to the argument that in practice liberalism, and particularly the neo-liberalism of Hayek, is largely indistinguishable from authoritarian conservatism.

Certainly Willetts is right to point to the importance of free markets to Conservative governments in the past as well as the present. Thatcher herself argues that conservatism contains a connection to economic liberalism even within its most eminent figures such as Burke. As MacPherson points out, the debate concerning how best to define Burke's political and social thought has a long history. Marx, Laski and others have interpreted Burke as a liberal thinker and MacPherson himself points to the importance of liberal political economy in shaping Burke's perspective on the free market (MacPherson, 1980: 53). In fact, there are no serious differences on the desired role of the function of government between Adam Smith and Burke. Both agree that the government should be strictly limited: 'laissez-faire and decentralisation are sovereign in Burke' (Nisbet, 1986: 58), or as Eccleshall puts it, 'there was no more ardent exponent than Burke of the advantages of unregulated capitalism' (Eccleshall, 1984b: 84).

Other important Conservative figures have shown their support for economic liberalism. The Thatcherite free-market agenda had some roots in other free-market Conservatives such as Enoch Powell in the post-war period, and in the 1930s Neville Chamberlain was a strong advocate of laissez-faire economics (Glynn, 1991: 130). As far back as the 1880s and 1890s the Conservative Party was committed to a notion of limited state interference with property, and minimal intervention in the market (Gamble, 1994: 154–7). Even the so-called one-nation Tory Disraeli was in essence a free marketeer. As Ryan argues, 'the Tory left goes on about Disraeli being the great "one nation" person, but he believed straightforwardly in laissez-faire everywhere' (Ryan, 1986: 31). Nisbet argues that Disraeli's (limited) social reforms were motivated by the need to secure working class votes rather than any commitment to social rights. Because of the changing political circumstance of the late nineteenth century Disraeli was forced to 'trim his sails to the [social] liberal wind' (Nisbet, 1986: 59). This is an important point since it illustrates the contingent nature of conservatism in government and shows how such government will be necessarily shaped by structural factors and social change.

Thatcher herself acknowledges even her immediate predecessor Edward Heath had predated many of her policies in the so-called 'Selsdon programme' adopted in the first part of his government between 1970 and 1974. As Thatcher comments, the Selsdon programme, which stressed essentially neo-liberal economic management, 'seemed to foreshadow much of what we later came to call Thatcherism' (Thatcher, 1993: 13).

I would argue that, contrary to Willetts, in practice conservatism has much more in common with liberalism than is usually acknowledged. Even a Conservative sympathiser Norman Barry has argued that 'liberals and conservatives have a lot more in common than the leading spokesmen of either tendency are prepared to admit' (Barry, 1987: preface, ii).

THATCHERISM AS AUTHORITARIAN LIBERALISM?

The neo-liberalism of Hayek provides an important link between classical liberalism and conservatism and was adopted by the Conservative Party under Thatcher in the mid 1970s. Particularly important ideas shared by Thatcherism and the neo-liberalism of Hayek are the centrality of the individual, the dismissal of abstract notions of society, the importance of inequality in providing incentives to people, a rejection of collectivism, the need for a strong state to uphold the rule of law, and the superiority of the market in creating and maintaining prosperity and freedom. I wish to argue that the ideological core of Thatcherism was neo-liberal and its conception of citizenship was consistent with the political theory of writers like Hayek.

Thatcherism had at root the defence of individual liberty and the protection of the free market as the best source of that freedom and economic prosperity. Thatcher famously said in 1987 that 'there is no such thing as society' (interview in *Woman's Own*, 31 October 1987), thus echoing the criticisms by neo-liberals of abstract notions of society. Willetts argues unconvincingly that this statement was not an illustration of Thatcher's commitment to liberalism. Rather she was concerned with showing that 'we could not evade personal responsibility for our actions by saying that everything we did wrong was really society's fault' (Willetts, 1992: 48). This argument does not however refute the fact that Thatcher essentially saw the duties of citizenship as being individualised. As we shall see in Chapters 7 and 8, for the Thatcherites the primary duty of individuals was to themselves: duty to others was not an act of citizenship, but of charity. Thatcherism asserted the Hayekian rejection of citizenship as a status that denotes the interdependence of individuals in a political community.

Letwin has argued that individualism was at the heart of the Thatcherite project, which had as its main goal the promotion of the 'vigorous virtues' of self-sufficiency, energy, and robust opposition to enemies (Letwin, 1992: 32–3). Thatcherism, according to Letwin, can best be viewed as an attempt to achieve 'a paradigm shift in the relation between the government and the governed'. In this sense Thatcherite policies were more about reinvigorating citizenship through the promotion of individual autonomy than an economic project. Personal ownership, through the privatisation programmes, was promoted because it encouraged independence. High inflation was a target because it undermined savings, which also promote independence. Trade union and local government reforms were carried out because both were seen as potential seed beds for socialism, and as undermining the vigorous virtues of choice and independent thought. Even the poll tax is interpreted by Letwin as 'an experiment in autonomy' (Letwin, 1992: 198).

Letwin, however, rejects the nihilistic view of individualism offered by libertarians. She argues that Thatcherism reasserted an age-old 'distinctive but unidentified British morality', which had been undermined by continental influences in the nineteenth century and which had at its centre an individualism that is 'untainted by nihilism; it is a sceptical morality because it lays no claims to be based on truths beyond human questioning' (Letwin, 1992: 352). For Letwin such an individualism is moral and rooted in tradition and the nation. Therefore, Thatcherism represented a restoration of traditional conservative truths.

Whilst Letwin is right to emphasise the importance to Thatcherism of reasserting individualism as an ideological goal, her case is open to criticism. It is difficult to differentiate between vigorous virtues and a selfish authoritarianism which asserts the needs of the 'strong' against the weak and powerless. Her definition of British individualism as being based on scepticism and a lack of fundamental truths does not square with the Thatcherite insistence on the 'rightfulness' of their polices and their intolerance of deviations from the 'norm'. Letwin is right that Thatcherism was to some extent a moral crusade; but it was a project which utilised a very narrow set of criteria to assess individual success or failure. Those who cannot succeed on those narrow terms were condemned in deeply moralistic terms. Also, as Giddens has argued, the Thatcherite emphasis on markets actually undermined the fabric of the nation and unleashed 'detraditionalising forces of a quite far reaching kind' (Giddens, 1994: 40).

Letwin is unconvincing in her defence of a distinctive Thatcherite individuality. Thatcherism had little time for those who could not succeed on their merits, and Thatcher herself made it clear that her policies would not be hindered by what she called 'bourgeois guilt', which she identified as a distinctly upper class failing.

Thatcherism, like neo–liberalism, celebrated inequality in society as natural and as a reflection of people's worth. In *The Path to Power* Thatcher makes clear her belief that many people fail in society because they are unworthy and should find little sympathy from the rest of 'society'. With such a view Thatcherism carried to its logical conclusion the abstract and elitist logic of the individualism in neo–liberal political theory.

Because of their perspective on the relationship between society and the individual, Thatcherites argued that individuals were best left to make free choices in the market place and to take responsibility for their own actions and mistakes. Thatcherism ignored the importance of social structures in shaping people's lives and increasing or decreasing their opportunities. In terms of public policy this agency-based approach unifies liberals and conservatives who refuse to explain social behaviour in any terms other than personal choice. Indeed, although the Thatcherite emphasis on 'Victorian values' is sometimes contrasted with a rationalist liberal position (Letwin, 1992), the differences between liberalism and conservatism are greatly exaggerated. Essentially Victorian values amounted to the doctrines of self-help and thrift, which are as much liberal values, as they are conservative (Eccleshall, 1984b: 86). As we saw in Chapter 3, the social liberalism of Mill and Green is essentially concerned with the development of 'character', which has an image of an 'ideal' individual, the characteristics of which are very close to the vigorous virtues of Thatcherism (Bellamy, 1992: 9–58).

Also, the Thatcherite notion that individuals who failed in the market system were in some way to blame for that failure had its roots, not in conservatism, but in various forms of liberalism. For example, Locke justified extremely draconian treatment of the poor on the grounds that social problems such as unemployment were due to 'moral depravity' (MacPherson, 1962: 222–9). Spencer's views were perhaps even more extreme. He spoke of 'the poverty of the incapable, the disasters that come upon the imprudent, the starvation of the idle, and those shoulderings aside of the weak by the strong' (cited in Perkin, 1989: 142–3). Despite theoretical tensions, in practice the difference between conservatism and certain forms of liberalism are minimal.

An element of traditional conservatism normally identified by commentators is the notion of a natural social hierarchy (Nisbet, 1986: 34–46), and this is normally opposed to the classical liberal idea of formal equality between individuals. In Thatcherism, however, liberalism and conservatism were united. First, when in power Thatcher made clear her personal distaste and hostility to 'High Tories' and she had an infamously bad relationship with other established hierarchies such as the Royal Family. In general, Thatcher and her followers asserted the importance of individual effort (rather than privilege) in achieving success. As Wilson points out, however, Thatcher was seemingly oblivious to her own privileged background (Wilson, 1992: 61–7). Second, and more fundamentally, in Hayek's work the conservative and neo-liberal views of inequality are brought together. Inequality is inevitable and therefore the consequence for public policy under Thatcherism was to 'let our children grow tall and some grow taller than others' (Hayek, cited in Wilson, 1992: 33).

Thatcherism embraced the doctrines of free markets as the best incentive to bring out natural differences between people and to provide a motor for innovation and invention. Therefore, Thatcherism rejected collectivism and particularly socialist solutions. Thatcher made it clear throughout her reign that her aim was not merely to defeat the Labour Party at the ballot box but to crush socialism forever. The market was seen as vastly superior to state planning and interestingly Thatcherism, like Hayek's political thought, made little or no distinction between the 'mild' collectivism of the social liberal consensus, which developed after the second world war, and communism. In Thatcher's eyes 'guilt-ridden' aristocratic Tories, who advocated state intervention, were just as dangerous as 'socialists' in other political parties. As Wilson contends, central to Thatcherism was the need to free individuals from state interference and from too much concern for those less fortunate than themselves. As Wilson puts it:

> Instead of the deadly levelling climate of collectivism and chronic guilt feelings about the needs of others, there is warrant for triumphant competitive

individualism, enterprise, a buccaneering (or Samurai) spirit and a robust refusal of
the strong either to shoulder the problems of the world or to be ashamed of not
doing so. (Wilson, 1992: 34)

The Thatcherites, reflecting the influence of Hayek, showed little desire
to encourage the kind of compromises involved with democracy. We shall
see (in Chapter 6) how the institutions of British politics enabled
Thatcherism to govern with little mandate to do so, and it is worth
noting that the anti-democratic elements of Hayek's work outlined in
Chapter 4 are also common in traditional forms of conservatism, both in
the theoretical and political sense (Wilson, 1992: 15; Nisbet, 1986: 43–6).

Regarding the role of the state, I would argue that the logic of the neo-
liberal position was put in place under Thatcherism. We have seen how
the institution of the state is a problematic one for all liberals, and this
problem is particularly acute in neo-liberal theory. I will briefly return to
the neo-liberal perspective on the state to illustrate why the logic of
Thatcherism required a strong state.

Neo-liberals, like Hayek and Nozick, argue that the state should be
strictly limited, providing a framework for the working of the market
place. It should protect natural rights, in the case of Nozick, or the Rule of
Law in the case of Hayek. Hayek discusses the state as if it is a given, and
ironically Nozick is criticised from an anarchist position for providing a
defence of the state (Holmes, 1982). In this sense neo-liberalism seems
very close to authoritarian conservatism since both thinkers accept the
notion of the state as an inevitable institution which may act in a coercive
fashion.

Nozick's attempt to protect individuals from an over powerful state
through the doctrine of natural rights is weak because he does not accept
the classical liberal notions of a state of nature and the social contract,
which lends some weight to the theory of natural rights. Once the
commitment to an idea of individuals contracting themselves out of a
state of nature is abandoned, the idea of natural rights seems to rest on
little more than an assertion by Nozick of the need to protect the wealthy
and successful from claims by the less successful members of society.

Neo-liberalism is also weak in its analysis of the relationship between
the state and the market. Both Hayek and Nozick want to argue that the
market should dominate, but allow for the fact that in practice it may not.
For example, we have seen how Nozick's theory is weakened by the fact
that he accepts that in his native America inequality may have more to do
with racism, class and sexism than ability. By accepting this fact he
accepts the need for a strong state to eradicate unjust inequality and to
create the conditions for markets to work properly. Hayek also recognises

that many societies have developed in ways contrary to his desired spontaneous order. He does not make it clear how in practice collectivism could be reversed. Again the need for a strong state emerges to create the conditions for a spontaneous order to exist. Hayek's theory is contradictory because he accepts, indeed he defends, the importance of tradition in the evolution of societies but then rails against this when it produces 'traditions', like the development of social rights in post-war Britain, which he does not agree with.

What emerges from the logic of neo-liberalism is that to create a 'free economy', a strong state is required to create the conditions for the operation of the market. This may not be as contradictory as it sounds, for a distinctive feature of neo-liberalism is its highly abstract approach to notions of the market and the state. Thatcherism was faced with the difficulties of putting an abstract theory into practice. The problems and consequences of the Thatcherite experiment can be interpreted, not as a weak commitment on the behalf of Thatcherites to neo-liberal ideas, but rather they illustrate the flawed assumptions of such theories when applied to the real world. Gamble (1994: 42) has pointed to the apparent contradictions of a commitment to a free market and a strong state: 'citizens have to be forced to be free, otherwise there is no guarantee they will be so'. Thus Thatcherism was 'laissez-faire in its attitude to the private sector' but also the 'Thatcher government [was involved in] highly interventionist and centralist policies' (Gamble, 1994: Ch. 5). However, as I have argued, such apparent contradictions reflect a deep problem in liberal theory. The very logic of a neo-liberal perspective, with its emphasis on inequality, individual responsibility and market forces, necessitates a strong state to undermine the importance of institutions which mediate between the individual citizen and the state such as trade unions, pressure groups, local government and the media (Gilmour, 1992: 198–220). A strong state is also required to police those individuals who do not take their 'failure' in the market place in their stride and instead turn to crime, disorder and forms of 'deviant' behaviour which threaten private property and the capitalist market. Gilmour summarises well the consistent logic of Thatcherism:

> There was no paradox in rhetoric about 'liberty' and the rolling back of the state being combined in practice with centralisation and the expansion of the state's frontiers. The establishment of individualism and a free-market state is an unbending if not dictatorial venture which demands the prevention of collective action and the submission of dissenting institutions and individuals. (Gilmour, 1992: 223)

For conservatives like Gilmour, this philosophy is deeply unconservative since it attacks the 'little platoons' of social life which mediate between the individual and the state. As Nisbet argues, the 'chief accusation' made against liberalism by conservatives is that liberalism necessarily involves a systematic erosion of the social structure by dissolving collective consciousness into individualism (Nisbet, 1986: 50). The logic of Thatcherism in this regard was again more liberal than conservative.

The apparent contradiction between a strong state and a free market brings out a fundamental tension within liberal theory which can be expressed as a dualism between the abstract liberal view of freedom (which is, according to liberals, best delivered by the market) and equality, which applies only to the political sphere and should be strictly limited to avoid interference with the market. In neo-liberalism this tension between the economic and the political becomes particularly acute. The supposed superiority of the market in increasing freedom is contrasted with 'political' solutions to problems which involve the suppression of freedom in the name the 'common good' or 'social justice'. In neo-liberal theory politics is equated solely with statism: politics, the state and government are seen, in effect, as one and the same, and are viewed as equally harmful to the spontaneous order of the market. However, a paradox arises in neo-liberal theory because of its acceptance of the state. The state on the one hand is seen as hostile to the market, with its tendency to grow through democratic pressures and to take on functions which undermine the market, but on the other hand it is seen as a tool to protect the market and enforce market principles. The logic of this position is to reduce democracy and decisions taken in a political rather than economic manner, whilst maintaining a strong coercive state to prevent interference in the market by the 'envious', 'lazy', 'criminally minded', or 'weak'. This is the position of Hayek, which was adopted by Thatcherism. Such a defence of the strong state means that inevitably such a state will work in the interests of powerful elites who have institutionalised their power through the state machine.

What emerges from an analysis of neo-liberalism is its elitist view of democracy and the fear of the 'masses' usurping the natural order of things. The neo-liberals' confusion over the desirability of a truly participatory society and the nature of the state places it, in practice, very close to authoritarian conservatism. I would argue that these problems surfaced in the form of Thatcherism. Under Thatcherism the state became a tool to promote economic liberalism, and to protect the foundations of a market economy, such as private property, from individuals who failed to succeed on their own merits. Essentially, from this perspective, the state exists to serve the interests of inequality in civil society. Neo-liberalism wants to limit the state but, as we have witnessed under Thatcherism, the failings of other aspects of neo-liberal policy require the state to be strong.

The final area where conservatism and liberalism are often seen to diverge is in the relative importance placed upon the concept of the nation. As Willetts (1992: 65–79) argues, the centrality of the nation is something that Thatcher shared with her conservative predecessors from all wings of the party, and was an important part of Thatcherism's popular appeal, as a unifying symbol used against enemies without and within. Liberalism, however, with its emphasis on free trade seems to offer the transcendence of the nation.

However, in reality liberalism has accepted that the nation is the only legitimate political community. Even those liberals such as Cobden and Bright, who were highly optimistic about the prospects of free trade uniting rather than dividing people, did not foresee the end of the nation (Read, 1967: 233–49). Rather, they saw a world order based upon sovereign nation-states engaged in co-operation through market mechanisms which would generate harmony and peace. Indeed, as has been argued throughout this book, liberalism has an essentially abstract, elitist and exclusive view of citizenship, which in practice has been strongly identified with the nation from the French Revolution onwards (Brubaker, 1992).

Liberal democracies like Britain have been economically successful largely because (ironically, given the supposedly progressive nature of liberal democracy) they have been able to exploit other nations through the maintenance of an empire or through the inequalities of world trade. In practice, then, liberalism and conservatism have converged on this issue of the nation, particularly in the twentieth century. Of particular importance in uniting conservative and liberals on the need for a strong nation was the reality of international relations, which saw the development of enemies common to liberalism and conservatism; that is, the rise of the collectivist ideologies of communism and fascism in the early part of the century. These common enemies provided an even greater rationale for a strong state. Classical liberalism and conservatism converged in works like Hayek's *The Road to Serfdom*, which also identified social liberalism as a threat to the capitalist nations. Rivalries between communism and the so-called 'free' world were institutionalised in the cold war from the end of the second world war.

The development of an increasingly global economy in the 1970s also pushed conservatives closer to liberalism in their embrace of free-market economics. As Gamble argues, 'for many British conservatives the free economy came to signify not just a national but an international economic space' (Gamble, 1994: 38).

The commitment to the nation by the Thatcherite governments from 1979 onwards became increasingly bound up with the place of the British nation within the wider global economy; indeed the dictums of free markets and deregulation became equated with the interests of the nation. Those opposed to free markets were, therefore, opposed to the nation and were identified as 'enemies within', subverting the struggle against communism and undermining the 'free' world led by America, with Britain at its side.

Overall, Thatcherism was most certainly a doctrine of radicalism that attempted to reverse the traditions and values of the post-war period, which remained strong in people's minds throughout the Thatcherite years. Thatcher declared her intention to follow a path of conviction rather than consensus and to alter fundamentally the relationship between individual citizens and the state. It has been argued here that liberalism and conservatism were united in Thatcherism through a common commitment to a coherent set of beliefs and doctrines. To summarise, these were:

- An assertion of a hierarchy of inequality, which was seen as natural and desirable, and the rejection of the claims of 'society' upon the will of individual agents.
- The superiority of the free market over state planning in providing for individual freedom and prosperity.
- A rejection of social explanations for 'deviant behaviour'. Such acts were due to individual failings, rather than structured inequality.
- Support for a strong state that protected individuals' market rights.
- A rejection of collectivism, and particularly socialist or social liberal variants.
- A suspicion of democracy and the growth of social rights resulting from the extension of political rights.
- Support for a nation that was liberal and capitalist as a bulwark against 'collectivist' enemies, whether they be internal or external to the nation.
- A view of social organisation that saw order as being created by a free economy and strong state, and was intolerant to those who threatened the dominant individualistic and market values.

The implications of Thatcherism for citizenship reflected the neo-liberal perspective discussed in Chapter 4. Citizenship was a legal status denoting membership of Britain, which must be limited to ensure the continuing purity of 'Englishness' as an example of the 'superior' values of Western civilisation (Hayek, 1944). Thatcherism rejected the 'collectivist' social rights which developed under the post-war consensus, asserted the doctrines of personal responsibility and defended abstract market rights to protect the operations of the market and private property.

Citizenship, then, was seen by the Thatcherites as best delivered through the market. As Gamble argues, the Thatcherite vision of citizenship was one where freedom would best be achieved through 'the daily plebiscite in the market' rather than through the 'infrequent plebiscite in the political system' (Gamble, 1994: 57).

Before we turn to the political and economic context of the development of Thatcherism, it is necessary to ask the question, to what extent did the fall of Margaret Thatcher mean the end of Thatcherism? It is to that question I will now turn.

THATCHERISM AFTER THATCHER?

In 1990 Margaret Thatcher was thrown out of office by a combination of nervous backbenchers, fearing they would lose their seats at the next general election, and cabinet ministers who had fallen out personally with Thatcher and/or had ambitions of their own which could not be fulfilled under her premiership. A key question that was asked was whether Thatcherism would survive the fall from office of its main creator.

I would argue that in essence the replacement of Thatcher with Major did not herald a new distinctive era of 'Majorism' but instead saw the continuation of Thatcherism by other means (Evans and Taylor, 1996: 247). The neo-liberal ideology of Thatcherism pervaded and dominated the Major agenda. Apparent deviations from its central values can be shown to be either shifts in style rather than in substance, or a shift in tactics rather than strategy. The Thatcherite vision of a new relationship between state and citizen continued to be applied after her demise.

Certainly, Thatcher herself, if not welcoming her own fall from power, expressed support for the Conservative Party in its choice for succession. Commenting on Major's election she made clear that he had, for some time, been her personal choice for succession: 'it's what I always dreamed of and hoped for' (cited in Hogg and Hill, 1995: 3). Other prominent Thatcherites endorsed Major's Thatcherite credentials. For example, Norman Tebbit, commenting on the radicalism of the 1992 election manifesto, said that 'it does not depart from Thatcherite fundamentals but finds new ways of adapting them into everyday life' (cited in Hogg and Hill, 1995: 220).

The relative lack of academic books and articles exploring the tenets of

'Majorism' is itself evidence that Major's premiership did not signal a radical departure from the policies of his predecessor. In their lengthy study *The Major Effect* published in 1994, Kavanagh and Seldon conclude that the first four years of the Major government was characterised much more by continuity than change. In the twenty-five areas of policy surveyed by the various authors in their book, the overwhelming number of key policy areas can be characterised as Thatcherite. Kavanagh argues that 'it is difficult to discover a distinctive Major effect on the [political] agenda . . . he has largely accepted the Thatcher inheritance (Kavanagh, 1994: 4–5).

The differences between the Major agenda and the Thatcher agenda were largely in terms of policy style, personality and marketing of the Thatcherite approach. Smith argues that 'changes in policy were a matter of pragmatism rather than ideology' (M. Smith, 1995: 2–3). Although in 1994 Gamble wrote that Thatcher had not transformed the Conservatives into a 'Thatcherite Party' (Gamble, 1994: 213), he acknowledged in 1995 that there had indeed been a 'substantial ideological shift' within the party and that this shift has proved to be permanent (Gamble, 1995: 35). Ludlam and Smith argue that 'Major's direction has been one of implementing Thatcherism rather than challenging its key precepts. In policy area after policy area, Major has maintained the Thatcherite agenda' (Ludlam and Smith, 1995: 279).

Major, in his dealings with fellow cabinet ministers may have been more consensual than Thatcher, though this was largely forced upon him by circumstance (Hutton, 1996: 34), but in the important policy areas he was a clear Thatcherite: 'the overwhelming thrust of his policy was Thatcherite, he was found to have nothing big or new to say' (H. Young, 1994: 22). In important areas, for example civil service and local government reform, the Thatcherite agenda was speeded up (Willman, 1994: 64, K. Young, 1994: 84, 96).

The economic approach of Major was pure Thatcherism, with its emphasis on privatisation, deregulation, and tight control of inflation and commitment to lower taxes to increase individuals' incentives. In pursuit of the desired relationship between the state and citizen, and between the state and the market, Major's governments pursued policies consistent with Thatcherism. As Jay argues, Major was a 'genuinely passionate believer in free trade principles' (Jay, 1994: 197).

In the area of employment and industrial relations policy, Major also remained loyal to the Thatcherite agenda. As Taylor argues, 'Thatcher's labour market strategy was safe in their [Major's government's] hands' (Taylor, 1994: 246–65). This approach entailed increasing the flexibility of Britain's labour market, making it more responsive to market conditions: there was to be 'no obvious policy-making role for the trade unions' (Taylor, 1994: 247). The 1994 White Paper on competitiveness in British industry ruled out interventionist policies. The 1993 Trade Union and Employment Act increased restrictions upon trade unions, including the insistence upon at least seven days' warning to employers before strikes could occur, and the weakening of legislation preventing employers from discriminating against union members in conditions and pay (Hutton, 1996: 33).

In social policy the Conservatives' agenda was distinctively neo-liberal, with its emphasis on individual responsibility and the implementation of market-based strategies such as the creation of National Health Service trusts and fund holding for doctors (Pierson, 1995). Market mechanisms were increasingly applied to education and health services with hospitals, and schools and colleges encouraged to compete for patients and students on the open market (Sullivan, 1992: 183–201). Even in the final months of the Major government radical Thatcherite policies were being planned that would introduce a voucher scheme to pay for the care of elderly citizens and to reform the state pension scheme to encourage more private provision (*The Times*, 13 March 1997).

In the area of community care, Lewis concludes that 'there has been no slackening in the government's resolve to introduce market mechanisms into the public sector; Major's policy has not deviated substantially from its Thatcherite origins' (Lewis, 1994: 377). In policy towards the family, Lister contends that 'the impact on working women of his enthusiastic embrace of Thatcherite deregulation policies outweighed his more sympathetic stance towards working mothers' (Lister, 1994: 363).

Regarding European integration, it can also be argued that Major largely followed the logic of the Thatcherite agenda. In what has been called his 'Heart of Europe' speech in 1991, Major confirmed a commitment to a free market Europe of autonomous nation-states. Although Thatcher stated she would not have signed the Maastricht agreement of 1992, in fact Major managed to negotiate an opt-out from the Social Chapter (which would have increased social citizenship), and chose not to support a common currency for Europe. Debate within the Conservative Party over the issue tended not to concern the rights or wrongs of the free market but whether the market would be best served within or without the European Union.

A detailed assessment of the overall impact of Major upon British politics is beyond the scope of this work, but what is clear from the evidence above is that a high degree of continuity existed between the Thatcher and Major governments. The framework for the policies of the Major governments was provided by the Thatcher era. There was no such thing as 'Majorism' as a distinct set of policies or approaches to politics in general, and citizenship specifically. As Hogg and Hill (1995: 203–22) have argued, Major's 1992 election manifesto was radical in a Thatcherite sense and Major possessed 'strong convictions about the dignity of personal ownership'. He was wary of bureaucracy, had a 'hatred' of inflation, and remained committed to privatisation and open markets.

The few new policies or initiatives that Major instituted were essentially neo-liberal and Thatcherite (see Chapters 7 and 8). Major himself summarised his neo-liberal perspective on citizenship in several speeches prior to the 1992 general election. For instance, at the 1991 Conservative Party Conference, he spoke of 'the power to choose and the right to own'. On launching the 1992 manifesto he commended the Thatcher years, and expressed his commitment to continue along the Thatcherite path when he said, 'a new generation is coming along now – which wants to open the door wider. A generation that takes what's been done for granted, and now wants more choice. More ownership. More responsibility. And more opportunity' (cited in Hogg and Hill, 1995: 219). Perhaps we could add 'more Thatcherism'.

Stylistic differences between Thatcher and Major were evident. However, more important is the fact that Major was faced, particularly after 1992, with a more united and effective opposition. His majority in the House of Commons after the 1992 election was relatively small (21 seats) and fell regularly during his last years in office. Public opinion still rejected much of the Thatcherite agenda, and overall his room for manoeuvre was much less than Thatcher enjoyed for most of her premiership.

More fundamentally, Major inherited a position whereby British politics had radically shifted from social liberalism to neo-liberalism as the dominant model of government. This would have been difficult to reverse even if the will existed to do so. Under the Thatcher governments there had been considerable change in the way Britain was governed that can only be understood in relation to widespread social changes, which will be explored in Chapter 6.

Both the Thatcher and Major governments had at the heart of their programmes the desire to radically transform citizenship in modern Britain. The Thatcherite governments rejected the kind of citizenship advocated by social liberals like Marshall and instead sought their inspiration from the neo-liberalism of Hayek. However, in keeping with the argument that citizenship can only be understood in relation to the changing nature of British society, it is necessary to explain why the social liberal consensus was replaced by a neo-liberal vision of citizenship. In order to understand the rise of neo-liberalism one has to ask the following questions: what was it about the political culture and institutions of British politics that allowed for the advent of Thatcherism and the narrowing of citizenship? What economic factors led to its adoption by the Conservative Party in the mid-1970s? It is these questions that Chapter 6 will address.

6

THE CONTEXT OF
CITIZENSHIP IN BRITAIN

One of the primary criticisms of liberal theories of citizenship identified in this book is that they have conceived of citizenship in a way that fails to address the relationship between citizenship and the political economy of Britain in a satisfactory fashion. For example, we saw in Chapter 3 how Marshall's account of the development of citizenship in Britain contained within it an evolutionary logic. Although Marshall's account is historical, he fails to explore the relationship between social change, capitalism and citizenship and therefore fails to generate a convincing theory of citizenship grounded in the structural inequalities of British society.

The problem of generating a convincing account of the development of citizenship also bedevils other liberal theories. A key problem with the contract theory of Locke and Paine is that it is abstracted from real historical developments. Neo-liberal thinkers like Nozick also analyse citizen–state relations in an abstract way. In neo-liberalism, the state is 'naturalised', and consequently neo-liberals do not adequately explore the relationship between the state and capitalism. This chapter represents an attempt to transcend abstract liberal accounts by presenting a theory of citizenship that places its development in political and economic context.

CAPITALISM, THE STATE AND CITIZENSHIP

In recent years many writers, in trying to explain the ascendancy of Thatcherism, have drawn upon the work of Gramsci (1971) to develop frameworks for understanding change in the British state and economy. Such an approach is also useful in explaining the reasons why citizenship has developed in the way that it has in Britain, and therefore will be the starting point for the theory of citizenship developed in this work.

One such theory, which has been highly influential, has been developed by the regulation school of thought associated with figures like Aglietta (1979) and Lipietz (1985). This approach analyses the way in which the inherently unstable capitalist system attempts to maintain its profitability by adapting its 'regime of accumulation' and its associated 'mode of social and political regulation' to the changes brought about through recession, competition and political struggle, all of which may undermine the profitability of private enterprise.

As Harvey argues, there are two main areas within a capitalist economy which need to be successfully managed. These are 'the anarchic qualities of price-fixing markets' and the need to 'exert sufficient control over the way labour is deployed' (Harvey, 1990: 122). In practice, because the 'anarchic' market is unable by itself to guarantee stability in these areas, both problems require state intervention to regulate the market.

At certain historical junctures, increased state intervention has been necessary to maintain the stability of capitalist accumulation, and the nature and extent of this intervention will be shaped by the particularities of the crisis faced, the political culture of the particular nation, the place of the state in the wider international economy, and the homogeneity and cohesiveness of the various social classes involved in the struggle for resources and power. There is an identifiable tension between the liberal rhetoric of the free market and the reality faced by states in managing capitalism and overcoming its inherent instabilities.

It will be argued that the way in which citizenship is defined is bound up with the tension between the capitalist free market and the need for states to regulate, legitimise and stabilise their regimes. The way in which citizenship is defined in any historical period is determined by the resolution of this tension. However, because of the unstable nature of capitalist accumulation, these tensions will re-emerge in any state reliant upon capitalist production and the meaning and extent of citizenship will again be contested.

Writers like Gamble (1994), Coates (1984) and Jessop (1990) have made use of the Gramscian notion of hegemony in explaining how the dominant social forces in society use particular ideological strategies to legitimise a particular regime of accumulation and its appropriate mode of social and political relations. The term hegemony is used by such writers in a wide sense to express the economic and ideological domination by economic and political elites and their use of political ideas to 'engineer consensus' for a particular strategy of government. For example, neo-liberalism was adopted by the Conservative Party as the ideology best suited to the changing conditions faced by Britain since the 1970s. Its adoption, argued the Thatcherites, was in the best interests of capitalism, as well as improving the political fortunes of the Conservative Party. Accordingly, Britain's state and economy were restructured in an attempt to ensure Britain's continued competitiveness in the global economy.

In this context citizenship appears to have a Janus-like quality. It can be interpreted as a goal for which exploited groups fight to extend their rights to equal treatment, or it can be seen as an important legitimising force which can be redefined by the powerful to justify a new set of social and economic arrangements. However, an analysis of the development of citizenship in Britain shows how these two aspects have not always been mutually exclusive but have sometimes been complementary. At certain historical junctures citizenship has been both a goal for oppressed social groups in their struggle for the extension of rights, and an ideological tool (used by ruling elites) to pacify the exploited classes or to legitimise inequalities. In this sense citizenship can act as a 'trade off' between competing social forces (MacPherson, 1985: Ch. 4). As Gramsci argues:

> Undoubtedly the fact of hegemony presupposes that account be taken of the interests and the tendencies of the groups over which hegemony is to be exercised, and that a certain compromise equilibrium should be formed; in other words, that the leading group should make sacrifices of an economic-corporate kind. (Gramsci, 1971: 161)

In the approach to social change developed in this chapter, the liberal notion of agents competing in a meritocracy for influence and resources is rejected. Power is distributed unevenly in society due to the existence of social structures such as class, gender and 'race'. These structures shape social behaviour and help to explain social inequality and division, and therefore definitions of citizenship tend to reflect the needs and interests of political and economic elites.

A useful methodological tool for analysing economic and political changes in capitalist societies has been provided by the work of Lash and Urry (1987). Such authors provide a neo–Marxist model of three stages of capitalist development, and it will be argued here that the three stages of liberalism outlined in Part I of this work correspond to these three periods of capitalist development. This correlation is expressed in Table 6.1.

Table 6.1 Stages in capitalism and the development of citizenship

	Capital	Labour	State	Military	Economy	Citizenship
Anarchic capitalism c. 1750–1870s	Small-scale competitive firms.	Mobile labour unorganised.	Repressive: *Classical Liberal State.*	Limited war. Embryonic conscription.	Laissez-faire capitalist accumulation.	Limited civil or market rights.
Managed capitalism c. 1870–1970s	Large-scale monopolistic corporations.	Organised labour movement.	Consensual: *Social Liberalism.*	Development of industrial 'total war'.	Fordism/empire. Economies of scale.	Political and social rights.
Deregulated capitalism c. 1970s–1990s	Multinational corporations. International competition.	Declining class organisation. Flexible employment.	Coercive: *Neo-Liberalism.*	High-tech warfare. Specialised professional army.	Post-Fordism. Globalisation.	Individual duties and market rights vs. social rights.

Source: Adapted from Fulcher (1991: 2).

ANARCHIC CAPITALISM

The first stage of the development of citizenship began with the evolution of capitalist modes of production in Britain from around 1750 to the 1870s. At this stage of development, companies were small, competitive operations employing a relatively small, mobile and atomised work force. This period can be seen to run parallel with the development of 'civil rights', which Marshall argues grew in the eighteenth and nineteenth centuries. Before the eighteenth century citizenship in Britain was all but non-existent, particularly for the average person. As Colley argues, the masses were expected to be 'orderly, obedient and above all passive' (Colley, 1992: 370).

British people were subjects under the Crown and not defined as citizens. Oliver and Heater argue that 'the idea of subjecthood involved the notion that the governed . . . were ignorant, unreliable and incapable of making valid judgements' (Oliver and Heater, 1994: 60). The fact that Britain remained a constitutional monarchy throughout its history has continued to have repercussions for the development of citizenship into the twentieth century. The monarch has remained a symbol of passive obedience, rather than active citizenship. It clearly signifies the dominance of England within the union, and ties British identity closely to English institutions such as the Church of England.

It was only with the development of industrialisation and urbanisation from around the 1750s onwards that the conditions were created for the extension of civil and political citizenship beyond a narrow aristocratic elite. The development of limited civil rights in the eighteenth century was linked, above all, to the rise of the bourgeoisie as an economic force and its desire to extend its freedom to trade and make safe contracts in the market. What is clear, however, is that the extent of these rights was highly limited and worked in favour of the owners of property rather than workers and women.

Industrialisation and urbanisation were crucial factors in shaping the nature of citizenship. In classical liberal political theory one of its principal assumptions was that all adult males could assert their natural rights through ownership of land either in Britain or in the new world, but with the coming of industrial society this was no longer the case, and the problem of what to do with the mass of landless people was to be a major problem for the liberal state.

The main tactic adopted by the state during this period was to oppress the 'lower' orders. Trade unions were banned and there was little or no regulation to protect the work force from exploitation, unemployment and poverty. The state reinforced patriarchy by confining women to the private sphere. As was argued in Part I of this book, the rights that developed during this period may be better termed market rights than civil rights because they were deliberately apolitical and were ideologically structured along class and gender lines. They excluded many rights which would be considered to be basic civil rights, for example freedom of association. They existed primarily to facilitate capitalist accumulation and the notion of a 'free' market was dependent upon the exploitation of the working class and the unpaid domestic labour of women.

The fact that the bourgeoisie was able, after the civil war, to extend market rights in a relatively evolutionary and peaceful way meant that Britain, unlike France or America, did not undergo a complete bourgeois revolution (Gamble, 1981: Ch. 3). This meant that although Britain was the first capitalist nation, its people paradoxically were defined from 1688 onwards as subjects rather than citizens. This has led Turner (1990: 191–214) to define British citizenship as essentially passive.

Mann (1987) has pointed to the strategic decisions of the ruling class in maintaining social cohesion by extending citizenship gradually. The ruling class has been able to maintain its hegemony by reconstituting itself through alliances and mergers between the aristocracy and bourgeoisie, and by creating coalitions or 'historic blocs' which have prevented revolution from below. This evolutionary approach to citizenship meant that, as Mosca puts it, by the 'nineteenth century England adopted peacefully and without violent shocks all the basic political and civil reforms that France paid so heavily to achieve through the Great Revolution' (Mosca, 1939: 119).

However, as Colley points out, it would be a mistake to characterise the development of citizenship during this period as completely passive because social struggle was also important in extending rights. In particular, the history of citizenship rights can be linked to class struggle against the background of war, and the period of anarchic capitalism was no exception. The expansion of rights resulted from a bargain between the interests of the ruling class and those who were excluded from full citizenship. At times of 'unprecedentedly large scale and recurrent warfare', Britain's rulers were forced to 'demand far more from the people from below' (Colley, 1992: 370) leading to the partial extension of citizenship. By the nineteenth century, the ruling class had more cause to call upon the masses for warfare and 'higher and more rigorous wartime taxation fostered political awareness among the mass of ordinary Britons' (Colley, 1992: 371).

After the Napoleonic wars Colley shows how calls for citizenship were strengthened by participation in the war, and how campaigns for civil rights centred on the anti-slavery movement, the demand for Catholic emancipation and the 1832 Reform Act were linked to victory in the war over France (Colley, 1992: Ch. 8). With the move from limited war to total war in the twentieth century, the leverage of the masses to extend rights in exchange for military duty was increased still further into the social field. However, the key development in extending rights for the masses into the political and social spheres was the shift to a new stage of capitalism.

MANAGED CAPITALISM

By the 1870s Britain moved increasingly to a new stage of capitalism and the British state began to be increasingly influenced by the social liberal view of citizenship which advocated the gradual extension of political and social rights. It was the years from 1870 to 1914 'that produced the outlines of a society based on large organisations' (Crouch, 1993: 78).

Schwarz and Hall (1985) have argued that Britain experienced a severe crisis beginning in the 1880s which necessitated an ideological shift to accommodate new economic and social conditions. Out of this crisis there came a shift away from the individualism of classical liberalism towards a more interventionist approach to politics and the economy, as 'the nightwatchman role of the state began to be steadily eroded' (Schwarz and Hall, 1985: 10). Schwarz and Hall draw comparisons between the situation in the 1880s and the position in the 1980s. In the 1980s Thatcherism represented a deep ideological shift away from social liberalism, and in the 1880s a similar 'crisis of hegemony in the whole social formation' led to the demise of the classical liberal state and a crisis in liberalism itself.

The shift away from laissez-faire economics towards state intervention occurred for several important reasons (Schwarz and Hall, 1985: 7–33). The most fundamental of these was the change in the regime of accumulation to a managed system of production. This was due partly to falling rates of economic growth and profitability from 1873 onwards (Mathius, 1969: 468, 486) and a subsequent rise in unemployment. The reasons for these developments are complex and numerous, but perhaps the main factor was increased competition from America and Germany, who had the advantage of learning from Britain's mistakes and who had developed more advanced and efficient technology and production systems. Increased competition led some economies to adopt protectionist measures, but more importantly, there was a realisation by the ruling class of the need for a more strategic approach to managing the economy and its parallel social and political relations than had been the case before the 1870s.

The dynamic of capitalism is of course the search for profits, and it was the desire to increase these that led to the development of managed capitalism. Economies of scale demanded larger and larger units of production. This simple economic fact is crucial to our understanding of the development of citizenship rights in Britain since it was the growing concentration of production that created the conditions which made the temporary extension of social rights inevitable and functional for capitalist accumulation.

The concentration of production meant the development of distinct regional economies organised around growing urban centres. This had the effect of greatly increasing the profitability of industry but also allowed for the development of labour organisation since workers were grouped together in close-knit communities and in massive factories where solidarity could grow. In 1871 the Trade Union Act granted legal protection for union funds, and in 1875 peaceful picketing was al-lowed. Crouch shows how union membership and influence grew from the period of the 1870s onwards, so that by 1900 12.5 per cent of the labour force was unionised (Crouch, 1993: 96).

With the development of the Trade Union Congress and the Labour Party in 1900, calls for the extension of citizenship could not be resisted. Therefore, in the interests of profit, the ruling class had to concede first political rights and then social rights.

The key point, however, is that this represented a trade-off between the cost of extending rights and the increase in profits that managed capitalism could deliver. By the turn of the century, there was a realisation by the governing class that the economy, by itself, was not regulating the labour market in an effective way. Neither was it providing capitalists with the reproduction of 'labour power of a particular quality' (Schwarz and Hall, 1985: 19). State intervention therefore was seen by many capitalists as a necessary development to 'overcome blockages in the labour market'. Such developments created their own momentum with the development of the tools of regulation in the form of a more developed bureaucracy, which, once established, greatly increased its spheres of influence. The second half of the nineteenth century increasingly saw the rise of the identification and categorisation of social problems by experts and administrators.

Pressure for greater state involvement also came from employers, who increasingly required a more educated work force. Britain's clearest industrial rivals, America and Germany, had much more developed public education systems and this was felt to be a factor in their increased profitability. There was also the feeling amongst the governing elite that after the 1867 Reform Act, which had extended the vote to include some working-class people, there was a need to ensure that these votes were used 'wisely', hence the need to instil suitable values through the provision of public education. From the 1870s onwards government passed a series of Acts to increase the availability of state education, which in practice was geared to the needs of industry and provided little in the way of citizenship education.

The feeling amongst business and industry that some reforms were necessary to maintain the market was also in evidence with regard to trade unions. Some employers began, by the 1880s, to realise there were certain advantages to be gained by dealing with organised, rather than disorganised, workers. Profit could be greatly increased and at the same time class conflict reduced by providing legitimate channels of expression through the trade union and labour movements, which could be contained within the system. The extension of social rights, in the form of embryonic state education and limited trade union rights, was in practice to the benefit of capitalism.

In the first half of the twentieth century the pace towards a more organised capitalism was increased by the Liberal Party reforms of 1906–14, by the effects of the Great Depression, and by the development of total industrial warfare of the first and second world wars.

The reforms of the Liberals between 1906 and 1914 continued the trend towards the development of social citizenship by 'laying the foundations of what later came to be called the welfare state' (Powell, 1992: 40; Scott, 1994: 64–8). The reforms were the result of the increased influence of the labour movement upon the Liberal Party (the 1906 general election saw thirty Labour MPs gaining seats), a greater awareness for the need for social reform following the poverty studies of Booth (1984) and Rowntree (1901), the pressure from employers for a more educated and fitter work force, and the influence of social liberal thinkers within the party. The liberals' reforms included a pension scheme and a contributory national insurance system covering health and unemployment insurance.

The first world war increased the drive towards a more inclusive citizenship by creating pressure for the further extension of the franchise. The Representation of the People Act of 1918 extended the vote to all men over 21 and all women over 30, again illustrating Colley's argument that 'the fact that votes for women and universal manhood suffrage had to wait until 1918 confirmed what the post-Waterloo period also demonstrated . . . the winning of radical constitutional and social change was also intimately bound up with the impact of war (Colley, 1992: 361–2).

The second world war gave further support to Colley's argument, for it was partly as a result of this event that an extensive welfare state was constructed. The inter-war depression had provided further evidence that markets were inherently unstable and could guarantee neither profitability nor social cohesion, and the war-time experience of Britain reinforced further the need for government intervention (Thomas, 1992: 23–35). The war also increased the influence and prestige of the Labour Party, with Bevin as one of its most powerful and respected ministers. The need for state planning and conscription increased the state's knowledge of the poor health and education of its conscripts. The collective act of the war effort led to increased demands for a more collectivist approach to peace. Between 1945 and 1951 the Attlee governments went some way to achieving this through the creation of the modern welfare state and the extension of social rights.

By the 1950s social liberalism had become the 'dominant paradigm' (Roche, 1992: 11–38), and was seen by policy makers as the best approach to create a prosperous and socially cohesive society. The notion of a strong concept of citizenship as outlined by Marshall was accepted by all political parties and was maintained up until the 1970s by broad agreement on the correct relationship between the state and the citizen (Lowe, 1993: 22–3). It is important to note that the era of consensus did not mark the end of ideological differences between the main political parties; the 'consensus era' resulted from a particular set of economic and political constraints. However, regarding citizenship, all governments forged policies which maintained the welfare state as a deliverer of social rights through the provision of universal education, social security and health care, and kept full employment as a key policy aim throughout the period, therefore, in effect defending a right to work.

Increasingly the labour movement gained influence on policy making. As early as the 1920s, Middlemas (1979) argues that one could detect a shift towards corporatism, but the incorporation of the labour movement was at its height in the 1960s and 1970s under the Labour governments of Wilson and Callaghan. This involved the state working with both employers and trade unions to operate economic policy (Thomas, 1992: 237–305).

By the mid-1970s, however, as we have seen in the previous chapter, the relationship between the state, the market and the citizenry was challenged by the ideology of neo-liberalism, which found a champion in the Conservative Party under Thatcher. When managed capitalism began to fail it was largely blamed (by the Conservative Party and press) upon the corporatism of the Labour governments, which was seen as giving far too much power to the unions. The true extent of trade union power in making policy is highly debatable (Marsh, 1992), but it would seem that its influence was largely a negative one; that is, through the power of the strike and other industrial action. However, unions became, for many, the symbol of the socialistic distortion of the market.

In the 1970s, as in the 1870s, Britain faced a major crisis, which the Thatcher governments attempted to solve through a new hegemonic project with a clear redefinition of the relationship between the state and the individual at its centre. This development was shaped by a shift in the regime of accumulation pursued by capitalism in the light of changes in the international economy from the 1960s onwards. The conditions created by these changes opened up the opportunity for the reassertion of economic liberalism and a limited conception of citizenship in the guise of Thatcherism.

DEREGULATED CAPITALISM

With the onset of deregulated capitalism there have been fundamental changes in the nature of capitalism which have had implications for citizenship. Most importantly there has been a dispersal of production which has led to a process of de-urbanisation whereby people have moved out of the larger cities into suburbs, new towns and rural areas (*The Independent*, 6 September 1993). This helped to undermine labour organisation by reducing collectivism. Many old communities based around a particular industry, for example coal and steel, have been undermined, and these had been the bastions of the labour movement. This has led to an increased atomisation of the individual (Mulgan, 1994b). Individuals have become increasingly reliant upon the family for leisure; communal pursuits have declined, and the worker has become ever more 'privatised'. This has undoubtedly led to an increase in the influence of the mass media, which contains a detectable anti-labour and trade union message (Glasgow Media Group, 1976, 1980).

Linked to the dispersal of production is the decline of manufacturing industry and a move towards smaller plants and factories whose primary aim is to create an ever-growing number of consumer goods. For example, whereas in 1955 48 per cent of the British work force was employed in industry, by 1984 this had fallen to 34 per cent. In terms of size of production units in 1974 there were 1,018 factories employing over 1,000 workers. By 1983 this had dropped by 42 per cent to just 589. In keeping with the growth of the consumer society the service sector has greatly expanded. This is reflected in the growth of white-collar work, which rose from 6.25 to 11.5 millions between 1948 and 1979 (Kelly 1988: 283–90). Lash and Urry (1987: 269–84) argue that these changes in the occupational structure have led to a decline in working-class organisation with a subsequent loss in political influence.

Lash and Urry's arguments have, however, been criticised by Kelly (1988). He argues that Lash and Urry correctly observe some important changes in capitalist society but mistakenly assume that these changes, and particularly the decline of class organisation, are irreversible. Kelly makes comparisons with the 1930s where there also occurred a depression in the old manufacturing industries but this was later reversed. Trade unions managed to adapt to the growth of new industries in the Midlands and South and the labour movement survived. Kelly argues that the changes in the 1980s will also be cyclical in their nature. Once economic recovery begins, and the capitalist world moves out of the recession which began in the 1970s, the decline of trade unions will be turned around and the new service industries will become increasingly unionised.

In his criticisms of Lash and Urry, Kelly underestimates the impact of globalisation (Waters, 1995), which seems unlikely to be reversed. With the availability of cheap labour in the third world, it is unlikely that the conditions necessary for full employment will return. It is therefore unlikely that unions will regain the position of power they enjoyed up to the 1980s. Kelly's argument also depends on a change in government: 'there is every reason to suppose that a pro-trade union government will again be elected in Britain and that its policies will facilitate union growth in many sectors of the economy' (Kelly, 1988: 143).

In the light of four consecutive Conservative election victories and the sharp move to the right by the Labour Party under the respective leadership of Kinnock, Smith and Blair, Kelly's hope of a pro-trade union government seems unlikely to be realised. Labour organisation does seem, as Lash and Urry have argued, to have declined in a more permanent and fundamental fashion than Kelly allows for. Therefore, pressure from organised labour is unlikely to be powerful enough on its own to reverse the decline of social citizenship.

As was argued earlier, the development of citizenship rights was not in any case merely the product of struggle from below. It was also the product of the needs of the ruling class to maintain the market which had proved to be unstable and unable to maintain labour suitable to the needs of modern production. The expansion of social citizenship in the period of managed capitalism was due to the mutual benefits it secured for capital and labour. Social rights in Britain were the result of a combination of pressures from 'above' and 'below' and this has helped to shape the unstable nature of social citizenship:

> In combination these two streams – those which looked to the state for an organic solution to the crisis of reproduction, from 'above', and those which looked to the state to intervene in the name of the collective good against the imperatives of the free market – not only powered the transition to collectivism, but helped to form the contradictory parameters which, ever since, have enclosed modern welfare programmes. (Schwarz and Hall, 1985: 20)

Writers such as Marshall have tended to see the growth of state intervention through Keynesian economic management, nationalisation, and the development of a welfare state as overwhelmingly in favour of the working class and as developments which were largely irreversible. In fact many of these developments can be seen as maintaining social cohesion and social control and developing the necessary infrastructure for the needs of capitalism. For instance, public education was only introduced when industry reached levels of complexity that required a semi-literate and numerate work force.

Many commentators have overemphasised the process of struggle by the working class to gain these concessions (Giddens, 1982: 166–80; Lockwood, 1974). In reality managed capitalism represented a phase where the interests of capitalism happened to coincide with those of the working class for a relatively brief historical period and this led to a temporary extension of social rights. These rights could be dismantled when the needs of capitalism changed in the 1970s. The reasons for this change need to be examined in some detail.

THE TRANSITION FROM
MANAGED TO DEREGULATED CAPITALISM

The restructuring of capitalism was caused primarily by a crisis in the old industrial societies involving a rapid decline in profitability. In Britain the net profit rate of manufacturing industry fell from 17.5 per cent in 1960 to 2 per cent in 1981 (Armstrong et al., 1984: 464). The reason for this decline was a series of events, several of which had their origins in the stage of managed capitalism which preceded deregulated capitalism.

During the period of managed capitalism, profits were increased by the industrial powers of the West dominating the world through the building of empires, of which Britain is the prime example. Colonisation meant captive markets and cheap raw materials for the industries of the developed world to turn into manufactured goods. These developments helped to reduce competition and the uncertainties of the market place and allowed for predictable profit. Ironically Britain's industrial success and its ability to compromise with the forces of labour at home were to some extent dependent on the distinctively 'unfree' markets of the empire. Britain's imperial history has also meant that it has been, more than any other nation, bound up with the fortunes of the world economy, and international finance capitalism has been dominant in the British capitalist class (Overbeek, 1990: 31–2; Hutton, 1996).

One of the key factors in Britain's long-term economic problems was the decline and eventual disintegration of the empire, and the inability of British capitalism to adapt to that decline in a way which would increase the performance of the British economy (Gamble, 1994: 32–3; Coates, 1994). The main reason for the disintegration of empire was the impact of the two world wars, which weakened, and then destroyed, the ties between the imperial countries and their colonies. The fact that the wars were total wars, in the sense that the whole economy of the countries involved became part of the war effort, reduced trade with the empires and in turn encouraged the process of industrialisation in countries across the globe. The old industrial societies gradually faced the growth of new competition from Asia, Latin America and other developing economies, which meant that increased international competition sharply reduced profits.

Thus, despite the apparent success of managed capitalism, there were clearly underlying problems which became apparent in the 1970s. The trigger event which sent the world into recession was the oil crisis of 1973. The oil-producing countries tired of being paid relatively little for their produce and forced world oil prices up by a factor of four. This caused havoc in the capitalist world as oil is fundamental to most manufacturing industry, particularly during the 1970s when alternative energy sources were relatively underdeveloped. A further oil crisis following the Iranian revolution in 1979 again raised oil prices and sent further shock waves through the capitalist system (Gamble, 1994: 47).

A number of other factors were also important in the demise of managed capitalism. For example, the relative decline of the main capitalist economy, the United States of America, was due largely to overspending on arms as a result of America's new-found role as policeman of the world and defender of the capitalist countries. This increased in the 1980s as the cold war began to intensify following the Soviet invasion of Afghanistan (Green and Sutcliffe, 1987: 76–9).

The relative decline of America was of particular significance because ever since the agreement at Bretton Woods in 1944, the capitalist economy was tied to the US dollar. The growing interdependence of the world economy meant that the poor performance of the American economy would cause problems throughout the whole capitalist system. The growing power of multinational companies also restricted governments' ability to influence their economies through counter cyclical measures. The result was a defiance of the Philips curve, as inflation and unemployment rose sharply at the same time. In the UK inflation reached 28.7 per cent in 1974 with unemployment hitting the million mark (Wilson, 1992: 5).

By the end of the 1970s the 'long boom' which had characterised the post-war period was clearly at an end. This had implications for the relationship between the old industrial states and their citizens, since the balance of power that had existed between capital and labour, which helped to guarantee the maintenance of social rights, was drastically changed (Green and Sutcliffe, 1987).

Of crucial importance to the changing nature of capitalism has been the growing influence of multinational corporations. These can be defined as large companies which produce goods and services in more than one country. These corporations have immense wealth; the sales of the top 200 companies in the world in 1986 amounted to one-third of the total production of the world and the sales of General Motors in 1983 were equal to that of the GNP of Thailand, Pakistan and Uruguay combined (Weatherby, 1986: 13–26). As these companies become more truly global in their nature, they will become an increasing threat to the nation-state and the maintenance of social citizenship.

The growth of multinational corporations has been made possible by technological change and the vast improvements in communications. Due to these changes it is possible to move capital the length and breadth of the globe at the push of a button. Satellites have allowed companies to link up with their plants and offices over the world. These companies can gain many advantages from this. Transport costs are drastically reduced and the penetration of tariff barriers is made possible by the ability to produce in the countries where the company's product will be sold. It allows companies more control of the market and perhaps most importantly of all it gives the opportunity for the exploitation of advantageous local conditions in the form of deregulated areas or low-wage costs (Sengenberger and Wilkinson, 1995). A new international division of labour has emerged since the 1970s (Nyilas, 1982). Instead of exporting raw materials from the third world and transforming these into manufactured goods, the old industrial nations now export capital and receive cheap labour from the third world nations. This has consequences for the working classes in the old industrial nations in the form of mass unemployment and changes in occupational structure.

De-Industrialisation has occurred in the first world and a growth in service industries, rather than manufacturing, is evident. This has resulted in a changing composition of the work force with an increase in female, part-time and temporary labour, which have lower levels of union density (Mitter, 1986: 83–104). High levels of largely male unemployment have also become common. This fact alone has weakened labour organisation by providing a readily available pool of labour. As this unemployment has occurred largely in the old industrial areas such as ship building, coal and steel production, union power and membership have been greatly reduced. Union membership in Britain reached its height in the late 1970s. A total of 8,940,000 workers were in unions in 1978 compared to 7,458,000 in 1985 (Hyman, 1989: 231–9).

Changes in capitalist production have also weakened the labour movement's bargaining position with capital. The period of managed capitalism can be characterised as Fordist in its nature (Kumar, 1995: Ch. 3). This system placed its emphasis upon large-scale standardised production based on scientific management. Production tasks were specialised and the division of labour was highly developed, with each worker working on a small part of the final product. Management was centralised and removed from the shop floor. One of the problems of the Fordist system was that there were high levels of industrial conflict revolving mainly around organised strike action, and this contributed to the eventual decline of the system.

Deregulated capitalism has seen a gradual shift towards a post-Fordist model. This has given rise to the 'flexible firm' (Atkinson, 1984). Advances in technology have enabled manufacturing to become more flexible: goods can be made in smaller numbers and still be cost effective. This allows capitalism to feed the ever-growing demand for new and more varied products. In these firms workers are divided into a well-paid 'core' who are expected to perform multiple production tasks, and an increasingly insecure and deskilled 'periphery'. The rationale of these changes is to encourage innovation by reducing alienation amongst skilled workers, whilst the movement towards the use of peripheral workers has been encouraged by the policy of contracting out and the privatisation of state services where union membership is discouraged and wages are kept to a minimum (Coates, 1989: 145–59).

The increase in flexible firms has also meant changes in industrial relations. There has been a growth in single union agreements that has reduced the right of unions to recruit members anywhere they choose. There are now many more 'no strike agreements' with disputes being settled more and more by arbitration, rather than conflict. Companies have also encouraged consultation with workers to create the feeling of involvement by the workers in the company. It is doubtful how much of this has really meant a move towards industrial democracy as workers are excluded from the key areas of decision making, for example concerning when and where to invest capital (Bassett, 1987: 87–99).

The growing flexibility of capital and the increasing global nature of the international economy has had some extremely important effects on the governments of states. States have become much less able to determine their own economic policies. The state has become 'porous'; unable to ignore the needs of international capital: 'national boundaries no longer act as fairly "watertight" containers of the production process; rather they resemble sieves through which extensive leakage occurs' (Dicken, 1986: 32). States have been forced to compete for investment by the multinational corporations. These companies have as their overriding goal the maintenance of profit. They require certain conditions to prevail in order to invest in a country.

In Britain, government policies since 1979 have clearly been geared to attracting capital investment from abroad and facilitating the operations of multinational corporations (Fulcher, 1995). Exchange controls were abolished to allow the smooth transference of capital. The government followed a policy of deregulation, removing many obstacles to the capitalist class. A good example of this was the creation of enterprise zones where regulations on planning permission were greatly relaxed. Credit was made much easier to obtain and this helped to encourage consumption of the products of the multinationals. Policies of privatisation, rather than giving any significant power to the many small investors in shares, increased the power of multinational companies, who often gained controlling interests in the newly privatised industries (Hutton, 1996: 56–169).

Deregulated capitalism can, in many ways, be seen as return to the anarchic stage of capitalism; with smaller units of production, less labour organisation, the decline of state regulation in the economic field and a revival of market forces. The implications for citizenship have been as follows. A weak concept of citizenship associated with the anarchic stage of capitalism has re-emerged. Social rights have been eroded and market rights and individual duties asserted.

SUMMARY:
THE UNEVEN DEVELOPMENT OF CITIZENSHIP IN BRITAIN

The advantage of the Gramscian approach adopted here is that the concept of hegemony allows us to analyse developments in citizenship by exploring the relationship between the ideology of liberalism, economic conditions, state forms and class cohesiveness. As Gamble (1994: 207–8) rightly points out, hegemony is often misrepresented as simply ideological, but in fact it involves the relationship between ideological, economic and political factors. If military factors and class organisation are added, we can get much closer to understanding why citizenship has developed as it has in modern Britain.

In the early stages of capitalism the growth of market rights were a precondition to the capitalist mode of production. The feudal order, with its emphasis upon ascribed status, was incompatible with the market system that had begun to develop. These rights were limited and in the interests of the owners of capital; the right of workers to associate together to protect themselves was denied.

At this stage the state was transformed into its classical liberal form.

Labour was atomised and repressed by the state. Mass production had not yet developed to the stage where the conditions existed for the development of class consciousness. Warfare was limited in its objectives and fought, for the most part, by professional soldiers. Consequently the ruling class did not need to engage in a substantial trade-off with the masses, whose demands could be largely suppressed by force. The dominant ideology of the time was classical liberalism with its emphasis on individuals struggling in the market place for advantage, a limited statism and an agency-based approach to social problems, where the poor were castigated for their own failings.

With the development of managed capitalism the ruling class became much more dependent upon the working class. This was because of international as well as domestic factors. First, increased competition from other European countries and America required the development of larger units of production in an attempt to maintain profits through economies of scale. This led to greater labour organisation. Second, increased international rivalries and the need to maintain the empire as a bulwark against foreign economic and military strength saw the industrialisation of warfare, which, by the twentieth century, required mass armies of conscripts drawn from the working class.

The realities of Fordist mass-production techniques and industrial warfare meant that a laissez-faire approach to the labour problem was no longer possible. State-funded education and health programmes became necessary for the reproduction of a suitable labour force. The working class could no longer be controlled purely by force and a more consensual approach was necessary by the state. Social liberalism provided the ideological logic for the extension of social rights.

As in the 1870s, the 1970s saw a number of economic and political changes which provided the background for another hegemonic shift: away from social liberalism towards neo-liberalism. With the movement towards post-Fordist production techniques, unemployment increased massively and division between core and peripheral workers grew. Because of high unemployment, the development of a new international division of labour, and the dependence of Britain on nuclear rather than conventional armed forces, the balance of power between labour and capital, on which the development of social rights was based, has shifted away from labour.

FROM SOCIAL LIBERALISM TO NEO-LIBERALISM

In order to understand the failure of social liberalism and the hegemonic shift towards neo-liberalism, it is necessary to show how the foundations of the social liberal consensus were undermined or challenged in the 1970s. These developments can be analysed in terms of the relationships between the economic changes explored above, the nature of Britain's political institutions, and the way in which the ideology of Thatcherism articulated a response to the crisis of the 1970s. These developments occurred against a background of Britain's long-established political values and a changing class system.

POLITICAL FACTORS

The central political right gained during the period of managed capitalism was the extension of the franchise, which by 1928 extended to all citizens equally. Class conflict was, to some extent, institutionalised. The development of the Labour Party into a respectable political force gave a parliamentary voice to the working class, and trade unions were seen by the main political parties as legitimate institutions. From the second world war onwards there was an increase in the development of universal social rights and the Labour governments of 1945–51 were largely the vehicle for this. The 1945 Labour government created the framework for the welfare state and helped to establish the era of consensus politics lasting until the 1970s (Kavanagh and Morris, 1989). The power of the labour movement appeared to increase with the development of corporatism in the 1960s and 1970s, and Labour began to be looked upon as the natural party of government because it was the architect of the social liberal consensus, and was closely associated with the development of social citizenship.

However, the development of citizenship rights had less to do with the success of the Labour Party and more to with the nature of Fordist production techniques, which by definition gave more power to the labour movement. As has been argued, in order to maintain profit it was necessary to pursue policies which gave concessions to the working class. Thus limited social rights were put into place partly to buy off and partly to incorporate the working class into capitalist society. This explains why the political champion of the capitalist classes, namely the Conservative Party, was content to follow the social liberal consensus since it was in the interest of the business class which it represented.

The argument that class conflict on a mass scale was largely latent during the post-war period up to the crisis of the 1970s is borne out by the fact that the Conservatives were in power for most of the period. This balance of power between labour and capital however was a short-term occurrence. As we have seen, once the economic basis for this social bargain was eroded by developments in capitalism, social citizenship became vulnerable to change.

However, the reversal of social rights and the narrowing of citizenship have to be understood in terms of political as well as economic factors. One of the reasons why the development of social rights was reversible was that these rights were not cemented in the form of a bill of rights, which may have made them more difficult to undermine (Brazier, 1991: Ch. 7; Benn and Hood, 1993: Ch. 4). Citizenship was never founded upon legally protected rights but instead largely existed in a normative or prescriptive form. This proved to be a problem not just for social rights but also for certain kinds of civil rights (see Chapter 8), which parliament could change at will. Britain's constitution proved to be highly malleable when the Thatcherite governments sought to narrow and redefine citizenship. The lack of a codified constitution also means the government of Britain has relied on political conventions which rest upon the good will of particular governments to respect these traditions. The Thatcher governments proved that a radical government could by-pass many of these conventions, and this flexibility allowed for many of the policies which helped to fundamentally alter the relationship between the citizen and the state. For example, no constitutional barrier existed to prevent the scrapping of a whole tier of local government, the marginalisation of certain pressure groups, or the introduction of the poll tax: radical policies, all of which can be interpreted as undermining citizenship.

The myth of parliamentary sovereignty (Kingdom, 1991: Ch. 10) also greatly increased the power of government because since the nineteenth century, when parties became increasingly disciplined, any government which possessed a clear parliamentary majority was more able to carry out its policies at will. In 1979, but particularly in 1983 and 1987, the Thatcher government held a large majority in the House of Commons which enabled it to carry through its legislative programme.

Within the cabinet Thatcher showed her willingness to shape its judgements through a number of methods. In her first term of office Tory 'wets' were sacked and Thatcherites put in their place. Thatcher often broke with convention by by-passing cabinet all together. The Thatcher years were characterised by 'political' appointments to top civil service jobs, the growth in importance of ad hoc committees controlled by the Prime Minister directly, and the growth of advisors outside of cabinet structures (Hutton, 1996: Ch. 2).

Wilson has argued that from 1979 onwards, Thatcherism gradually developed a 'courtier' state 'more akin to a feudal monarch's court than to the office of an elected head of state' (Wilson, 1992: 99). Thatcher, as she points out in her memoirs (Thatcher, 1993, 1995), relied increasingly on two or three Thatcherite figures within the cabinet to help her to push through her agenda. By her own admission, once she had alienated such key Thatcherites as Norman Tebbit, Geoffrey Howe and Nigel Lawson, her position as Prime Minister was vulnerable. In short, the vague nature of the British constitution allowed the Thatcher governments to implement a radical programme which continued under the premiership of John Major (see Chapter 5).

Another weakness of the political system which allowed the Thatcherite project to occur was the first-past-the-post voting system, which allowed the government a huge parliamentary majority in 1983 and 1987 with well under 50 per cent of those who voted. Thatcherism also prospered from an opposition, in the form of the Labour Party, which failed to construct an alternative response to the crisis of accumulation of the 1970s. Labour suffered from the fact that it was closely associated with this crisis in the eyes of the public, who were constantly reminded by the Tory press of the 'winter of discontent', the failure of Labour's economic management, and the humiliation of having to go 'cap in hand' to the International Monetary Fund for a loan to bail out the economy (Coates, 1980: 39–43).

A significant factor in the progress of Thatcherism was that corporatism was never embedded in the decision-making process (Overbeek, 1990: 126). The period of British government which may be described as corporatist was short lived, and trade unions and employers were from the start suspicious of its aims. The weakness of corporatism is illustrated by the ease with which the Thatcher governments marginalised the unions from 1979 onwards. Politically then, citizenship stood on shaky foundations and could be redefined by an alternative hegemonic project, namely Thatcherism.

IDEOLOGICAL AND CLASS FACTORS

As we have seen, the ideology of neo-liberalism provided a clear diagnosis of and cure for Britain's problems. The social liberal approach to citizenship, and particularly its insistence on the need for social rights, was rejected as subverting, rather than civilising, capitalism.

It has been argued that the Thatcherite project deliberately chose a hegemonic strategy that resonated with the population at large. O'Shea (1984) argues that Thatcherism combined two forms of populism which seemed to go a long way to explaining Britain's decline in the post-war period. One form of populism emphasised individualism and attacked collectivism, particularly in the form of the welfare state and trade unions, as being at the root of Britain's problems. Second, Thatcherism stressed the need to reinvigorate a morally diluted nation which had been undermined by 'enemies within' and by a mass immigration which had brought to Britain cultures 'alien to our streets'. Thatcherism, then, seemed to identify a plausible set of reasons for Britain's economic problems which concurred with a 'commonsense' appraisal of the situation, and by doing so it tapped into values embedded in British society.

Notions of individualism and nationhood are deeply engrained in Britain's political culture. In our earlier analysis of classical liberalism we have seen how individualism has been central to Britain's political theory in a way which is very different from the continental tradition, which has seen collectivism and state intervention in a much more positive light (Lukes, 1973: 3–39). The mix of fact and myth which is involved in the historical development of Britain as the first industrial country, the largest empire in the world, and the 'civiliser' of other nations, continues to feed into Britain's political culture (Coates, 1991: 159–5). Large defence spending, the maintenance of an 'autonomous' nuclear deterrent, and the jingoistic reaction to such events as the Falklands war and the problems of Northern Ireland are symptoms of this and cannot be discounted in assessing conceptions of citizenship.

It is important to recognise that the concept of the British nation is an 'imagined community' (Anderson, 1983), which in fact is defined in a gendered and 'racialised' form. The state is always characterised in masculine terms: it is required to be 'strong', able to defend its population and ensure security. As we have seen, citizenship is bound up with warfare and military duty, which has been the almost exclusive domain of men. Similarly the important link between the empire and the nation has ensured that black and Irish immigrants have been defined as dependants rather than citizens, and experience life in the historical context of the domination of a white Protestant Britain over black Africa or Catholic Ireland. These deep-seated ideological preconceptions of the nature of the citizen have continued to resonate through Britain's political culture and have played a part in the Thatcherite project.

However, ideological factors have to be seen alongside economic and political circumstances in order to understand the combination of factors which led to a Thatcherite hegemonic strategy. The shift in capitalism to its deregulated stage meant that in the 1970s, governments of all shades of political opinion were faced with a new set of economic conditions. The crisis of capitalism from the 1960s onwards, the decline of profitability and the increased global competition for investment meant that by the 1970s governments were under pressure to offer suitable conditions to capital. Labour's abortive attempts at trade union reform in 1969, the Selsdon programme of Heath in the early 1970s, and the monetarist policies of the Labour Party in the late 1970s can all be seen as a response to these pressures. Citizenship as it had developed in the era of consensus politics seemed, particularly in its social form, to be an impediment to Britain's competitiveness in the world economy.

Neo-liberalism appeared to offer a solution to these problems but again its rise to power has to be understood in political context. Throughout the Thatcher years, support for social rights was strong amongst the electorate, but it was the peculiarities of Britain's electoral system that enabled the Thatcherite revolution to take place. The internal divisions of the Labour Party ensured the Thatcher governments could remain in power despite a distinct lack of support for many of their policies amongst the electorate (Edgell and Duke, 1991: Ch. 4; Crewe, 1988).

Another concept of Gramsci's is useful in understanding the coalition of interests constructed by the Thatcherite governments. The notion of historic blocs describes the construction of an alliance between social groups in order to maintain or institute a particular set of policies which sustain a hegemonic project. The advantage of this approach is that it allows us to go beyond the rather abstract and stale debate concerning the relationship between the state and capitalism. One does not need to demonstrate that the state *always* operates in the interest of the capitalist class to realise that the need to maintain profitability and economic growth will exert tremendous pressure on governments to pursue policies which facilitate this end.

Capitalism is by its nature a competitive system which means that a political system can never serve the interests of *all* capitalists *all of the time*. More sophisticated accounts of the relationship between state and capitalism have recognised the often diverse interests of industrial and finance capitalism (Coates, 1984), and in the field of state theory there has been a clear convergence of pluralist and Marxist perspectives (Etzioni-Halevy, 1993).

Neo-Marxists like Jessop have increasingly put more emphasis on particular state strategies which are shaped by previous political conflict and compromise, as well as economic factors. Different nation-states, with separate histories and political institutions, will react to economic change in a variety of ways as economic transformations are mediated through particular political and state forms. As Jessop states, 'the form of the state is the crystallisation of past strategies as well as privileging some other current strategies. As a strategic terrain the state is located within a complex dialectic of structures and strategies' (Jessop, 1990: 260). We have seen that as political, ideological and economic factors converged in Britain during the 1970s, a conjuncture of these forces made the resurgence of a form of classical liberalism, constituted in the interests of capital, likely.

In the case of Britain it is not difficult to make a clear correlation between the interests of capital and the policies and ideology of the Conservative Party. From at least the nineteenth century onwards, the Conservative Party has identified its interests with the maintenance and promotion of capitalism (Belchem, 1990: Ch. 3; Ross, 1983). This identification has occurred for several reasons. Ideologically capitalism seemed to many Conservatives to be the best guarantee of individual freedom and the prosperity of the nation. Also more directly, a large literature has developed around the business and financial interests of Conservative Party ministers and MPs (Ross, 1983; Scott, 1982, 1991; Miliband, 1969). Such studies have led some commentators to the conclusion that a high degree of homogeneity exists between the economic elite and the Conservative Party, which is cemented by similar cultural pursuits, educational background and marriage. John Scott argues that 'Britain is ruled by a capitalist class whose economic dominance is sustained by the operations of the state and whose members are disproportionately represented in the power elite which rules the state apparatus. That is to say, Britain does have a ruling class' (Scott, 1991: 151).

This ruling class is united, above all, by a commitment to capitalist values and anti-socialist beliefs. This view does not deny that tactical differences occur regularly between different sectors of the economy or within the political elite, but strategically these differences are overridden by a common commitment to the maintenance of capitalism. The form that capitalism takes has shifted as the result of crisis, technological change and political factors (such as military conquests and the development of empire), and this has shaped the substance of policy. Hence during the period of managed capitalism the Conservative Party largely accepted the social liberal consensus.

As Gramsci argues, in order for a particular hegemony to succeed the ruling class needs to galvanise support from a cross section of the population so that a historic bloc can be formed and consent secured. In Britain under Thatcherism this has been achieved for a variety of interrelated factors.

Capitalists, from all sections of the economy, had, by the 1970s, become disenchanted with the Labour Party's efforts to modernise the British economy. The Wilson and Callaghan governments were seen to have been frustrated by their close links with the trade unions and by an outdated commitment to social citizenship which the faltering economy could no longer sustain.

Writers from the left, as well as the right of the political spectrum, have argued that Britain was becoming 'ungovernable'. Habermas (1976) argues that the maintenance of social rights, through the institutions of the welfare state, and the pursuit of economic profitability are incompatible. With the development of corporatism the government became increasingly identified with economic problems and this led to a 'legitimation crisis'. In an analysis from the right, Samuel Brittan writes that 'liberal representative democracy suffers from internal contradictions' (Brittan, 1976: 96), these contradictions being essentially the tension between the inequalities of capitalism and the egalitarian logic of citizenship and democracy.

The economic crisis of the 1970s meant that the capitalist class in Britain required a solution to these problems by asserting the primacy of economic inequality over political equality. Thatcherism was clearly an attempt to adjust to the new realities of capitalism by reducing impediments to capitalist investment, such as trade union and social rights, and opening up Britain's economy to increasing globalisation.

In order to achieve its aims, the Conservative Party had to win power through the ballot box and achieve a coalition of interests large enough to sustain it in power. One factor that facilitated this was the changing nature of the working class in Britain. As we have seen, changes in the working class can be tied to the changing nature of capitalism in the late 1960s and 1970s. By the 1980s, a combination of high unemployment, the increasing causalisation of work and government legislation undermining union power meant that the working class became increasingly unable to organise effectively (Coates, 1989).

Some commentators have put forward the argument that the working class has become divided in terms of housing, union membership, region and sector of work (Crewe, 1992). This has meant that the 'new' working class, who are home owners, non-union members who work in the South and in the private sector, no longer have a strong class allegiance to the Labour Party. Crewe may be right that a degree of fragmentation has taken place. Certainly, government policies such as the privatisation of council houses did prove popular with more affluent working-class people (Wilson, 1992: 169), but as Heath et al. (1985: Ch. 2) have argued, changes in the occupational structure, with a shift away from manufacturing industry, also meant that the traditional working class has declined as a percentage of the work force. Another factor that Heath and his colleagues point to is the failure of the Labour Party to unify behind a set of coherent policies, thereby offering little alternative to the Conservative government.

The realities of Britain's political system, coupled with changes in the working class, allowed the Conservative government to pursue a two-nation strategy (Jessop et al., 1988: Ch. 4), which achieved a coalition of support from a variety of sources, including a large section of the working class. The interests of the nation became identified with a section of those who benefited or believed that they benefited from policies of free trade, a strong state, tight immigration laws and so on. Those members of the nation who did not agree with this vision were branded as 'enemies within', 'traitors' or 'do-gooders' (see Chapter 8).

Thatcherism, then, can be interpreted as a hegemonic project based on the ideology of neo-liberalism, which asserted values that had deep roots in Britain's political culture, and which were adopted by the Conservative Party as a strategy to deal with the economic and political problems faced by Britain in the 1970s. It was able to become dominant because of its apparent symmetry with the new economic conditions of deregulated capitalism, the nature of Britain's political system and the absence of a coherent alternative hegemonic project. Central to the aims of Thatcherism was the redefinition of citizenship, which, in its social liberal form, was thought to have failed to reconcile the contradictions of Britain's liberal democracy.

The next two chapters of this book will explore the attempts by the Thatcherite governments to overcome the problems of the relationship between citizens and the state through a neo-liberal conception of citizenship.

7

ACTIVE CITIZENS?

It was through the neo-liberal approach of the Thatcherite governments that the dualistic nature of citizenship in the liberal tradition was emphasised. This chapter, and the chapter that follows it, therefore analyses the elitist and exclusive nature of liberal citizenship through an examination of a selection of government policies and discourses. These two chapters do not attempt to offer a detailed overview of all of the major policies of the Thatcherite governments which have impacted upon the relationship between the citizen and the state, but instead seek to illustrate and support the theoretical arguments of this book via a case-study approach (for an overall assessment of these policies, and the Thatcherite years in general, see Wilson, 1992; Green, 1987: Part Two; Kavanagh and Seldon, 1990, 1994; Ludlam and Smith, 1995; Hay, 1996).

A clear theme that emerges from Thatcherite definitions of citizenship is the division between active citizens and the passive or undeserving citizen. Therefore the main concern of this part of the book will be an analysis of this dualism, which, as was argued in Part I, is inherent in the liberal tradition, and is particularly evident in its neo-liberal variant. It will be argued that the failure of Thatcherism to increase the security, liberty and autonomy of *all* citizens in Britain can be understood as a symptom of the more profound failure of liberalism to generate a meaningful and inclusive citizenship. The Thatcherite project, by further polarising the dualisms of liberalism explored in Part I of this work, served only to emphasise and illuminate its essentially incoherent nature. The failure of Thatcherism therefore points to the need to develop a post-liberal theory of citizenship if the potentially radical notions of equality and anti-statism contained in classical liberalism are to be realised.

LIBERALISM, THATCHERISM
AND THE LOGIC OF ELITISM

Within liberal citizenship theory a tension exists, not just between rights and duties, but also between different kinds of rights. One of the primary reasons for the development of social liberalism was the realisation by writers like Green and Marshall that civil rights and political rights, as advocated by classical liberals, were not enough by themselves to achieve a just and ordered society. Social rights were needed which created the resources for people to make use of their rights in practice. However, as has been argued, because of the other dualisms inherent in liberalism, social rights are in a state of tension with market rights. Particularly significant is the way that liberalism privileges the market and the 'liberty of the individual' against the claims of equality and democracy. Social rights were vulnerable in Britain because they developed as claims for equality (of opportunity) and were the result (indirectly) of democratic compromise. The basis of this compromise, as we have seen, rested mainly on economic conditions and therefore could be reversed when these conditions changed. Theoretically social rights always stood uneasily within liberalism, with its emphasis on inequality in civil society, competitive individualism and the defence of free markets. With the advent of deregulated capitalism and the rise of neo-liberalism, citizenship was redefined as part of the attempt by the Thatcherites to restructure British society to meet the changing needs of the market.

Thatcherite policies and pronouncements attempted to shift the balance between rights and duties away from rights and towards the duties citizens were expected to carry out. Basic social rights, which had come to be seen as the norm by the population in the post-war period, were greatly reduced, with a subsequent reduction of the ability of many members of society to play a full part in the wider community (Sullivan, 1992: Ch. 6). The duties that citizens were expected to undertake were essentially to themselves; compassion for others was an optional extra.

As well as individual responsibilities, Thatcherism also reasserted market rights defined as freedom to choose, freedom to own property and have that property protected, the freedom to spend one's money as one sees fit, and the right to be unequal. These market rights were asserted against the claims of social rights, which were seen by the Thatcherites as having undermined market rights, and were unnecessary, unaffordable and contrary to the vigorous virtues of Thatcherism.

However, such a definition of citizenship reduced not only the freedoms of groups already marginalised in society, but crucially it also had a detrimental effect upon the overall quality of citizenship for *all* people in

Britain. By moving many groups such as ethnic minorities, the poor, the long-term unemployed, single parents and travellers ever closer to the edge of society, the community as a whole was disadvantaged. This is so, first, by the loss of diversity in society, and second by the fear that the anger felt by such groups may spill over into increased violence and disorder thus undermining security and liberty for all.

As we have seen in Chapter 6, many rights that existed in Britain prior to the 1980s, particularly those rights relating to the social field, were never codified or protected through constitutional mechanisms. However, these rights had in the post-war period become, in a Burkian sense, central to the expectations of the population at large. According to Burke such prescriptive rights (that come to us through our historical ancestry) are the only source of real rights as opposed to the abstract liberal notion of natural rights. Since, according to Burke, human nature is socially determined and thus essentially diverse, there can be no rights that can be applied to all societies at all times: only those rights that have developed within a particular social and historical setting.

Traditional conservatives argue that radicals attack prescriptive rights at their peril because these rights are firmly engrained in people's hearts and minds as their historical entitlement. This of course is reinforced when such rights have been gained in return for duties rendered. Indeed, this was the case in Britain after the second world war where the duties of conscription were expected to bring an increase in social rights. This expectation has been summed up by various contemporary commentators through the use of such clichés as the *People's Peace* (Morgan, 1990) or the idea that *Never Again* (Hennesey, 1992) would people live in squalor in the post-war world. According to such a view, social cohesion can only be maintained if proper reference is made to the expectations and norms of the recent past (Nisbet, 1986: 23).

However, Thatcherism (in a highly unconservative fashion) showed scant regard for these traditions. The aspirations of universal social citizenship, and the hopes for an ever-widening and inclusive concept of citizenship (which had characterised much of the post-war period), were replaced in the 1980s and 1990s by a redefinition of citizenship articulated by a government with a highly particularistic and prejudiced view of who constituted a 'good' citizen in modern Britain. The resulting exclusion of large segments of British society who did not fit the ideal of the 'Thatcherite citizen' left many of Britain's citizens with a deep sense of powerlessness, which was a major factor in numerous social problems such as the rise in crime and public order offences throughout the 1980s and 1990s (Central Statistical Office, 1994a: 151; Box, 1987; Lea and Young, 1984).

Many of these social problems were linked to the fact that the prescriptive rights that had developed during the period of consensus politics had become embedded in the minds of the people. Throughout the Thatcherite years the public was generally supportive of the welfare state, and was prepared to pay for it; for example in 1985 only 6 per cent of the population favoured tax cuts if they would lead to reductions in welfare (Bosanquet, 1986: 135). Undoubtedly this public support made a direct assault upon social citizenship politically highly risky for the Thatcherite governments. Therefore, it was mainly through a combination of piecemeal reform of social rights and the development, through various discourses, of the active citizen–passive citizen dichotomy that the Conservative governments attempted to shift the country away from support for social citizenship.

The shift towards an emphasis on personal responsibility and market rights and away from social rights was underpinned by the Thatcher and Major governments' view of the apparent growth of social problems associated with a perceived moral decline. Throughout the 1980s and 1990s Conservative ministers have been concerned by the supposed moral breakdown of society associated with the permissive social values of the 1960s and 1970s. It was argued that British citizens had forgotten how to express civic virtue, and more importantly the vigorous virtues necessary to preserve a wealthy and stable society had been undermined (Letwin, 1992).

There appears, at first sight, to be a fundamental contradiction between the neo-liberal element of the Thatcherite governments and the more traditional social conservative element of the Conservative Party concerning such issues as social order, crime and social responsibilities. The two elements within the Conservative Party are, it is argued, often in conflict (Ludlam and Smith, 1995: 11). I would contend, however, that in terms of explaining social behaviour both liberals and conservatives place the emphasis on the individual in terms of responsibility for one's actions. That is, both traditional conservatism and neo-liberalism privilege the individual social agent actor above the structures of society, such as class and gender, which constrain or influence personal behaviour. It is the resistance to structural explanations for people's behaviour that pervades conservatism and liberalism. The argument being made here is that the Thatcherite approach to social problems was consistent with the logic of liberalism. In liberal approaches to citizenship a dualism is created between active and passive citizens. In other words, because of its assumptions, liberal citizenship is inherently elitist. This follows logically from liberalism, first because of its agency-based approach to social problems, and second because of its failure to acknowledge the often coercive and unjust outcomes of market forces.

Because of the neo-liberal approach of the Thatcherite governments and their lack of acknowledgement of the inability of markets to deliver an inclusive sense of citizenship, they turned to moralistic explanations of anti-social behaviour (King, 1987). Citizenship had to be redefined in terms of Thatcherite values to counter the following problems:

- A generalised breakdown of respect for private property, authority and the hierarchical structures of British society which required a renewal of active citizenship to revive individual responsibility and duty. The core values of Britishness were seen to be under attack from assorted anti-social groups.
- Following the second world war citizens became increasingly dependent upon the state to solve their problems, and this dependency rendered citizens impotent in the performance of their responsibilities.

The Thatcherite governments attempted to change the meaning of citizenship by redefining the relationship between the state as a guarantor of rights and the individual citizen as a recipient of these rights; particularly in the arena of social rights and public service. This development can be linked to the major changes in the capitalist economy that altered the balance between classes in Britain since the 1970s (see Chapter 6). The development of social rights was a key component of the consensus politics of the post-war period, but was seen as unnecessary and unaffordable following the crisis of capitalism in the 1970s. As we shall see in Chapter 8, the Thatcherites attempted to limit, not just social rights, but also to curtail basic political and civil rights for those deemed to be unworthy citizens. This division between active and passive citizens is embedded in the logic of liberalism and was extended in practice by the Thatcherites.

ACTIVE CITIZENSHIP

The first explicit use of the notion of citizenship by Conservative ministers in the 1980s was by the Home Secretary Douglas Hurd, who introduced the concept of active citizenship in 1988 in a speech at Tamworth celebrating the anniversary of the death of Sir Robert Peel. The idea was given official endorsement at the 1988 Conservative Party Conference by Prime Minister Thatcher and remained an explicit theme in Conservative discourse until 1990, and an implicit one throughout John Major's government (echoed, for example, by Major in his so-called 'back to basics' campaign in 1993).

The active citizen was, according to the Thatcherites, a dynamic individual who was self-reliant, responsible for his or her own actions, and yet possessed a sense of civic virtue and pride in both country and local community. Active citizenship was a mixture of self-help and voluntarism whereby the competition and rigour of market relations would supposedly be 'civilised' by concern for one's community and country.

The notion of active citizenship was underpinned by the perceived need for shared values and a set of networks of reciprocal obligations and loyalties: 'freedom can only flourish within a community where shared values, common loyalties and mutual obligations provide a framework of order and self-discipline' (Hurd, 1989).

The main arena for the development of these loyalties and obligations was to be the local community in which citizens lived and worked. The active citizen was likely to be a school governor, involved in a neighbourhood watch scheme, perhaps a scout troop leader, and active in local charities and social issues affecting the local environment:

> Greater opportunities for active citizenship are being offered and being taken up. Parents are having more say over the way their children's school is being run. Council tenants have new powers to share in the management of their estates. Our action against crime and against drugs relies increasingly on a partnership between statutory agencies, the relevant professions and public-spirited citizens. (Hurd, 1989)

The tone of the active citizenship campaign appeared, at first sight, to draw its inspiration from the traditional conservative ideas of Burke, who envisaged that the basis for civic virtue to develop was through the overlapping loyalties contained within the so-called little platoons of society. These platoons, such as the brass band movement or the women's institute, because of their focus upon local communities and shared interests, provide the social networks and therefore the social fabric on which individuals' identities, as well as their security, is maintained and ordered. I wish to argue, however, that the active citizenship campaign was consistent with the neo-liberal agenda of Thatcherism, which was concerned more with the development of a citizenship based upon the assertion of the individual and the market, rather than a genuine concern for the promotion of community values. The kind of communities envisaged by traditional conservatives were actually undermined by Thatcherite policies, which increased social division, rather than created the basis for community spirit to emerge (see Chapter 8).

In terms of the Thatcherite aspiration of rolling back the (welfare) state, the evoking of active citizenship seemed consistent with that policy aim. As Gamble (1994) has pointed out, the rolling back of the state was a highly selective exercise and was really focused upon welfare or the 'nanny state', which the Thatcherites argued had created a dependency culture where many people lost all sense of individual responsibility, innovation, and self-reliance. Active citizenship can be seen as a corrective to this problem, which the Thatcherites saw as a product of the social liberal consensus on the need for universal social rights that emasculated rather than emancipated citizens.

By stressing self-reliance, people would again be effective, rather than apathetic, citizens. On a more practical level, active citizenship would take the strain off state services, health workers, police officers, teachers and social workers, who would all be greatly assisted by a more active citizenry. In this sense the notion of active citizenship can be related closely to the idea of 'character' building, which was the central aim of social liberals like Mill and Green. Implicit in its aims was the idea that it is individuals' actions that determine 'social' outcomes.

In keeping with the Thatcherite thesis that Britain from 1945 to 1979 had been overgoverned, the concept of active citizenship can also be seen as an attempt to take power away from the government. Of course this also meant that government could be less easily held to account for social problems if the stress was placed upon the need for individuals to solve their own problems.

According to the Conservative governments from 1979 onwards, yet another unfortunate by-product of the social liberal consensus was not only the creation of a dependency culture, but also the promotion of the 'permissive society'. It was argued that a combination of rising expectations, fuelled by the ever-expanding and self-perpetuating welfare state, plus the dominance of public services by left-wing activists had resulted by the 1970s in increasing delinquency and social disorder (Cox and Scruton, 1984). The 1960s and 1970s, according to the Thatcherites, saw the increase of licence rather than liberty, and a general attitude that 'society owes me a living' and that authority should be ridiculed rather than respected. The rising crime rates of the 1980s and the public disorder in Britain's inner cities were explained in these moralistic terms (Benyon, 1987: 30–5). Active citizenship would help to combat these problems by encouraging pride in one's local community, as well as combating such instances of anti-social behaviour through locally organised crime prevention activity such as the neighbourhood watch schemes.

The encouragement of active citizenship would also return a moral dimension to politics, missing in the social liberal era, where bureaucrats, leftist academics and teachers had reduced the causes of all society's problems to a set of impersonal structures. These structures (read excuses) allow for the abdication of responsibility, banish the concepts of sin, guilt and shame, and through sociological jargon explain away crime and hooliganism as 'understandable,' or even as a rational response to the inequalities of capitalist society (Benyon, 1987).

Active citizenship recast liberal values such as respect for the law and for private property in a new mould. Thus citizenship was evoked by the Conservatives as both an explanatory device, in the sense that society's ills could be put down to a lack of individual responsibility, and also as a wonder cure for such problems. Once citizens realised their responsibilities and began to be active in solving their own problems and, if the mood strikes them, other people's, many of society's ills would be solved. In this context the continuity of policy can be observed, from Thatcher's constant reference to Victorian values to John Major's 'back to basics' campaign (discussed below). The Conservative government showed its willingness to attribute the problems of British society to individual moral failings.

CRITICISMS OF ACTIVE CITIZENSHIP

The first criticism I wish to make of active citizenship is that historically citizenship has been essentially a political concept expressing a relationship between individuals and some form of political community, whether that be a city state, as in medieval Italy, or more recently the nation-state. Any notion of citizenship that tries to emphasise its social aspects in the form of duties, without proper reference to the political realm, is a narrowed and de-politicised definition which detracts from true active citizenship, which must involve collective policy making, consultation and the protection of basic rights associated with democratic forms of government.

Active citizenship requires empowerment in a political community. In the Thatcherite vision of active citizens, there was no reference to the defence of fundamental civil rights or democracy. The Thatcherite governments consistently neglected to provide basic reforms to the polity which would increase the information, access and protection which underpins a developed sense of citizenship.

A second criticism is made by Michael Ignatieff (1991: 26–37), who argues that the Thatcherite notion of a citizen was ultimately linked to property ownership and wealth. In a 'conservative home owning society' it is property ownership that enables citizens to be active. The Thatcherite vision of active citizenship was exclusive since, without property and wealth, some citizens are dependent upon the activities of others who do have such a stake in society. The 'active citizen' is really a social entrepreneur; an individual who is empowered, not by democracy, but by property ownership. Therefore, those who are not able to be active because of the constraints of money, resources and time are stigmatised as dependants and subjects. They are implicitly designated as second-class citizens, dependent upon the good will of other citizens. Douglas Hurd recognised the connection between money, time and active citizenship when writing in *The Independent* in September 1989 he argued:

> The idea of active citizenship is a necessary complement to that of the enterprise culture. Public service may once have been the duty of an elite, but today it is the responsibility of all who have the time or money to spare. Modern capitalism has democratised the ownership of property, and we are now witnessing the demo-cratisation of responsible citizenship. (Hurd, 1989)

The very fact that property in Britain is clearly not democratised (Scott, 1991: 145–76; 1994) prevents many people from having money to give to charities, or because they have to work for wages they have little time for the pursuit of active citizenship. The division in liberal theory between an unequal private sphere and a formally equal public sphere is crucial in understanding the elitist notion of the active citizen. The 'responsible citizenship' that Hurd desires amounts to mercy, compassion and pity by the propertied elite for the rest of society, rather than a recognition of the interdependence of all citizens. In this sense citizenship is depoliticised and privatised. By detaching economics from politics in such a way, the liberal theory on which Hurd draws necessarily creates a division between active and passive citizens because citizenship is ultimately connected to resources which allow for participation in both the public and private worlds.

Also, as Hill (1994: 20) points out, the good will of others may not be a secure foundation for the care of those in need. She estimates that only a seventh of charitable receipts comes from donations and fund-raising activity, with the rest coming from fees and charges for services rendered. By emphasising that the individual citizen is morally responsible for 'care,' it can be argued that this reduces collective responsibility expressed in more democratic forms than individual charity or isolated acts of voluntarism, such as through local government provision. In a society of the size and complexity of Britain it is difficult to see how the solutions of social problems can be left to be solved by spontaneous and unco-ordinated individual acts of charity (Miller, 1989: Ch. 4).

Finally, the strain of active citizenship cannot of course be shared evenly in a highly gendered society. The emphasis upon caring at home for elderly relatives, for example, undoubtedly puts a disproportionate strain upon women, who still tend to bear the brunt of such caring. Ironically this fact also works against the involvement of women in other activities normally associated with good citizenship such as participation in political parties, pressure groups, or even in the kind of voluntary activities envisaged by the Conservative ministers advocating active citizenship. Active citizenship, couched in such individualistic terms, actually tends towards undermining good citizenship and increases existing inequalities in the sexual division of labour. As Oliver has commented, 'it is these aspects of the emphasis on family responsibility that produces scepticism about the motivation of exponents of active citizenship: it is seen as a substitute for the state's responsibility for the social element of the citizenship of entitlement' (Oliver, 1991: 165).

The Thatcherites, by stressing responsibilities while at the same time reducing social entitlements, undermined citizenship because such provision is essential to enable people to carry out their duties. Use of the discourse of active citizenship shifted the emphasis of citizenship away from the political community and towards individual acts of moral behaviour, generosity, or charity. As Ignatieff argues, 'the history of citizenship has been the struggle to make freedom real, not to tie us all in the leading strings of therapeutic good intentions' (Ignatieff, 1991: 34).

The Conservative notion of active citizenship was a reflection of the duality of citizenship in liberal theory, which, because of its individualistic assumptions, creates a tension between rights and duties. It is only when the individual and political community are perceived as intimately connected, and rights and duties understood as two sides of the same coin, that this dualism can be dissolved and meaningful citizenship constituted.

THE CITIZEN'S CHARTER

With the fall of Margaret Thatcher in 1990, the explicit use of the active citizenship concept largely disappeared and her successor, John Major, introduced his so-called 'big idea', namely the Citizen's Charter, as a foundation stone of Tory policy on citizenship in the 1990s.

Some writers (Lewis, 1993) have implied that this policy represented a break with the neo-liberal policies of the Thatcher years with the Charter's emphasis on customer rights and public service provision. However, on closer examination, high levels of continuity exist between the concept of active citizenship and the Citizen's Charter as regards the vision of what characterises the good citizen.

The main themes of the Citizen's Charter programme were again, like those underpinning the active citizenship campaign, concerned with the problem of state overload, social citizenship and its associated (self-serving) bureaucracy. Throughout the official publications of the Charter, references can be found to inefficient bureaucrats, patronising local councillors, and bad practice in public service. For example:

By the early 1980s, the Government was seeking ways of improving the quality of public services without adding to their costs. Too often, public sector organisations seemed to deliver services that were designed to suit the providers rather than the recipients. (Citizen's Charter Unit, 1992: 7)

There must no longer be a hiding place for sloppy standards, lame excuses and attitudes that patronise the public. (John Major, cited in *The Independent*, 6 July 1991)

The key right envisaged in the Charter was the right to choose: individuals should be able to express preference and make decisions about the services they receive from the state or in the market place. The greater the choice, the better services would be, according to the simplistic logic of deregulated market economics. By making public service more like private industries service would be rendered more effective and efficient.

ORIGINS OF THE CITIZEN'S CHARTER

John Major claims to have begun to formulate the ideas of the Citizen's Charter in 1987. Indeed in 1991 a text appeared from 1987 when Major was Chief Secretary to the Treasury which summed up Major's desire to restructure the relationship between public service provision and the consumer. Major commented that 'for too long we have given excessive weight to the interests of the producers of public services and too little to those of the consumer' (*The Independent*, 6 July 1991).

The centrality of choice reflected the Conservatives' commitment to a neo-liberal ideology, which views the individual as the basic unit of any community. Individuals are seen as sovereign and autonomous, acting according to free choice. In this context the Citizen's Charter programme should be seen as part of a wider set of policy initiatives in the field of public service dating back to the 1980s. The Education Acts of 1988 and 1993, the Housing and Local Government Act of 1989, and the National Health Service and Community Care Act of 1990 were all attempts to increase personal responsibility and the basic market right of the citizen, as privileged by the Thatcherite governments; that is, the right to choose (see Sullivan, 1992: 185–207, for a discussion of these policies).

All of these Acts attempted to shift the balance of power away from the producers and providers of public service to the individual consumer. This was done by increasing choice between services by promoting internal and external competition in such fields as education and health service provision. The government was keen to ensure that people's duty to pay tax was balanced by a right to good and prompt service, so that citizens should have increased and more accessible information about public services. Citizens should be empowered by government to make choices in an environment of public service that was accountable to the people.

For the Conservative government, the best insurance of such accountability was to introduce the rigours of the market into public service. It was through healthy competition, rather than dogmatic state control, that citizens would be empowered. In education, for example, schools should be given the opportunity, through local management of their budgets, to by-pass local government bureaucrats and to compete directly with other schools for pupils and, therefore, resources.

Those schools who failed to deliver a quality service (and this should be monitored through the publication of information concerning pupils' achievements in exam performance and truancy rates) would ultimately pay the price by being forced to close. Teachers who failed to meet government standards would be removed from their jobs. By being opened to the forces of the market, schools would more effectively serve, not only parents and pupils, but also the whole country, as schools run in this way were more likely (it was argued) to be responsive to the needs of business.

It is clear that in the area of public services the principles underpinning the Citizen's Charter bear striking similarities to the concept of active citizenship since the flip side of the right to choose is of course the responsibility to exercise that choice in a thoughtful way. A good example of the duties associated with choice relates again to the area of education. As the Parent's Charter stated in 1994:

> The parent's charter will help you get the best education for your child. You can do this most successfully as an active partner with the school and its teachers . . . It is true that discipline begins at home . . . This means that parents, relatives and friends have a big responsibility. (Department for Education, 1994: 25)

The choice to send one's child to a school which best appeared to satisfy that child's needs also entailed a responsibility to carefully examine available evidence about the schools in any given area, as well the duty to ensure attendance at the school.

The Citizen's Charter, like active citizenship, saw individual responsibility as the key to good citizenship. Consumers, too, had to be active in maintaining pressure on public services to work more effectively.

KEY THEMES OF THE CHARTER

The original White Paper introducing the Citizen's Charter was first published on 22 July 1991. The themes of the Charter, which stemmed from the wider public policy areas already discussed above, were outlined in the various documents accompanying the launch of the Charter. They were quality, choice, standards, and value. The main mechanisms for achieving these objectives were to be:

- Privatisation, for example British Rail.
- Contracting out and more competitive tendering.
- Information on performance, such as the publication of leagues tables of schools' exam results.
- Performance-related pay.
- Effective complaints and compensation systems.

Major, and his various ministers involved in the formulation and implementation of the Charter, made clear its chief objectives in several speeches and pronouncements, and via the various government publications reporting on its principles and progress. For Major the Charter reflected a determination 'to raise the standard services up to and beyond the best at present available and to make them answer better to the needs of ordinary people' (Major, in Citizen's Charter Unit, 1992: 4). Junior minister Francis Maude believed the Charter to be 'simply the most comprehensive programme ever launched by any government anywhere to improve public service . . . the Citizen's Charter will improve the life of every citizen in the land' (cited in Connolly et al., 1994: 26).

The Charter aimed to improve citizenship in the following ways: quality and greater information and access to the citizen of public service; the need for public service to operate efficiently with the knowledge that government spending would be strictly limited; and the introduction of market mechanisms as the principal way of protecting the paramount citizenship right of choice. All of these provisions reflected the government's view that the individual, acting as a consumer, was more effective at maintaining standards than collective decision making in public sector bureaucracies.

Following the first Citizen's Charter, a whole host of separate but related charters appeared covering such diverse groups as students, patients, rail travellers, tenants, consumers and job seekers, all led by the basic market strategy outlined above. The aim of all of these charters was, in essence, to deliver to citizens consumer rights as part of a wider commitment to market rights, which would provide assurance of the quality of the services provided through government spending. The

Charter should not be seen as the foundation of a new ideology or set of beliefs known as Majorism; rather the Charter is more accurately seen as an extension of the Thatcherite policies of privatisation, contracting out government services, and the general programme of the deregulation of the economy, all of which were supposedly aimed at increasing the market rights of the people.

In the 1980s the government emphasised the need for tax payers' money to be spent in a responsible manner, and it sought mechanisms to ensure value for money in public service. The best role for government was in delivering market rights to people through the policies discussed, and thereby increasingly reducing the role of government as provider of other rights such as welfare and education. The Citizen's Charter was merely a continuation of these policies by other means.

INTERPRETING THE CHARTER

Davina Cooper (1993) has examined the possible reasons for the development of the Citizen's Charter. The first possibility was a party political one, namely that John Major as a recently elected Prime Minister felt the need for a so-called 'big idea' which would make his premiership distinctive from his predecessor, whose domination of the Conservative Party and, indeed British politics in the 1980s, had been exceptional. According to this view, the Citizen's Charter was a way for Major to establish his leadership of the Conservative Party and of the country as whole. Making public service more effective and accountable seemed like a popular theme to tackle as the 1980s had seen a persistent concern amongst politicians, commentators and the public about the amount of spending on state services and the supposed lack of efficiency, accountability and value for money that public services offered and delivered. In fact, Major's 'big idea' was based on an agenda created and popularised by his predecessor. As Barron and Scott (1992: 526) write, 'the Citizen's Charter programme maintained a policy of fiscal restraint and of seeking to replace bureaucratic public sector structures with marketised ones, and of replacing collectivised forms of decision making with forms of individual choice'. The Citizen's Charter, then, can be seen as a continuation of the policy of the rolling back of the welfare state.

A second possible reason for the creation of the Citizen's Charter was that it legitimised the restructuring of public service. Through the policy of the Citizen's Charter the government, by setting unrealistic targets for public service, could point to the advantages of the private sector, and therefore plan future policies of privatisation of aspects of the public sector. An advantage of this approach, for the government, was that the language of the Charter was difficult for critics to argue against, since who could complain that quality and standards were unimportant?

Third, the Citizen's Charter enabled the government to distance itself from the problems of public service. Through the mechanisms of the Charter, providers of the various public services consumed by citizens were identified as the problem which the government was curing through provisions in the Citizen's Charter. At the same time, problems in the system caused, or made worse, by lack of adequate government spending could be papered over with bold statements of services rendered to the consumer. The origins of the Charter can be seen to be entirely consistent with the Thatcherite agenda. Indeed, as Cooper argues, the Charter was another use (or misuse) of concepts of citizenship: it presented an opportunity to assert a neo-liberal conception of the relationship between the state and citizen.

Finally, Cooper puts forward the argument that the Charter can be seen as a movement away from the Thatcher era, which was perceived by the public as over centralised and authoritarian, by providing more power to the people through increased information and the opportunity to complain against poor service. However, an examination of the nature of the Charter and its relationship to citizens clearly shows that the empowering element of the Charter was severely limited. This limitation was due, not just to poor policy formulation, but to deeper and more fundamental problems which lay at the heart of the Thatcherite approach to citizenship in general, and social rights in particular.

Essentially the Citizen's Charter can be seen to be part of a major redefining of citizenship by the Thatcherite governments. Under Thatcherism, there occurred a movement away from citizenship, defined as rights and duties enjoyed by citizens who are political animals joined together in a common political purpose, to a definition where citizens were perceived as individual economic consumers in the market place. This has led Cooper to argue that:

> In reducing relations in civil society to those of the market-place, the Citizen's Charter entrenches a process of de-politicisation – there is no place for campaigns, protests and pickets in Major's Charter society. There is little room even for the 'active citizen', beloved of the right, in this relationship of citizen and state. (Cooper, 1993: 156)

Cooper is right to point to the market as the foundation of Thatcherite definitions of citizenship. However, the Citizen's Charter did not mark a break with active citizenship as she suggests. Both the Citizen's Charter and the active citizenship campaign shared the same assumptions of the desired nature of the citizen. Both were concerned with personal responsibility and individual choice in the market place rather than political participation. Both were part of a wider strategy to reduce citizens' reliance upon social rights provided by the state and they rested equally upon the assumption that citizens had the resources to be active consumers and vigorous members of society.

The Charter, like active citizenship, was informed by neo-liberal ideology dominant in the Conservative Party in the 1980s and 1990s. In particular, a critique of the operation of social rights lay behind both policies. Thatcherites assumed that all people were essentially egoistical actors, and this meant that any institution set up to serve some notion of the public good would in practice be driven by the self-interest of the provider, rather than the needs of the consumer. As bureaucracies are self-perpetuating and self-interested, they tend towards practices which maintain conditions for those who work in the bureaucracy, which are necessarily inefficient and costly. Public services are particularly prone to this as they are paid for by government and are natural monopolies.

The answer to this problem of self-interest, argued the Thatcherites, was to introduce market forces to public services. One way to promote such practice was through the introduction of the language contained in the Citizen's Charter; that is, a combination of neo-liberal terminology such as privatisation, efficiency and market forces, with new managerialism, with its emphasis on consumer care, quality, accountability and performance indicators. Through the combination of these complementary approaches the Conservatives aimed to redefine the relationship between the citizen and the state. The key rights of citizenship according to the Citizen's Charter were the right to choose between different kinds of provision and the right to receive good public service.

CRITICISMS OF THE CHARTER

The Citizen's Charter can be criticised in a number of ways. It has been accused of being an indirect attack on the concept of public provision guaranteed by the state, and therefore an attack on social rights. The Charter was also limited as a guarantee of the rights of citizenship, defined even in the narrow sense of consumer rights. I will consider the inconsistencies of the Charter, and examine its wider context in terms of general government policy and ideology.

The status of the various charters was unclear. They had no legal force and were not consistent in the guarantees, promises, aspirations and compensation they offered to the consumer. Some of the individual charters merely stated what was actually happening in that particular policy area, whereas others were more aspirational and ambitious. There is a danger in grouping lots of different kinds of services under the single umbrella of a Citizen's Charter because clearly services are very different in terms of who consumes them and the type of service given. In addition, the various charters are inconsistent in the provision they make for complaints and compensation. For example, the Job Seeker's Charter promised only that people would be treated with courtesy: little compensation for a person struggling to survive and overcome a clerical mistake which delays his or her benefit.

More fundamentally, the Citizen's Charter contained no meaningful provision for the guarantee of basic political or civil rights. Labour MP Chris Smith argued one of the problems not addressed by the Charter was freedom of information legislation: 'the government's legislative programme contains no commitment to provide for freedom of information legislation to give our citizens the right of access to information on what the government are up to' (Smith, 1991: column 1346). Tony Benn pointed out during the House of Commons debate on the introduction of the Citizen's Charter programme that because of the lack of a bill of rights the very use of the word 'citizen' was misplaced:

> The phrase 'Citizen's Charter' attracts my interest but those who advocate it do not have the slightest idea what they have started. We in this country are not citizens, we are subjects of the crown . . . If we are talking about citizens the government will have to consider constitutional reform. (Benn, 1991: column 1395)

As regards social rights, there existed only a vague commitment to fundamental services for all citizens but there was no systematic attempt to define the content of these. As has already been argued, the Charter in fact presented an attack on a notion of social rights guaranteed, and largely provided, by the state. As Benn argued, 'the Citizen's Charter has nothing to do with real rights. It is an attempt to mobilise public opinion against the public services' (Benn, 1991: column 1395).

A good example of the approach of the charters, and its implicit attack on public service, was the publication of exam league tables with the supposed aim of facilitating greater consumer choice, whilst also ensuring that the most 'responsible' parents would be able to judge whether any one school was suitable for their children. Without placing such statistics into their social and economic context the performance of any one school could easily be distorted. Also by focusing attention on only one 'performance indicator', much good work carried out in state schools such as community liaison, development of teamwork and preparation for adulthood were buried under a mountain of exam statistics.

The approach of the Charter was consistent with the neo–liberalism of

Hayek, with its emphasis upon freedom of choice in a competitive market. For the government of John Major the Citizen's Charter was an ideal way to introduce such ideas into public services, possibly as a prelude to turning some such services over to the private sector. By ensuring efficiency and freedom to choose, the government argued that this increased the liberty of citizens, as well as decreasing passive dependency upon the organs of the state.

Importantly the Citizen's Charter can be seen as an attempt to weaken the link between the state as a provider of welfare and the citizen. Services consumed by the citizen became the responsibility of the provider (the individual school or hospital for example) rather than the political responsibility of the government. The Charter was an attempt to empower the individual as a consumer rather than deliver more power to the citizen community, which is by its nature collective and cannot be reduced purely to individual preference or want.

In reality, the concept of the individual 'consumer citizen' choosing rationally from a diversity of public service is illusory. As Cooper (1993) argues, the Charter ignored the vast difference in the balance of the power between the provider of a service and the individual consumer of that service. Cooper argues that the government's policy perceived the very nature of civil society to be characterised by a conflict between the provider and the user of services. Certainly, in some of the language surrounding the Citizen's Charter evidence can be found to support this idea (Citizen's Charter Unit, Press Notice, 7 November 1991; see also *The Independent on Sunday*, 2 February 1992).

The problem is that individual choices in the market place are a poor way to run public service, particularly as social structures mean that not all individuals are as well placed as others to make use of these services. Public service itself is a reflection of community, shared needs and common purposes. It is doubtful, for example, whether such important agents of socialisation such as schools and colleges can be, or indeed should be, driven by customer preference. For instance, all citizens have a stake in the education of our children, not just parents.

The Thatcherite governments perceived social rights to be detrimental to the nation. Therefore, it was argued that public service should be made to resemble the private sector as closely as possible through the mechanisms of 'quality control' provided through the Charter. The fact that the Charter did not extend to the private sector reflected the liberal idea of the necessary division between the market and the public sphere. The private sector remained untouched by the Charter and therefore the citizen was denied control over this sector. As Benn contends, this opened the whole Citizen's Charter programme to the allegation that it operated only in the interest of capitalism and illustrated the incompatibility of citizenship and unregulated capitalism. As Benn puts it, 'the discipline of the market is challenged by the use of the word citizen' (Benn, 1991: column 1395).

For socialists like Benn, the notion of a citizen was incompatible with the Thatcherite model of the self-interested consumer operating in the market place. The very notion of the citizen implies a community where our interests are bound up with those of our fellow citizens: 'to go back to the book of Genesis, "Am I my brother's keeper?" That is the question raised by having a serious debate about citizens' rights' (Benn, 1991: column 1395).

One of the principal weaknesses of the Charter, then, was that it implicitly attacked citizenship as a concept that expresses membership of a collective political community. It detached citizenship from the political community and redefined it in terms of consumer values, which de-politicised and narrowed the concept. The fact that the Citizen's Charter was expressed as a charter for individuals, that it is the Citizen's Charter rather than a Citizens' Charter, reinforced the notion that citizenship could somehow be detached from the very community which rendered it possible.

It can be also be argued that even in terms of providing citizens with effective consumer rights, the Charter failed. This is because citizens passively received services that had already been shaped, organised and structured by government policy and the various policy networks involved in any given public service (Marsh and Rhodes, 1992). If we take education as an example, the consumer was offered no choice over what was studied by children between the ages of 5 and 14 (in state schools only of course) as this was centrally imposed by the government through the National Curriculum. The only option for parents faced by a National Curriculum they did not agree with, or found limited in some way, was to exit from the system and to pay for their children to go to a private school.

It can be seen that consumer choice of public services was limited, the only alternative being to opt out of the system altogether. This did not exist as a meaningful choice for the majority of citizens who did not possess the necessary financial means to turn to the private sector. A truly effective charter would provide much greater consultation and decision-making powers to consumers so that their preferences could actually be taken account of. The only mechanism to ensure this would be collective rather than individual, that is through some form of democratic process. The problem is that the government's focus was upon individual choices rather than collective decision making and democratic mechanisms.

The Charter made no attempt to increase the mechanisms to improve consultation with citizens. In fact, it can be argued that through such developments as the extension of enforced contracting out of local government services, real democratic accountability of services was undermined. In a speech to the Commons, concerning the setting up of independent housing trusts, Major summed up his view of the effectiveness of many local governments: 'no longer will the improvement of their estates be frustrated by the opposition of local councils . . . the Citizen's Charter will end, once and for all, the patronising of tenants by incompetent town halls' (*The Independent*, 23 July 1991).

Another problem was that the Conservative government made clear that any lack of quality within public service could not be rectified through making more tax payers' money available. Services would have to be made more effective through the largely superficial changes suggested by the rhetoric of the Citizen's Charter. However, as Malcolm Bruce has commented, for those in desperate need of essential services this was of little comfort: 'it is no consolation to people who are going to the housing department to be told politely, quickly, efficiently and courteously that there are no homes available to meet their demands' (cited in Connolly et al., 1994: 26).

Contrary to the Thatcherite vision of the sovereignty of the individual, clearly choices are limited if an individual is socially disadvantaged. The Charter made little provision for dealing with the problems of discrimination. All citizens were assumed to be equally able to consume public services without the need for special provision to counter unequal treatment by the white and male-dominated higher echelons of such services. The various charters operated at an abstract level of equal opportunity divorced from the reality of inequalities, which were based on social structures such as 'race', gender and class, rather than the 'natural' inequalities championed by Thatcherism.

Finally, many of the assumptions in the Charter were treated as uncontroversial and uncontested (Cooper, 1993). Much of the language contained in the charters assumed that the right to choose in the market place was the only way to solve many of the important issues of distribution of services and goods. For example, it was assumed in the Tenant's Charter that the right to buy was the guiding principle. However, it can be argued that such a policy reduced the number of houses available to future prospective tenants, encouraged those who could not afford to buy a house to try to do so, and also had implications for the homeless (see Chapter 8). How can citizens exercise their 'sense of responsibility' effectively without adequate shelter?

Through a critical examination of the Citizen's Charter programme, it can be argued that the Charter failed to extend citizenship in any significant way. The consumer rights that it offered were restricted to public services and did not impact upon the private sector. Also, customers were unable to influence the actual policies of public service in any direct fashion through the mechanisms of the Charter. The fact that the Charter was undemocratic and limited in its scope led many critics to argue that it was a convenient way of reducing government responsibility for the effectiveness of public service; rather than representing an extension of citizenship it attacks the concept of social rights.

This chapter has shown how the Thatcher and Major governments' essentially neo-liberal conception of citizenship was reflected in such policies as the Citizen's Charter and the active citizenship campaign. At the heart of these policies was the Thatcherite view that social rights were detrimental to the independence and self-reliance of individuals and were therefore harmful to the market that relies upon individuals to display the vigorous virtues of hard work, innovation and enterprise.

Implicit in the Thatcherites' approach was the division between those active citizens who were able to make provision for themselves, and those passive citizens who, for a variety of reasons, failed to make use of their market rights. These citizens should not, according to the Thatcherites, be allowed to drain the resources of the nation through either excessive claims for social rights or through displays of anti-social behaviour. Chapter 8 will explore the debate concerning these passive citizens.

8

PASSIVE CITIZENS?

During the years of the Thatcherite governments, citizenship in Britain became increasingly exclusive. This chapter will show how Conservative policies sought to change the relationship between the citizen and the state by attempting to increase the opportunity for people to make use of their market rights, which in practice served only to increase social division. It will be argued that these failed policies led the government to blame those social groups who lost out in the Thatcherite experiment for their own alleged inability to become active citizens. The Conservative government increasingly pathologised individuals who were characterised as passive and parasitic citizens, and such exclusive discourses helped the government to increase the coercive arm of the state in an attempt to combat the perceived threat of an emerging underclass. It will be argued that through policies like the Criminal Justice and Public Order Act 1994, citizenship in its civil and political forms was diluted.

THE ROOTS OF EXCLUSION

For the Thatcherites, the social rights of the post-war period were both morally wrong and a primary component in Britain's economic decline. With the developments associated with deregulated capitalism, Thatcherites argued that in order to remain competitive, social rights should be restricted and the inequality of the market promoted. As we saw in Chapter 3, writers like Barbalet (1988: 20) have argued that what happened was that the government asserted civil rights (perceived as rights against interference from the state) over claims for social rights that were guaranteed by the state and which therefore threatened individual civil rights. However what actually happened in Britain after 1979 was that market rights, rather than civil rights, were asserted against claims of social citizenship. The distinction between civil rights and the more narrow concept of market rights is a crucial one in this context, because the Thatcherite approach to citizenship not only undermined social rights but also attacked civil and political rights both directly and indirectly through its policies.

Linked to the undermining of civil and political rights was the willingness of Thatcherite governments to redefine exactly what attributes constituted a good citizen. They were not afraid to use the power of the state to curtail the rights of people perceived to be outside the defined norms of acceptable social behaviour. Linked to this was an attempt by the government after 1979 to implicitly dispute the legitimate membership of the British nation of certain social groups and to question their right to substantive citizenship. The presence of this moralistic tone has to be understood in terms of the dualistic nature of liberal citizenship presented in this book.

The dualism of active versus passive citizens arises naturally from the logic of liberal approaches to citizenship adopted by the Thatcherite governments. The emergence of a notion of passive or undeserving citizens is partly due to the theoretical assumptions of liberalism, and partly due to the realities of applying liberal policies in practice. In other words, the roots of exclusion are multifaceted, operating on both a practical and theoretical level.

A central problem which has been discussed throughout the book is the emphasis liberalism places upon the importance of individual action within the context of a free market for explaining social behaviour. This idea is a cornerstone of all liberal theories of citizenship, but is particularly emphasised by neo-liberals. This means that citizenship should be a strictly limited affair. It should enable the individual citizens to display the vigorous virtues of self-reliance, innovation and responsibility, and states should protect the negative rights of the market. Constraints upon individuals such as high taxes to pay for social rights should be minimalised. In this formulation the market is characterised as impersonal and non-coercive and therefore does not discriminate between individuals.

Neo-liberals oppose the neutrality, and therefore superiority, of the market to the coercive, discriminatory and arbitrary operations of democracy. Politics is characterised as threatening to the spontaneous order of the market. In this sense neo-liberal conceptions of citizenship strive to de-politicise citizenship in order to achieve maximum freedom for the economy and individuals. By the de-politicisation of citizenship I mean that neo-liberals seek to define citizenship in terms of a formal and negative status applying to the individual actor. They wish to undermine citizenship as a status denoting the interdependence and collective nature of a political community. In this way not only is freedom maintained but the whole community is enriched by the efforts of its most talented members. Society is made more prosperous by the dynamic of inequality because entrepreneurs create opportunities for all members of the nation. This was essentially the position of Thatcherite governments concerning the meaning of citizenship.

A problem however arises out of the failure of all citizens to perform the vigorous virtues or prosper by utilising their market rights. The logic of the agency-based approach of Thatcherism was, in short, to blame the agent for his or her failings. Such individuals must, therefore, be strongly dealt with by the state to ensure that their actions do not interfere with the freedom of others. The logic of a strong state is consistent with the neo-liberal assumptions of Thatcherism and in practice the state has been extremely coercive towards perceived 'enemies of the market'. In particular, the Thatcherite governments' perspectives upon issues of crime and public disorder were agency-based. The problem of disorder was therefore viewed as the sole responsibility of the criminal or rioter, and such people were variously labelled by Conservative ministers and right-wing ideologues as wicked, genetically inferior, permissive, workshy and so on. It is not social structures and processes which are to blame, but the individual, and this perspective derives directly from liberal theory. The problem for Thatcherite governments was that the frequency of such behaviour rose sharply during their period of office. For the first time for decades, mainland Britain witnessed full-scale riots, and crime escalated during the years following the election of Margaret Thatcher.

These problems of social order have been linked by many writers to rising levels of unemployment, poverty and deprivation during the Thatcherite years, and the key to these problems was the failure of Thatcherite economic policy to deliver the 'trickle down effect'. By actively encouraging inequality the Thatcherites hoped to achieve prosperity for all. However, a survey of the evidence on poverty and inequality in Thatcherite Britain indicates that this failed to occur, and that many citizens were in no position to display self-reliance, or to utilise their market rights.

THE DIMENSIONS OF EXCLUSION

Through their public policy, the Thatcherite governments showed a consistent approach to citizenship that aimed at a fundamental transformation in the relationship between the citizen and the state. By promoting the virtues of personal responsibility, underpinned by the extension of market rights, the economy and moral health of the nation would be improved and both virtue and wealth would spread downwards to all but the most feckless. In this sense, active citizenship, like economic success, would trickle down to encompass all citizens.

However, the evidence of the Thatcherite record clearly does support the view that citizenship was not enhanced by such policies. The result of many of these policies was to further exclude many citizens from the resources necessary to the practice of citizenship.

OWNERSHIP AS A FOUNDATION OF CITIZENSHIP

According to the Thatcherites, the basis for successful citizenship was ownership of property and an economic stake in society. As we have seen, the notion of active citizenship was underpinned by the ownership of property. Thatcherite governments believed that good citizenship was promoted by extending, to as many people as possible, market rights of ownership and choice. The policies of privatisation clearly reflected this view, particularly in relation to the sale of public utilities and council housing. In practice, the selling of shares has been of little significance in extending the influence of ordinary citizens over large companies and most of the shares sold went to extremely rich individuals or to large corporations (Central Statistical Office, 1992: 103). The small percentage of shares that did go to small investors were often quickly sold for short-term profit and therefore provided little in the way of a lasting foundation for citizenship (Scott, 1990: 362).

Of more lasting significance was the 'right to buy' programme. One of the first major Acts of the Thatcher government was the passing of the Housing Act of 1980, which attempted to increase the market rights of citizens by instituting a right to buy policy. The scheme involved large discounts of up to 50 per cent for long-standing council tenants, which between April 1979 to the end of 1991 led to the sale to tenants of some 1.8 million homes (Central Statistical Office, 1994b: 333). In addition to council house sales the early Thatcher governments took measures to ease the cost of home ownership, including various tax relief schemes on property ownership.

Such policies aimed to promote a commitment by people to the values of the market and to foster a sense of autonomy which had been undermined by dependence upon local authorities to provide and maintain housing. The 1992 Conservative manifesto stated that 'the opportunity to own a home and pass it on is one of the most important rights an individual has . . . it lies at the heart of our philosophy' (Conservative Party, 1992: 33).

However, many citizens were unable to establish for themselves the foundations of citizenship in property ownership. Government policy on housing increased insecurity for many citizens and decreased their opportunities to display active citizenship. Several negative outcomes can be detected:

- Increased levels of homelessness.
- Record levels of repossessions.
- Negative equity.
- An increased polarisation between property-owning active citizens and passive citizens.

The pressure group Shelter (1994) produced figures which put the level of homelessness in England at 420,000 people by the year 1991, and since 1979 it was estimated that homelessness had more than tripled. In addition the number of unofficial homeless people in the mid 1990s was thought to be well in excess of official figures (Oppenheim and Harker, 1996: 82–8). If we accept Marshall's definition of social rights as including 'a modicum of wealth and security' and as enabling citizens 'to live the life of a civilised being' (Marshall, 1963: 74), many people in Britain in the 1990s were clearly bereft of meaningful social rights. Homelessness decreases access to social security and employment; rights which are essential to the exercise of citizenship. In addition, homeless people are unable, without an address, to register to vote and are therefore deprived of a basic political right. Two of the key reasons for the increase in homelessness during the Thatcherite years was the lack of available and affordable rented accommodation and changes in social security benefits. These were taken away from 16- to 18-year-olds in the 1986 reform of the social security system.

By the mid-1990s many of those citizens who purchased housing were under financial pressure as levels of repossessions and the phenomena of negative equity illustrate. In 1993 60,000 houses had been repossessed by building societies and other mortgage lenders, and by 1993 around 1.3 million house owners were in the position of possessing homes which had a lower market value than the mortgage they were paying (Joseph Rowntree Foundation, 1994).

For many people the promise of security through the promotion of the right to own increased insecurity and failed to lay the foundation for active citizenship. The gap between those who could afford to build their sense of citizenship upon property ownership and those who did not have even the most basic of social rights such as secure housing was widened. The policy of council house sales, whilst increasing market rights for some, greatly decreased the social rights of others; remaining council housing, for obvious reasons, tended to be poor quality and concentrated in deprived inner-city areas, thereby increasing the sense of social exclusion felt by many tenants.

PROGRESSIVE TAXATION AS A BARRIER TO CITIZENSHIP

A significant area where market rights needed to be extended and incentive increased was, according to the Thatcherites, in personal taxation. One of the major problems with the post-war social liberal consensus had been the increasing levels of direct taxation that reduced the inequality which, it was argued, was necessary for a dynamic economy and enterprising citizens. Progressive taxation was seen not as an enhancer of citizenship but rather as a barrier to incentive and therefore active citizenship. Therefore, throughout the Thatcherite years, a key policy aim was the lowering of income tax.

Changes in levels of income tax have serious implications for citizenship since, as Marshall argues, progressive taxation had a central role in undermining social inequality in the post-war period and therefore increased the resources for the poorest citizens to take part in society. In the years following 1979 there was a shift from progressive income taxation to indirect taxation in the form of increased VAT rates, which take a greater proportion of the income of the poorest members of society than of wealthier citizens. Income tax rates were cut and the top rate of income tax was reduced from over 80 per cent to 40 per cent. Giles and Johnston (1994) found that between 1985 and 1995 the proportion of the overall tax burden shifted from the richest to the poorest citizens, so that the poorest 50 per cent of the population actually saw an increase in taxation whilst the rest of the population saw it reduced.

In addition, the government reformed the taxation of inheritance to decrease tax on inherited wealth. Other measures such as the introduction of the TESSA scheme and the stress on low inflation at the expense of high unemployment also benefited those citizens who had savings and owned property, again increasing the social divisions between citizens. However, for the Thatcherites, low inflation was the number one priority since this protected savings and investment and was essential to the long-term quality of citizenship. For this goal of low inflation, high unemployment, in the words of the ex-Chancellor Norman Lamont, was 'a price well worth paying' (*The Guardian*, 16 June 1993).

THE PROBLEM OF UNEMPLOYMENT

As was discussed in Chapter 6, the approach of the Thatcherite governments to employment issues was to reduce regulation and barriers to the operation of a free market in employment. According to this perspective, institutions like the wage councils, and particularly trade unions, were seen as infringing the operation of the market by maintaining artificially high wages. In this sense, the extensive legislation against trade union during the 1980s and 1990s (Rosamond, 1995) can be interpreted as increasing the right to work free from intimidation from pickets and the right to sell one's labour at a level determined by the market. While individual choice to engage in union activity may have been increased by such legislation, this has to be understood in relation to the reduction of collective bargaining, the increased vulnerability of workers to the imperatives of market forces, and the huge rise in unemployment.

High levels of unemployment throughout this time not only increased inequality, but also undermined important citizenship rights. Again if we take Marshall's definition of social rights, a right to work has to be considered as a cornerstone to citizenship. Marshall outlines the relative nature of social citizenship in his definition of social rights when he says that citizens have the right to a quality of life 'according to the standards prevailing in a society' (Marshall, 1963: 74). A clear expectation in Britain has, for some time, been the centrality of paid employment to the maintenance of personal dignity. In Britain throughout the 1980s and 1990s, this right was denied to as many as four million citizens at any one time. The reasons for the large increase in unemployment during the 1980s are complex and are outside of the focus of this work, but to a certain extent high levels of unemployment can be accounted for by structural changes in the economy due to the changing nature of capitalism discussed in Chapter 6. However, what is clear is that the trickle down effect hoped for by the government did not lead to a lowering of unemployment. The pursuit of lower inflation and a controlled money supply, coupled with an ideological aversion to state intervention in the economy, greatly increased levels of unemployment. As MacInnes (1987) has argued, Britain's record on unemployment in the 1980s was poor compared to other European countries. In addition, government figures on unemployment represented a large underestimate due to multiple changes in the way it was measured after 1979.

Mass unemployment has a number of consequences for citizenship. In terms of Thatcherite definitions of good citizenship, unemployment decreases the chance for citizens to make use of their market rights. The opportunity to purchase housing, or to be an active consumer, is greatly reduced. Also the vigorous virtues are undermined because, for the Thatcherites, unemployment reduced the opportunity for personal responsibility and created dependence upon the welfare state. Research into the psychological consequences of long-term unemployment also reveals a whole host of personal problems caused by being out of the work place for long periods. These include loss of personal esteem, feelings of isolation and depression, all of which undermine the ability of citizens to display active citizenship (Sinfield, 1981).

SOCIAL RIGHTS VERSUS MARKET RIGHTS

For the increasing number of unemployed people in the 1980s and 1990s the social rights provided by the social security system, despite their many flaws, were the only bulwark against further hardship and poverty. However, for the Thatcherite governments such social rights were the target of vigorous reform. Again the aim of reforming the social security system is consistent with a conception of citizenship which privileges market rights and personal responsibilities. The first problem with the social security system, it was argued, was that it placed an unaffordable strain upon the market, which is the real creator of wealth and, therefore, welfare. Second, excessive social security had the effect of creating a dependency culture, which undermined people's willingness to care for themselves.

The Conservatives argued that social security represented a massive strain upon the economy, which has led to high levels of borrowing by the government. However, the government, despite its rhetoric, failed to significantly reduce public borrowing and in fact the proportion of spending on the welfare state going on social security increased in the years following 1979 (Oppenheim, 1994: 6). The interpretation of why this occurred is of course crucial to finding the cure to this problem.

The Thatcherite's approach was to argue that the root of the problem lay in the inferiority of state social security compared to market solutions, and with individuals failing to perform their duties and to make use of the opportunities provided by the market. The Thatcherites therefore consistently argued for a radical reform of the social security system. However, as we have already noted, social rights were embedded in the consciousness of the nation and to dismantle them shiftily or completely would have been political suicide. Another barrier to reform has been the inherent inertia that is present in any policy area due to the complexity of the policy communities which developed to implement and influence policy and which will always inhibit radical change (Marsh and Rhodes, 1992).

However, inertia and political expediency should not be allowed to obscure the actual extent of radical reforms of the social security system, which undermined the citizenship of those forced to rely upon them. A detailed review of these is beyond the remit of this work but detailed studies of the social security system have been carried out by the Child Poverty Action Group. These show that the various reforms of the social security system added to the exclusion of many citizens and reduced their rights by depriving them of the adequate resources necessary to enact their citizenship effectively. Despite having low levels of social security benefits compared to many other countries in Europe, benefits were cut or access to them restricted (Oppenheim, 1994: 16–33).

Government reforms asserted the principles of greater means testing and more targeted benefits and reduced access to universal benefits as rights of citizenship. For example, some recent changes affecting universal benefits include:

- The replacement of the single payments scheme, which allowed people to claim for one-off grants for the purchase of essentials such as cookers and heaters, by the social fund in 1986. The social fund was discretionary and no appeals system was implemented.
- The Job Seeker's Allowance was introduced in 1996, which meant unemployment benefit was cut from one year to six months. Unemployment benefit and income support were joined together under the umbrella of the Job Seeker's Allowance, thereby blurring the distinction between means-tested and contributory benefits.
- Support for home owners who lost their job was decreased, further reducing the ability of people to ground their citizenship upon secure property ownership.
- The retirement age for women will be raised to 65 in the year 2010.

The attack on the principle of universal rights to benefit and the gradual shift to means-tested and targeted benefits were a serious threat to the citizenship of those dependent upon social rights to provide them with some stake in society. However, for the Thatcherites, a more secure base for citizenship would be provided by the market, which by encouraging the talents of individuals would benefit the whole of the nation. The rationale for the undermining of social rights was that fiscal constraints upon the market would be reduced, and more importantly the vigorous virtues of entrepreneurial citizenship suppressed by the nanny state would be liberated, to the benefit of all citizens.

The facts of the Thatcherite years, however, show no evidence in support of the success of trickle down economics. An examination of the extent of inequality in Britain in the mid 1990s shows that income and wealth inequality actually increased after 1979 and levels of poverty rose extensively.

WEALTH, INCOME AND POVERTY

In 1995 the Joseph Rowntree Foundation published the results of a major study into income and wealth distribution in Britain. Their findings illustrated the failure of Thatcherite policies to increase the opportunities for most citizens to assert their market rights. The inquiry found that the wealth gap between rich and poor had increased between 1977 and 1990, and that the pace of this growing inequality was higher than in any other European country. Income levels of many benefit claimants fell in real terms during the 1980s, and inequalities between rich and poor stopped declining. In a ringing condemnation of a central plank of the Thatcherite economic policy, the final report of the inquiry stated that:

> It might be possible to justify a growth in inequality – a widening gap between incomes of rich and poor – on the grounds that the beneficial effects on growth would raise the living standards of the poorest, but there is no evidence that this occurred in Britain: there is no sign of 'trickle down'. (Joseph Rowntree Foundation, 1995, vol. 1: 7)

This view of the trickle down effect concurs with that of ex-Tory minister Ian Gilmour. He states that 'the only trouble with the trickle-down theory . . . is that, as both the statistical and empirical evidence clearly show, it is not true' (Gilmour, 1992: 134).

Both the Child Poverty Action Group and the Rowntree Foundation concluded that because of the problems of homelessness, high unemployment, restricted benefits, a less progressive tax system, and excessive income inequality, levels of poverty in Britain dramatically increased during the Thatcherite years. The ability of people to be active citizens and to share in the cultural heritage of the country declined sharply. As the Rowntree inquiry concluded, 'one of our particular concerns is with the living standards and life opportunities of the poorest. In many areas of the UK these are simply unacceptably low in a society as rich as ours' (Joseph Rowntree Foundation, 1995, vol. 1: 8).

Although concentrated disproportionately amongst ethnic minorities and women and in certain geographical areas, poverty was widespread throughout the population. In 1992–3 between 13 and 14 million people in the UK were living in poverty, measured as those people who were either on or below levels of income support or who had levels of income below 50 per cent of the national average after housing costs (Oppenheim and Harker, 1996: 24). Oppenheim and Harker argue that in addition to absolute levels of income, poverty has to be understood as a measure of people's resources relative to other people in society. That is, poverty, like the extent of social rights, is best gauged by comparing the general standards prevailing in society with the plight of the poorest members of that society (Townsend, 1979). Oppenheim and Harker dispute government assertions that social rights were at the root of Britain's problems because they undermined personal responsibility and weakened the economy. The problems of the welfare state were due to the fact that during the Thatcherite years it was placed under increasing strain owing to poor economic performance, extreme levels of unemployment, the deregulation of the economy, lowering of health and safety standards and the scrapping of the wage councils. All these factors increased claims upon the welfare state. It was the failure of Conservative policy, rather than social rights, which placed the welfare state in crisis (Oppenheim, 1994).

By applying a relative definition to social citizenship it is clear that social rights in Britain were in a highly weakened state after eighteen years of Thatcherite government. Although the government was prevented by the strength of public opinion and the failure of their own economic policies from implementing even more radical reform, the effect of existing changes to social citizenship was detrimental to the quality of life for thousands of citizens in Britain.

TOWARDS A NEW CONTRACT STATE?

In the area of local government the Thatcherites also tried to increase the market rights and responsibilities of active citizens at the expense of those who relied on local services for their basic needs. Throughout the Thatcherite years, local government was viewed with suspicion by the government. It was seen as wasteful of public money and undemocratic (Boyne, 1993).

Under the Thatcherite governments, there was increasingly a shift towards the introduction of market forces and mechanisms into local government. Through such policies as compulsory competitive tendering, local authorities were forced to allow private companies to compete for such contracts as service cleaning or catering to local schools.

Some authors have argued that such developments were part of a wider shift to a new 'contract state' whereby government provided a framework (or contract) of rights and responsibilities for the relationship between the individual and the provider of services: the 'key aim underlying a number of recent central government policy shifts is to create a "market", that is, replace monolithic state services with numerous competing providers' (Hambleton, 1994: 3). The idea was to increase consumer rights and the right to choose. Again the flip side of the right to choose was the responsibility to choose wisely, and the duty to pay tax. This responsibility helps to explain the rationale for the poll tax, with every citizen expected to contribute to the cost of local services.

However, the advantages of a shift to such a contract state for many were hard to see. The failure of the poll tax is well known and proved to be one of most unpopular policies ever pursued by a British government. As Field has pointed out such policies as a poll tax were by their nature highly detrimental to political citizenship because people disappeared from the electoral register in an effort to evade the tax (Field, 1989: 96).

Authors also pointed to the problems of contracting out local services. The chief problems were the inflexibility of privatised service to the changing needs of citizens; the suspicion that because private companies were driven by an ethos of profit many jobs previously done by the council at cost would not be performed adequately, and that the poor wages and conditions of many workers in private cleaning and catering firms were unacceptable (Gyford, 1991). Those in most need of local services as social rights stood to lose, rather than gain, from a shift to market mechanisms.

Table 8.1 Thatcherite policies and citizenship

Policy	Supposed impact on market rights	Desired impact on vigorous virtues	Actual impact
Trade union reform	Right to sell labour at market price. Right to freedom from intimidation and compulsory membership.	Unions made more responsible for strike action and to members via ballots.	Some increase in individual choice over union activity. Weakening of collective bargaining and increased vulnerability to inequalities of market rights.
Reduced direct taxation	Right to enjoy inequality of outcome.	Promotes incentive, innovation and initiative.	Increased division between active and passive citizens.
Home ownership	Right to buy private property as a foundation of citizenship.	Encourages independence and forms basis for active citizenship.	Reduced social rights to housing. Linked active citizenship closer to ownership.
Poll tax	Right to accountable local services.	Duty for all citizens to contribute to local provision.	Undermined political citizenship. Increased local government incentive to reduce social rights.
Deregulation of local services	Right to effective services and right to choice.	Increases efficiency of local provision. Citizens have duty to choose responsibly.	Undermined quality and quantity of social rights. Reduced political citizenship by substituting market for political decisions.
Social security reform	Increases market rights by undermining universal state benefit and barriers to wealth-creating private sector.	Encourages duty to seek work, reduces dependency and increases personal responsibility through private insurance schemes.	Reduced social rights and stigmatised claimants. Undermined civil rights through increasingly coercive welfare state.

CITIZENSHIP AND THE THATCHERITE GOVERNMENTS

By viewing the Thatcherite project as an attempt to increase market rights and individual responsibilities, at the expense of universal social rights, the continuity in terms of aims and objectives from 1979 to 1997 is clear.

Limitations placed on policies by adverse public opinion, political expediency and the inertia or hostility of certain policy communities should not be allowed to mask continuity of purpose. Table 8.1 provides an outline of some of the policies discussed above and their desired and actual impact on citizenship.

'ENEMIES WITHIN': DISCOURSES OF EXCLUSION

It is clear from the evidence surveyed above that the policies pursued by the Thatcherite governments during the 1980s and 1990s led to an increasingly divided and unequal society. Growing poverty, unemployment and an increasing sense of exclusion were the experiences of many citizens in Britain during the Thatcherite years. Interpretations of these results are varied. Some authors have argued that high unemployment and a deregulated work force were actually policy aims of the Thatcherite years (Overbeek, 1990). According to this view, high unemployment and the restriction of social citizenship were seen as functional to the restructuring of the British economy because both high unemployment and the narrowing of citizenship increased insecurity amongst workers, thereby undermining trade union power and militancy.

Certainly pressure to deregulate the economy during the 1980s was strong due to the changing nature of capitalism during that period. Also the political institutions of Britain, and in particular the first-past-the-post system of election, meant that an electoral strategy that aimed at securing the support of an increasingly wealthy 40 per cent of the population at the expense of the rest was a rational one in terms of political success. However, this perspective probably underestimates the extent to which the Thatcherites passionately believed that through the redefinition of citizenship they pursued, Britain's fortunes would be transformed and the majority of citizens would eventually see their citizenship enhanced.

The problem for the Thatcherites was how to account for the large numbers of citizens who failed to make use of their market rights. Given the fact that the Thatcherite governments were convinced of the superiority of their economic policy (which was described by the Conservatives as an 'economic miracle'), and their refusal to accept structural explanations for the failure of individuals to succeed, the only logical explanation for the continuing problems of poverty, unemployment and increasing crime rates was individual failure. Underpinning this was a highly moralistic view of the nature of the good citizen and what did, and did not, constitute acceptable behaviour.

The antithesis of the active citizens of the Thatcherite vision explored in Chapter 7 was someone who possessed little incentive, sense of responsibility or entrepreneurial skill. The passive citizen was someone who undermined the prosperity of the nation by refusing to conform to the values of the market. As Lister points out, the Thatcherite years were marked by an approach to citizenship which attempted to reduce the universality of social rights while at the same time expecting a universal sense of obligations (Lister, 1990: 14). Because of this division between the active and the passive citizen, the Thatcherite era was characterised by a whole series of 'moral panics' concerning the undesirable and undeserving elements of society. A strong sense of continuity in these matters can be detected from the time when the Thatcherites began to take over the Conservative Party in 1975, through to the Major governments. The various targets throughout these years were many, and they included single parents, ethnic minorities, travellers and 'welfare scroungers'. In all of these cases common themes emerged in government discourses. Such people (it was argued) were unable to be active citizens because of their idleness and lack of personal responsibility, which was promoted by a dependency culture. Poverty was no excuse because the success of the Thatcherite experiment had largely rid the country of absolute poverty. Notions of relative poverty were dismissed by the Thatcherites because such a concept merely provided an excuse for envy of those who had been more successful (Oppenheim and Harker, 1996: 7–9).

The real problem according to the government was how to reduce the number of people who were becoming dependent upon social security payments, and were thereby undermining the moral fabric of their community. For the Thatcherites there was little doubt that many people living off the nanny state actively chose to do so. Very often, it was argued, such people took deliberate actions to avoid the responsibility of work or made fraudulent welfare claims. A constant theme for Conservative ministers in the 1980s and 1990s was the single mothers who chose to have children in an 'irresponsible' way to secure housing and increased benefits. In 1993 the then minister George Young announced that a law that prioritised the needs of teenage mothers in housing was to be scrapped. In a tone typical of the Thatcherite era he commented on such 'unjust' law:

> We must ask ourselves whether the signals sent by this legislation sit comfortably with the values we share; with the self reliant society we want to promote . . . How do we explain to the young couple . . . who want to wait for a home before they start a family . . . that they cannot be rehoused ahead of the unmarried teenager expecting her first, probably unplanned, child? (*The Independent*, 8 October, 1993)

In effect, the Thatcherites made clear their view that not all people were acting as good citizens and taking the opportunities that had been created. Therefore the answer was not to cushion such people from the consequences of their action (or inaction) but rather to condemn and coerce them into acting responsibly. Extensive social rights had removed the important link between poor choices and damaging consequences. In this sense an important part of the Thatcherite concept of citizenship was the right to fail, not the right to be cushioned from such failure.

Increasingly, for many writers in the 1990s, Britain's divided society has been reflected in and explained by the notion of an underclass. This concept has been used by commentators on both the political left and right. For writers like Field (1989) the concept has been used to express growing social divisions in structural terms. Thus for Field the underclass comprises those citizens, such as the long-term unemployed, lone parents and old-age pensioners on state benefit, who are excluded from the full rights of citizenship. This 'class' has supposedly developed because of structural change in the economy and through the failure of government economic and social policy. However, the notion of an underclass proved highly useful for those adopting a Thatcherite approach to social problems.

For those on the right, the underclass is precisely those citizens who have, through their own failings, failed to grasp the opportunities given to them. They are cultural and moral misfits who choose to be passive citizens. As Morris (1994) and Mann (1992) have noted, the notion of an underclass is a theme that has appeared in various forms since the beginnings of industrial society. From the notion of deserving and undeserving poor in the eighteenth and nineteenth centuries, to the 1960s debate concerning a 'culture of poverty', the idea of placing the blame for poverty or deprivation with the individual has been a recurring theme in liberal society.

In the 1990s the main figure on the right who has popularised the concept of an underclass was Charles Murray. Murray's ideas were embraced by parts of the Thatcherite press, and it was the publication of one of Murray's articles in *The Sunday Times* in 1989 that was largely responsible for his notoriety.

Whilst Conservative politicians have been wary of making explicit use of the term, an underclass approach was implicit in their attacks on those who broke their contract with society and refused to face up to their duties and responsibilities. In her memoirs, Thatcher wrote admiringly of Murray's bravery in facing up to the 'difficult problems' of a dependency culture (Thatcher, 1995: 543–54).

For right-wing advocates of the existence of an underclass like Murray

(1990) and Green (1992), issues of morality and individual failings are paramount. People choose to be poor citizens and this choice is made possible by socialist notions of 'social justice' institutionalised in the welfare state and social rights. Thus for Murray the key to understanding the underclass is not poverty or unemployment, but rather the unemployed and poor's reaction to their condition, which, for Murray, is too often characterised by envy and violent hostility to the dominant 'civilised' values of society. The problem with extensive welfare rights is that they worsen, rather than cure the problem. Projects like the creation of the welfare state in Britain or the Great Society programmes of the 1960s in America led to a situation where passive citizenship was encouraged through public policy: 'the first effect of the new rules [increasing welfare] was to make it more profitable for the poor to behave in the short term in ways that were destructive in the long term. Their second effect was to subsidise irretrievable mistakes' (Murray, 1984: 178–91).

David Green (1992) has argued that it is central to liberal society that the state should not aim at providing social justice regardless of people's attitudes and actions. The shift towards the nanny state is at the root of the creation of the underclass. He claims that even the social liberal tradition associated with J. S. Mill and T. H. Green was opposed to extensive social rights guaranteed by the state:

> For J. S. Mill, too, the state should be a liberator, seeking to set loose the energies and initiative of its people. But he was opposed to the state taking on the role of provider, making provision for all our principal material requirements. Such a state could only deny human potential. (Green, 1992: 71)

For right-wing underclass theorists, the state in post-war Britain deviated from its role as liberator and therefore undermined people's sense of personal responsibility. David Green is right to point to the limited deviation from this perspective by social liberals. As was argued in Chapter 3, because of their commitment to the market and their ambivalence to democracy, social liberals are wary of excessive state provision. Interesting work by Rees (1995) has shown that by the 1980s, even T. H. Marshall had become sceptical of the effects of the welfare state on the morality of its recipients. This reaction is akin to a doctor misdiagnosing an illness and then blaming the patient when the (wrong) medicine fails to work. The problem in social liberalism is that the social rights they defended were paternalistic and were part of the coercive state apparatus. Because they were divorced from political citizenship and participation, they were necessarily vulnerable to the criticism that they created a passive and dependent underclass.

The notion of an underclass, distinct from main-stream society in terms of values and morals, was particularly appealing to the Thatcherites and such a perspective underpinned their social policy. Thatcher asserted that the challenge for governments faced with a growing underclass was not to excuse their 'deplorable behaviour' or increase their access to social rights but rather, 'the most important task is simply to curb public spending in general and welfare state spending in particular'. This policy should be accompanied by the incentives of reduced 'regulation and taxes, so as to make it more worthwhile to work and earn' (Thatcher, 1995: 560). It is important to note the Thatcherite perspective was a reaction to the failure of social liberalism to generate a vision of social citizenship which was genuinely inclusive.

FROM CONSENSUS TO COERCION

However, the Conservatives were not content merely to reduce social rights and to increase incentives to deal with the problem of the underclass. The Thatcherite governments, throughout their time in office, took a tough approach to social problems associated with dependency culture. Of particular concern was increasing crime and social disorder, because 'the habitual criminal is the classic member of an underclass' (Murray, 1990: 13).

In keeping with their methodological approach to the nature of social behaviour Thatcherites argued that the increasing problem of crime could not be explained in terms of society, but was an outcome of individual moral failing. Discourses concerning the pathology of members of the underclass helped to prepare the ground for a shift towards increasingly coercive methods of dealing with crime and disorder. This is connected to a general shift away from the social liberal consensus where the development of social citizenship was seen by many policy makers as a way of increasing social inclusion and reducing social conflict. For the Thatcherites, this approach was both expensive and ineffective. Anti-social behaviour, it was argued, needed to be condemned and severely punished, rather than explained away in 'trendy sociological jargon'. Throughout the Thatcher years, social science (and sociology in particular) was attacked at party conferences precisely because of its (perceived) emphasis on structural explanations for social behaviour. Keith Joseph insisted on changing the name of the Social Science Research Council to the Economic and Social Research Council during his time as Education Minister, and social science was absent from the National Curriculum drawn up in 1988.

A good example of the agency-based approach of the Thatcherites can be found if one examines the reaction of the government to the urban riots of the early 1980s. In 1985 the Home Secretary, Douglas Hurd, clearly rejected structural explanations for the disorders:

> The excitement of forming and belonging to a mob, the evident excitement of violence leading to the fearsome crimes that we have seen reported and the greed that leads to looting . . . to explain all those things in terms of deprivation and suffering is to ignore some basic and ugly facts about human nature. (cited in Benyon, 1987: 30)

Once the deviant individual was identified as the root of disorder, the strategy for dealing with crime and disorder became clear. Social engineering such as more welfare, increased social services or training programmes would not work to cure the problem. In fact such reform may, through creating a lazy state-dependent underclass, worsen the problem as such people would have time on their hands and may be tempted to increase their income through illegal methods. The solution to disorder was through increased police powers, stiffer penalties for criminals and generally a harsher approach to juveniles and persistent offenders. This approach led to an undermining of basic civil freedoms for *all* citizens, since the effective exercise of political rights, such as the right to association, the right to free speech, and the right to demonstrate, requires a high degree of freedom from interference from the state. Such political rights cannot be seen purely as rights held by individuals without reference to other citizens because atomised societies cannot be effective political societies. True individuality and democracy are soon destroyed when people stop acting together in exercising their political rights.

An examination, however, of government policies after 1979 towards the policing of society does indicate a severe curtailing of the ability of citizens to exercise effectively their basic civil and political rights. In a seminal study of civil liberties under the Thatcher governments, Ewing and Gearty (1990) show how the fundamental rights of citizenship were eroded by a series of government policies designed to clamp down on deviant elements in society. We have seen in Chapter 6 how citizenship rights had little protection in the law, allowing radical governments to fundamentally undermine basic liberties. The Thatcher governments showed their willingness to make use of the flexibility of the constitution to assert highly oppressive measures in the area of public order. As Ewing and Gearty argue, 'civil liberties are in a state of crisis' (Ewing and Gearty, 1990: 255). As we shall see, the erosion of civil and political rights continued at an increased pace under the Major governments.

These attacks on fundamental rights are best understood in terms of the Thatcherite approach to citizenship in general, and in particular the active citizen–passive citizen dichotomy inherent in liberal approaches to citizenship. For the Thatcherites, active citizens had nothing to fear from an increasingly coercive state. Indeed their freedom was enhanced, not only by the extension of market rights, but also through the more effective control of deviant elements who refused to conform to the vigorous virtues. Rights to protest and criticise the government were portrayed by the government as undemocratic, rather than as examples of good citizenship. This view reflected the suspicion that Thatcherites had towards political rights which extended beyond voting or standing for office. The active citizen was perceived not as a political activist but as a property owner, consumer or volunteer. Paradoxically, therefore, restrictions on the civil rights of protest and assembly were explained in terms of increasing, rather than undermining, liberty.

The Thatcherites were particularly concerned with increasing police powers in their attempt to tackle rising crime and disorder. Kingdom has argued that under the Thatcher and Major governments, the police force in Britain underwent major changes which radically altered its traditional character. The police became more centralised through a process of amalgamation and the growth in strength of staff associations such as the Police Federation. The ability to co-ordinate police activity was increased by developments in information technology, the creation of specialist police squads, and the use, by the government, of ad hoc committees to create and direct police strategy as in the 1984–5 miners' strike (Kingdom, 1991: 551–9; Benyon and Bourn, 1986).

Kingdom argues that the police also became increasingly militarised, with the use of riot gear, firearms, and c.s. gas all becoming more common on the streets of mainland Britain. Kingdom detected an increasingly politicised police force; in the 1980s the Police Federation campaigned openly on a number of controversial and highly political issues such as the role of juries in society, increasing police powers and stiffer sentencing. With an accountability system which failed to allow anyone but the police to investigate complaints against themselves, the increasing power of the police service was of major concern to those attempting to preserve basic political rights.

Moreover, Kinsey et al. (1986) have argued that increasingly the police were actually failing to lower crime rates, largely because the processes identified by Kingdom alienated many citizens from the police. For example Lord Scarman, in his report of the riots in 1981, found that many young people 'had become indignant and resentful against the police, suspicious of everything they did' (cited in Benyon, 1987: 35). The Thatcher years saw the collapse of consensus policing. Rising crime rates were taken out of their social context by the government, who responded by moving to 'military policing'. This in turn alienated parts of the community, particularly young working-class males and ethnic minorities. Lack of co-operation by members of the community meant that the police were denied *the* essential part of their armoury in the fight against crime; that is, information from the public. This became a vicious circle as police turned to more draconian measures such as stop and search tactics to get information about criminal activity, which further alienated the community and reinforced hostility to the police.

Under the Conservatives political and civil rights were curtailed because of a stated commitment to protect market rights, which were seen to be under threat from unruly collections of anti-social groups. This provided the rationale for a series of government bills concerned with increasing police powers, which led to the narrowing of citizenship rights (Ewing and Gearty, 1990; Benyon and Solomos, 1987). One of most significant of these recent reforms was the Criminal Justice and Public Order Act, which came into force in 1995.

THE POLITICS OF EXCLUSION

From the government's perspective, the Criminal Justice Act was part of a series of reforms which asserted market rights against rights of a more collective nature. In a similar vein the Criminal Justice Act sought to further protect market rights, particularly property rights, against the perceived threat of deviant individuals and groups.

The Criminal Justice Act has to be understood in the context of the language and discourses of exclusion which were a feature of the Thatcher and Major years. Such discourses cannot be dismissed as mere rhetoric for, as Laclau and Mouffe (1985) have argued, the articulation of a particular set of values by a powerful social group is an important element in galvanising support for policy changes. The Thatcherite governments were keen to utilise a set of discourses around the notion of the nation, which was made up of independent and responsible individuals. These individuals were, according to the Thatcherite vision, individualists rather than collectivists: they believed in loyalty to the nation, and duty to themselves and their families. This vision was a racialised and gendered one because it had at its core a notion of 'Englishness' and traditional patriarchical family structures. Those who did not conform to this vision were increasingly excluded via such notions as the underclass or 'enemies within'. Howarth has pointed out that the success of an ideological project like Thatcherism rests upon the need to construct scapegoats for Britain's problems. As Howarth contends, 'the creation of an antagonistic relationship, which always involves the production of an "enemy" or "other", is vital for the establishment of political frontiers' (Howarth, 1995: 121).

For instance, an example of this tactic was displayed in a television interview in 1978 when Margaret Thatcher spoke of 'alien cultures' swamping Britain. According to Thatcher, ordinary people were 'really rather afraid that this country might be swamped by people with a different culture' (cited in Barker, 1981: 15). This fear was also reflected by Sir Peter Emery, Conservative MP, in his interpretation of the riots of the 1980s in many of England's inner cities: 'the vast majority of people expect the precepts of Anglo–Saxon behaviour and of law and order to be maintained. These standards must be maintained, despite what other ethnic minorities want' (cited in Benyon, 1987: 25). The assumptions underpinning such statements were that people from other countries, and more specifically black people, had standards of conduct that were much lower than whites.

Under the Thatcherites, groups which challenged the government views explicitly or even implicitly were seen as outsiders. People were perceived as either 'one of us' or as the 'enemy within'. For example, Norman Tebbit spoke in the early 1990s of those citizens who failed the 'cricket test' as being outside the dominant culture, and therefore not truly British. They were 'partial' citizens because they failed to prove their 'Britishness' by supporting the national cricket team against the teams from their original or cultural homeland, for example India, Pakistan, Sri Lanka or the West Indies (*The Guardian*, 19 November 1992).

Policies like the Criminal Justice Act can be seen as being tied to the perceived crisis of the British state in the 1970s and the feeling amongst Conservative politicians that the health of the nation was at an all time low during the 1960s and 1970s: the time of supposedly high trade union power, corporatism, high public spending, welfare dependency, mass immigration and permissive social values. Many Conservative politicians had not come to terms with Britain's position in international affairs, and in particular its decline in importance since the second world war as symbolised by the Suez debacle of 1956.

One of Margaret Thatcher's self-proclaimed roles was to make Britain great again and place it back at the centre of the world stage as a major influence. However, before this was possible, the social groups allegedly responsible for Britain's decline needed to be identified and dealt with. Thus the Thatcher years saw an unprecedented number of moral panics and the creation of numerous and varied 'folk devils', including single mothers, travellers, youth, the underclass, gays, or ravers. All of these groups were seen to be a threat to the 'dominant', 'normal' Thatcherite citizen (Murray, 1986).

A yearning for a long-lost golden age, a mythological past of British

greatness and social harmony, was a feature also of the Major governments, and indeed was at the heart of his so-called 'back to basics'
campaign, launched in October 1993 in a speech at the Conservative Party
Conference. In that speech Major summarised many of the anxieties of
the Conservative Party since Mrs Thatcher came to power in 1979, and
indeed provided a clear statement of the values underpinning the main
policies which, under the Thatcherite governments, impacted on citizenship in modern Britain:

> Let me tell you what I believe. For two generations too many people have been
> belittling the things that made this country. We have allowed things to happen we
> should never have tolerated. We have listened too often and too long to people
> whose ideas are light years away from common sense . . . Some said the family was
> out of date and that it was better to rely on the council and social workers than
> family and friends. I passionately believe that was wrong. Others told us that every
> criminal needed treatment, not punishment. Criminal behaviour was society's
> fault, not the individuals. Fashionable, but wrong, very wrong . . . It is time to
> return to core values, time to get back to basics, to self-discipline and respect for the
> law, to consideration for others, to accepting responsibility for yourself – and not
> shuffling it off on other people and the state. (*The Guardian*, 9 October 1993)

In this speech we saw a clear rejection of structural explanations of social
problems. Individual deviancy was stressed as the key to understanding
Britain's problems in the last two decades. Criminals should not be
understood but punished. People needed to take responsibility for their
actions, and families (heterosexual nuclear or extended families that is)
needed to be encouraged, while alternatives, for instance single-parent
families, should be condemned. The appeal to 'common sense' can be
interpreted as an attempt by the Conservatives to appeal to prejudices and
fears of the 'ordinary people', who had their views shaped to a large extent
by the discourses concerning the problems caused by the outsider or
deviant groups discussed above.

From such a perspective, Acts like the Criminal Justice Act were
portrayed as greatly enhancing liberty and the ability of citizens to enjoy
their citizenship rights without fear of trespass, crime and unruliness, by
deviant and outsider groups who threatened 'decent' values. By clamping
down on deviant individuals the Conservative view was that law-abiding
citizens would be more able to exert their rights of citizenship.

THE PROVISIONS OF THE
CRIMINAL JUSTICE AND PUBLIC ORDER ACT 1994

The significance of the Criminal Justice and Public Order Act (Home
Office, 1994) in relation to citizens' rights was that it proved the

commitment the Thatcherites had to redefining citizenship in a way which compromised not just social rights, but also fundamental civil and political freedoms. In the government's view these rights were either helping to protect undesirable criminal elements, or were providing the opportunity for illegitimate protest by what were seen by the government as militant anti-democratic forces.

The Act was part of a general campaign by the Major government against rising crime rates culminating in a wholesale attack on 'soft' approaches to criminals at the 1993 Party Conference. Indeed the Act cannot be understood outside the context of that conference, which saw numerous Thatcherite discourses attacking those already on the margins of society. There was a concerted assault upon single-parent families and Home Secretary Michael Howard asserted that such families were more likely to create criminals. A number of measures to reduce single-parent families were discussed, including restricting access to council houses, and John Patten called for parents 'not to walk away from their children and their responsibilities' (*The Independent*, 7 October 1993).

It was against this background, and despite the Prime Minister's alleged desire for a nation at peace with itself, that the Conservative Party backed Michael Howard's 27-point point plan to 'take the handcuffs off the police and put them on the criminals where they belong' (*The Independent*, 7 October 1993). It was a plan which unashamedly asserted the rights of 'the angry majority'. Howard attacked social workers, judges and clergymen for being soft on crime and promised that 'young thugs' would receive punishment not sympathy.

Many of Howard's 27 points were included in the Criminal Justice Act, and this bill seriously undermined citizenship. The pressure group for civil liberties Liberty argues that the Act potentially violated 23 international articles on civil and political rights. These can be grouped into three main attacks on citizenship: the Act undermined the right to justice; it reduced the rights to assembly and free expression; and it attempted to stigmatise a significant number of minority groups.

In 'Citizenship and Social Class' Marshall defines the right of justice as a civil right, protected largely by the courts system. Marshall rightly asserts the centrality of the right to justice in any meaningful notion of an equal and common citizenship. He comments that the right to justice is 'of a different order from the others because it is the right to defend and assert all one's rights on terms of equality with others and by due process of law' (Marshall, 1963: 74). The Criminal Justice Bill weakened this right in numerous ways.

Section 26 of the Act, by changing the rules on the eligibility of bail, challenged the fundamental assumption that one is innocent until proven guilty. Those persons charged with a new offence could be denied bail if they were due to appear in court charged with another crime. This section of the Bill contravened several articles of the European Convention on Human Rights (ECHR) (Robertson, 1977: 1–21).

The right to justice was also threatened by Section 38, which effectively removed the right to silence for those people taken into custody. This was perhaps the most controversial part of the Bill and provoked outrage amongst a wide cross-section of the population (*The Independent*, 7 October 1993).

Leading barristers, the bar council and civil rights groups condemned the ending of the right to silence. The rationale for this section of the Act was to prevent 'professional criminals' from hiding behind the right to say nothing, thereby frustrating the efforts of the police to get a prosecution. However, once again the Thatcherites ignored the real-life experiences of many citizens in dealing with the police. Studies of the way deviance is defined and implemented by the law-enforcement agencies clearly show that often there is a link between social class and the likelihood of prosecution and conviction (Cicourel, 1976). The process of questioning suspects is a negotiated process which discriminates against those from low-income families and particularly ethnic minorities. By removing the right to silence, an important safeguard against discrimination disappeared. The reality of oppressive police questioning has been evident in the Birmingham Six and Guildford Four cases. This legislation was more likely to have the effect of further intimidating innocent members of the public, rather than effectively tackling persistent offenders who were more used to the pressure-cooker atmosphere of the interview room.

The removal of the right to silence meant that courts could take into account, that is 'draw adverse inference' from, the actions of a defendant who remained silent. Again, this section of the Bill contravened the ECHR that states that the burden of proof of guilt should be with the prosecution not the defence. Charles Glass has argued that this threat to the right to silence was 'as coercive, though not as brutal, as torture . . . the threat of imprisonment [if one refuses to speak] is replacing torture and subtle means of coercion' (*The Independent*, 9 November 1994).

The ECHR also states that a defendant or suspect should not be compelled to testify against themselves or to confess guilt. As Helena Kennedy has pointed out, the ending of the right to silence was 'about an erosion of the presumption of innocence. It's an emblem of how we have stopped caring about liberty. The right to silence was to protect the vulnerable and the innocent' (*The Independent*, 14 November 1994).

Other sections of the Bill also undermined the right to justice. Section

32 removed the obligatory warning to juries that it may be hazardous to convict someone on the uncorroborated evidence of an accomplice in an alleged crime. Sections 54 to 59 extended police powers to collect DNA samples from suspects, allowing the use of 'reasonable force' to acquire these samples. Liberty has argued that because the Act allowed the police to keep records of these samples, regardless of the subsequent outcome of a case, it also infringed basic rights of privacy (Liberty, 1995: 12–17). The use of force in obtaining such samples may also contravene the International Covenant on Human Rights (to which Britain is a signatory), which states that when citizens are deprived of their liberty, they should be treated with humanity and respect for the integrity and dignity of their person (Feldman, 1993: 41–7).

The second fundamental way in which the Act undermined citizenship was through its various sections dealing with the issues of protest and assembly. The fact that Section 26 of the Act allowed police, and not the courts, to grant conditional bail to people who were facing charges, not only attacked rights of justice, but it also allowed the police to impose bail restrictions on political protesters, thereby preventing them from taking part in further demonstrations in a particular place. This part of the legislation was used by the police in 1995 to control campaigners against the live veal trade at British ports.

Section 60 of the Act effectively returned to the police the power to stop and search members of the public on suspicion that they were carrying a weapon: the notorious 'sus' laws which were so severely criticised by Lord Scarman in his report on the Brixton riots of 1981. Scarman argued that the law was being used to discriminate against young blacks. This helped to create the conditions of antagonism and bitterness that led to rioting. The 'sus' laws were abolished by the Criminal Attempts Act of 1981 in reaction to Scarman's report, but the Criminal Justice Act of 1994 reversed this legislation. As Liberty argues, Section 60 also restricted the right to freedom of expression because 'people from ethnic minorities, people engaged in political, environmental or industrial protests and people whose live style differs from the most of the rest of society are likely to be particularly targeted' (Liberty, 1995: 17).

The Criminal Justice Act also dealt extensively with issues of public order which undermined basic rights to protest and free speech. In particular, the Act created the offence of aggravated trespass. The aim of this part of the Act was to deal with protests against the use of land, for example for fox hunting. Section 70 of the Act effectively banned political protests when it stated that assemblies could be prevented or broken up where they were deemed to have caused 'serious disruption to the life of the community' (Liberty, 1995: 24). This allowed the authorities to prevent protest which was deemed by them to be outside of the interests of the 'community' and therefore to act as judges of what constitutes acceptable protest. Police were also given the power, in Section 71, to stop people who might be considered to be travelling to an illegal protest (as defined in Section 70). In combination, these two sections of the Act outlawed rights which are crucial to the practice of political citizenship.

The third major way in which citizenship was undermined was through the Act's attack on diversity. The Act was clearly designed to protect the perceived needs of the 'angry majority' against those citizens who did not confirm to the Thatcherite vision of the active citizen. In particular it attacked many of the weaker members of society, who through circumstance beyond their control had little political voice. These groups included travellers and squatters.

Travellers were consistently at the top of the list of folk devils of the Conservative Party in the 1990s. They were seen as the antithesis of the active citizen: they refused to be tied to the notion of home ownership, they abdicated their duty to work, and were a threat to the wider community. All of these criticisms were levelled at such people at the annual Conservative Party Conference. For example, in 1992 Peter Lilley spoke of new age travellers, 'descending like locusts, demanding benefits with menaces' (*The Guardian*, 8 October 1992).

Sections 61, 77, 78 and 80 made the right to choose a travelling lifestyle extremely difficult. As Liberty points out, Section 61 made it a criminal offence if travellers did not leave land when ordered to do so by the police. The grounds for them being asked to leave included 'damage' to land. This has been interpreted by courts in the past as including walking across a field (Liberty, 1995: 28).

The Act was also tough on squatters, reflecting Michael Howard's view that 'squatting can never be justified' (*The Guardian*, 15 April 1994). This harsh approach failed to accept that many people squatted because they had little other choice. This problem was made worse by government housing policy which prevented councils using revenue from the right to buy campaign to build new accommodation or to accommodate the homeless in the estimated 846,000 homes that stood empty in Britain (*The Independent on Sunday*, 24 April 1994). Sections 75 and 76 incriminated the activities of squatters by making it an offence not to leave a property when a landlord had secured an Interim Possession Order. Even senior police figures were sceptical about the government's approach to the problem, who felt that such harsh treatment would distract police from their real job of fighting serious crime (Liberty, 1995: 32).

Liberty also pointed out that such legislation could be used by unscrupulous landlords against legal tenants. Such legislation also has to be linked to the decline of legal aid in recent years, which means that squatters and travellers were unable to fight their case in the courts. Legal aid has gradually become less available to all but a few citizens, and as many squatters do not draw benefits, they do not qualify. The erosion of legal aid was itself a major attack on the right to justice. As noted earlier, it is difficult to speak meaningfully of common citizenship when many cannot even afford to defend their rights in court. As Atiyah argues, the government has treated the process of litigation as 'a commodity in the market, like other commodities' (Atiyah, 1995: 65).

Further attacks on alternative lifestyles could be found in Sections 64–7 of the Act. These sections of the Act dealt with the moral panic surrounding ravers. They increased police powers to prevent the right to assembly and thereby the potential for misuse of these powers, to prevent demonstrations for example, was ever present.

Overall, the Criminal Justice Act represented a major attack on basic civil and political rights of citizenship. It marginalised still further many groups in society already suffering from reduced social rights, homelessness and poverty. As the Chair of the Metropolitan Police Federation commented, 'it appears to be legislation against a certain section of the population and that is a recipe for disaster . . . why are they dreaming of legislating against people whose lifestyle, culture and attitude to life differs from other people?' (*The Independent*, 4 November 1994).

CONCLUSION

It has been argued in this chapter that the Thatcherite attempt to redefine citizenship in Britain involved a fundamental division between those citizens who were willing to take responsibility for their lives and take the opportunities presented by the extension of market rights, and those passive citizens who had, for too long, relied on social rights to provide their needs and relieve them from their responsibilities. Government policy was therefore determined by a 'carrot and stick' approach to citizenship. It has been shown how the government provided incentives to active citizens through a variety of policies, but at the same time it reduced social rights and increased the coercive role of the state. This approach was been highly prejudiced and moralistic. Many citizens already excluded through their poverty were condemned as parasites upon the nation. Conservative policies failed to create a secure citizenship for most citizens. The result of the erosion of basic citizenship rights was an increasingly divided and unjust society, which in turn (through the increase in social problems such as crime, and the draconian measures taken by the government to tackle these problems) created a vicious circle which undermined the citizenship of *all* citizens.

However, it has been argued that the Thatcherite position was consistent with the logic of liberalism, which refuses to accept structural explanations for social problems, and therefore condemns individuals for their own failings. The extension of state power, which undermined basic civil and political rights, can be understood as a defence of market rights, which were seen by the Thatcherites as the best guarantee of active citizenship. It was also, from a Thatcherite perspective, the logical reaction to the outcome of government policies. By failing to acknowledge the interdependence of all citizens and the egalitarian logic of citizenship, the Thatcherites took the flawed assumptions of liberalism to their logical conclusion. This resulted in an outcome that was the opposite of all of the promises and claims of liberal theories of citizenship.

The result of this was a highly irrational situation whereby the government increasingly sought to pathologise and exclude millions of its own citizens. The reality of citizenship in modern Britain continues to be problematic and paradoxical because of its basis in the dualistic nature of liberalism. The Thatcherites merely extended the inherently abstract, elitist and exclusive logic of liberal citizenship, thereby creating a situation where many individuals were increasingly marginalised as passive citizens. What is more, the liberal state, supposedly founded upon the notion of a contract for common security, has been shown to be an instrument of coercion that perpetrates acts of violence against the very people who need its protection most.

PART III

BEYOND
LIBERAL CITIZENSHIP?

9

ASSESSMENT, CHALLENGES AND PROSPECTS

This final chapter has three main aims. First, it will summarise the main criticisms of liberal theories of citizenship presented in this book. It will be concluded that the problems identified in classical theories of citizenship are not overcome by the social liberal and neo-liberal variants. The Thatcherite project to redefine citizenship in modern Britain, and its failure to deliver meaningful citizenship to all citizens, is interpreted as a logical, but irrational, outcome of the general failures of liberalism.

In the second part of the chapter some recent challenges to the basis of liberal citizenship, that is the nation-state, will be explored. It will be argued that the dialectical processes of globalisation and localisation require a radical reconsideration of the relationship between citizens and the political communities they inhabit; the development of the European Union as one possible approach to these challenges will be analysed.

The final part of the chapter will tentatively explore the possibilities and prospects for citizenship in Britain beyond liberalism and the liberal state. It will be argued that the concept of citizenship *can* maintain its significance as an ethical ideal for radicals who seek a unifying concept around which to base their policies and principles in a post-liberal world.

AN ASSESSMENT OF LIBERAL CITIZENSHIP

The main aim of this book has been to present a critique of liberal theories of citizenship and their application to the practice of citizenship in modern Britain. It has sought to show how liberal theory can be understood in terms of a series of dualisms arising from its methodological assumptions. Liberalism treats the individual abstractly, and its conception of social order is founded upon a problematic and contradictory relationship between the state, the market and the individual.

In liberalism, the wealth-producing market is seen as inherently superior to the potentially oppressive and discriminatory nature of political decision making. Therefore, liberals have sought to limit the interference of politics in the market in the name of safeguarding the 'liberty' of the individual. Paradoxically, though, the state has been seen as both a necessary organisation for the maintenance of order *and* a threat to the freedom of the individual. Because of this basic contradiction, liberals argue that the inequality of the private sphere should not be allowed to be subsumed into the public sphere, where individuals are formally equal in status. Given such assumptions, liberal theories of citizenship have stressed the protection of the citizen from the power of the state, and indeed from other individuals through a theoretical defence of citizens' rights. The promise of liberal citizenship is that it will produce security for all citizens, whilst maintaining their autonomy, freedom and individuality. The liberal state is conceived as the best possible framework for a rational society, and the market as the best guarantee of prosperity for all citizens. Three key problems have been identified with the liberal approach to citizenship. The first problem is that liberalism has a highly abstract conception of citizenship. Citizenship is divorced from the historical development of the relationship between the state, the economy and the individual. It has been argued in this book that citizenship, and the extent to which it denotes an equal status for all citizens, has to be understood in terms of the nature of social and political change. In Chapter 6 it was shown how citizenship in Britain should be understood, not as a slow evolutionary growth towards a more inclusive status, but in terms of a series of social struggles against the background of developments in capitalism, military conflict and the form that the state takes in any given historical period. Citizenship as a status which enables participation in the community is founded upon economic and social circumstance. When such circumstances are changed, citizenship may be rendered less, as well as more, inclusive.

Second, liberal theories are weak in their analysis of social power. Because of their abstract individualism, liberals tend towards an agency-based account of social behaviour which underestimates the constraints placed upon individuals by an unequal distribution of power. As Lukes (1974) asserts, in order to understand the progress of citizenship, a more sophisticated explanation of social power is required. Lukes argues that it is not enough to focus upon the decision-making aspects of power that are the outcomes of rational interaction between social forces. We also need to consider two further dimensions of power, non-decision making and the shaping of desires. Extending Lukes's analysis, it can be argued that agency-based accounts of the nature of power are inherently flawed. In reality, contrary to liberal assumptions, individuals do not exert power in an isolated, rational way. Power in modern societies is always institutionalised in formal and informal structures. Groups with social power are able to exercise that power, not only by obtaining favourable outcomes in terms of decision making, but also by preventing others (for example voters) from considering all the possible alternatives. Powerful groups can also use deception, persuasion and manipulation to shape the attitudes of groups with less power than themselves (Gramsci, 1971: 323–43, 419–25).

In classical liberalism the state is seen as a neutral arbiter between individual interests which control the state through the mechanisms of representative democracy and pressure-group politics. Capitalism is interpreted as a non-coercive regulator of individuals' desires, wants and effort. However, it has been shown in this book that such a view neglects the structured inequality of capitalist society. Thus, the third fundamental problem of liberal theories of citizenship is their essentially exclusive nature. Some citizens are able, because of their success in the market, to assert more successfully their citizenship rights. This success is in turn shaped by a citizen's place in the class structure, his or her gender, or ethnic origin and so on. Because of these divisions, which have little to do with individual ability or meritocracy, the classical liberal society is characterised historically by vast inequality of opportunity, poverty and social problems. Citizenship is in fact defined in terms of the interests of a small minority of property-owning white, middle- and upper-class males. This problem led some liberals to reconsider classical liberalism and its assumptions concerning the relationship between the individual citizen and the state.

In Chapter 3 we considered how social liberals like Marshall argue that with the development of social rights the inequality of liberal society is 'legitimised'. However a number of problems with the social liberal approach have been identified. It was shown in Chapter 3 how Marshall fails to overcome the problems of abstraction, elitism and exclusivity. By treating categories such as civil rights in an unproblematic way, Marshall, like Locke, ignores the ideological construction of such rights. The civil rights which Marshall argues developed in the eighteenth century were really exclusive market rights that were defined in class and gender terms. Civil rights which may threaten the ruling class, such as rights to protest and assembly, were ruthlessly suppressed.

Marshall is overoptimistic about the extent to which social rights represent, by themselves, a meaningful increase in citizenship for all citizens. Indeed, it can be argued that rather than emerging as a potent critic of classical liberalism, Marshall sees the development of social rights as being evidence that only liberal society, through its emphasis on capitalist economic growth, can provide the means to deliver social citizenship. Thus for Marshall the extension of social rights is proof of the superiority of liberal-capitalist society rather than evidence of its failure, and Marshall's notion of a hyphenated society, with an ever-present tension between democracy and the market, can be seen as an explicit acceptance of the dualistic nature of liberal societies (Marshall, 1981).

It is ironic that the perceived failure of social rights was at the heart of the reassertion of a form of classical liberalism by neo-liberals in the late twentieth century. It is precisely because social rights failed to eradicate poverty that neo-liberals are able to assert the need to further polarise the dualisms of liberal theory. Thatcherism represented a contemporary attempt to institute a neo-liberal definition of citizenship with a reassertion of market rights and personal responsibility at its core. Social rights were rejected as an aberration from classical liberalism, which (it was argued) damaged citizenship by placing strains on the market (the real creator of welfare for neo-liberals) and reducing individual responsibility and initiative.

Thatcherism's attempts to enhance citizenship are best interpreted as the logical extension of the contradictory nature of liberal citizenship. It was shown in Chapters 7 and 8 how Thatcherism meant that autonomy and individual freedom were decreased for *all* citizens because an increasingly divided and disordered society undermined the security of rich, as well as poor, citizens. Thus the schizoid nature of the liberal state was complete in the Thatcherite form. Because of the failure of the market to deliver meaningful citizenship, the state was turned upon the very citizens it is supposed to protect. As we have seen, the very logic of liberalism led the Thatcherite governments to increase state violence against citizens who were deemed to have failed in what is perceived by liberals as the most desirable set of social arrangements: namely an 'uncoercive' market protected by a strong, but limited state.

The irony of the liberal position is that in its desire for a society constructed upon rationalism, freedom and security, its logic necessitates the highly irrational situation of a government using state power to marginalise and coerce whole sections of society, which in turn reduces autonomy and liberty for all citizens. To summarise, liberal citizenship fails to deliver its promises for the following reasons:

- By abstracting the individual from his or her social context and privileging the individual against the demands of society, liberalism denies the relational and interdependent relationships of individuals to each other and their communities.
- In reality power is distributed unevenly in society due to the existence of social structures such as class, gender and 'race'. These structures shape social behaviour and help to explain social

inequality and division. The notion of liberal societies as meritocracies is, therefore, naive and misplaced.

- Contrary to the abstract and evolutionary logic of liberalism, the extension or reduction of citizenship rights and the balance between rights and duties in any given society are shaped by struggles between social groups with different interests. These social struggles occur against a background of social and economic change. The liberal notion of the equality of social groups is flawed because in these various social struggles, political and economic elites are well placed to define the extent of citizenship according their own interests.

- Deregulated capitalism is incompatible with meaningful citizenship for all individuals. The vast inequalities associated with unfettered capitalism cannot sustain a common citizenship. Contrary to the liberal position, markets are not uncoercive and neutral in their outcomes; their often damaging effects upon society can be clearly detected by the social sciences.

- Liberalism has, because of its emphasis upon individual freedom in the market, a sceptical view of politics and therefore seeks to limit the operation and influence of democracy. Because of this, democracy in the Britain has been partial and limited to the public sphere. This public sphere has been in practice dominated largely by a white, male and middle-class elite and has resulted in a highly exclusive and elitist concept of citizenship premised upon the ability of individuals to accumulate property and wealth in an unjust market.

- Citizenship in liberal theory is bound up with the development of modernity and the modern state. However, liberalism fails to show convincingly that the state rests upon the consent of many of its citizens, or that it can generate an inclusive citizenship. The state has often maintained, rather than undermined, social inequality and in this sense the state can be defined as inherently patriarchal, racialised and class based.

CHALLENGES TO THE
DOMINANT LIBERAL PARADIGM

The prospects for citizenship in Britain in the future revolve around solutions to the dilemmas of liberal citizenship presented in this book. However, before we explore some possible solutions to these problems, it is necessary to consider some recent social and political changes which have themselves presented a challenge to the foundations of liberal citizenship, and which may present the opportunity to move beyond liberal conceptions. In order to analyse recent social changes and their impact upon citizenship, I will structure my analysis in terms of the globalisation–localisation dichotomy. Both these developments challenge the statist assumptions of much of the liberal tradition. Processes of globalisation have to some extent challenged the dominance of the nation-state as it has developed in the modern era, whilst through the criticisms advanced by new social movements, the homogeneity of the nation-state and its competence to resolve the problems of diverse and pluralist societies have been questioned. In a sense the liberal state, as it emerged from 1789 onwards, is being challenged by processes from both above and below the level of national states. As Daniel Bell has written, it may be that 'the nation-state is becoming too small for the big problems of life, and too big for the small problems of life' (cited in Waters, 1995: 96). If the foundation of liberal citizenship has begun to disappear, the question is raised as to whether liberalism itself is outmoded.

GLOBALISATION

The concept of globalisation has become one of the most debated social processes in recent years (Waters, 1995; Sklair, 1995; Hirst and Thompson, 1996). Both legal and political definitions of citizenship have stressed citizenship as a relationship between individuals and the nation-state, the assumption being that states are sovereign bodies. However, globalisation has called that relationship into question.

Globalisation is a set of processes which involves the increasing interdependence of nation-states (Sklair, 1995: 1–6). This, it can be argued, has meant that national boundaries and nation-states are becoming less significant in social life, and that nation-states are losing their autonomy in terms of decision making. Waters (1995: 9) argues that processes of globalisation are economic, political and cultural. Changes in the global economy have weakened the ability of governments to control their economic arrangements and therefore to provide the economic base for aspects of citizenship, particularly in the social field such as welfare, education and social security (Horsman and Marshall, 1995). Politically, globalisation has meant that international organisations such as the United Nations and the European Union have challenged the sovereignty of nation-states. Culturally, it can be argued that the values of consumer capitalism and the free market have been promoted through the globalisation of the mass media. The question arises as to whether a nation-based liberal citizenship is relevant to the (post)modern world.

One of the ironies of liberalism is its commitment to free markets on the one hand and its commitment to the nation-state on the other. In this book it has been argued that recent liberal theories have increasingly ignored the anti-statist logic present in the work of the classical liberals and have instead accepted the state as a necessary expression of nationalism, a reconciler of opposed social interests and a protector of private property. Because of this paradox, it is not surprising to find that challenges to the nation-state can be interpreted both as a triumph for and the end of liberalism. For example, one optimistic view of liberalism can be found in *The End of History and the Last Man* by Fukuyama (1992). He argues that a 'new world order' has been constituted out of the ashes of the defeat of communism and the increasing internationalisation of the economy. Liberal democracy is being championed from Russia to Africa, and the free market has been embraced as the only alternative to authoritarian command economies.

Other authors have also questioned the interpretation of globalisation as a fatal blow to the liberal nation-state. Hirst (1993), Hutton (1995, 1996) and A. D. Smith (1995) have questioned the extent and impact of globalisation. Hutton interprets globalisation as a convenient excuse for right-wing governments like Britain's to deregulate their economies and social policy in the name of competitiveness. According to this view globalisation provides a rationale for the rolling back of citizenship rights and cuts in public spending. Through an examination of global trade flows, Hutton concludes that the great bulk of world trade is still between the leading industrialised countries, and in 1994 total portfolio investment in developing countries amounted to only 0.3 per cent of world output. Hirst stresses that the world is in fact a long way from being a globalised economy. He argues that to speak of a truly globalised economy the following developments would have needed to have taken place:

- State governments would be subordinate to the imperatives of multinational companies and the free market.
- Multinational companies would be truly international in terms of their management and would no longer operate from a national base.
- Labour organisation would have become redundant as capital could demand the minimal social protection necessary for efficient production.
- Capitalist corporations, rather than states, would be the major players in international relations. Economic, rather than military sanctions, would hold states firmly in a subordinate role.

Since none of the above apply in any large degree to reality, Hirst argues that 'this ideal type indicates that we are nowhere near a fully globalised economy, and are unlikely to get there' (Hirst, 1993). Smith, like Hirst, suggests that the nation-state remains the key actor in international affairs, and what is more this is normatively desirable. For Smith, nationalism has been the most important unifying ideology in the modern era, and is the only identity able to transcend other differences and identities. It is socially functional and historically embedded. Smith asserts that 'the nation and nationalism provide the only realistic socio-cultural framework for a modern world' (Smith, 1995: 159).

The criticisms of globalisation offered by people such as Hirst, Hutton and Smith are important in tempering exaggerated accounts of the end of the liberal nation-state and the triumph of a rootless global capital. However, globalisation does nevertheless present a real challenge to liberal citizenship in countries like Britain in a number of ways.

The existence of structural and long-term unemployment, which has weakened the ability of many citizens to make use of their rights and perform their duties is one major development. As was argued in Chapter 8, writers like Hutton are right to point to the importance of government policy as a major factor in explaining the decline of manufacturing industry in Britain, but there can be little doubt that structural un-employment has grown in all major European countries. This has much to do with the restructuring of the European economies in reaction to the economic crisis of the 1970s and the actual and perceived threat of increased global competition. The result of this in Britain has been a declining manufacturing base and an increase in the flexibility of the work force. Such developments have undermined the ability of the labour movement to resist the dilution of social rights.

The real threat of internationalised financial markets has undermined some aspects of economic policy making. Failures to control currency speculation and insider dealing can have a major impact on national inflation rates. This is turn has had the effect of undermining savings and the sense of economic security felt by ordinary citizens. A good example of the destabilising affects of currency speculation occurred in Britain on 16 September 1992 when Britain was forced to withdraw from the European Exchange Rate Mechanism (Cable, 1996: 134).

An increasing awareness of the global nature of threats to security and health is also an important aspect of globalisation. Developments in global communications have done much to spread the knowledge of potential global threats. These include nuclear proliferation, ecological disasters, world population growth and infectious disease. All of these threats may well render nation-based citizenship outdated as the world seeks solutions to problems which have no respect for national boundaries (Beck, 1995).

Linked to increasing awareness of global threats is what Giddens has called the growth of 'social reflexivity', which has been made possible mainly through processes of globalisation:

> Social reflexivity is both condition and outcome of post-traditional society. Decisions have to be taken on the basis of a more or less continuous reflection on the conditions of one's action. 'Reflexivity' here refers to the use of information about the condition of activity as a means of regularly reordering and redefining what that activity is. (Giddens, 1994: 86)

Through this growth of reflexivity people develop ever more critical stances towards old 'certainties' like the ability of the state and its associated experts to solve the complex problems of modern society. In this sense people increasingly do not believe that their citizenship status will ensure social protection.

It is through the notion of growing reflexivity that the globalisation – localisation dichotomy is linked. Indeed, Giddens argues that the two are in a dialectical relationship. Thus changes at the level of 'sub politics' are inextricably linked to the changing global context. Indeed Giddens defines globalisation itself in terms of 'the intensification of world-wide social relations which link distant localities', and he goes on to suggest that 'this is a dialectical process . . . local transformation is as much a part of globalisation as the lateral extension of social connections across time and space' (Giddens, 1990: 64).

One of the key developments in the area of 'sub politics' is the growth of new social movements, which have had important implications for the future of liberal citizenship.

NEW SOCIAL MOVEMENTS

Contrary to Fukuyama's optimism about the health of liberal institutions and traditions at the end of the twentieth century many citizens in industrialised countries like Britain have increasingly turned away from traditional politics in favour of a 'new' politics which in essence is characterised by ethical, rather than material concerns (Offe, 1985: 832). As Hallsworth argues, the term new social movement refers to those movements which 'pose new challenges to the established cultural economic and political orders of advanced capitalist society' (Hallsworth, 1994: 7).

In part the rise of new social movements in the 1960s and 1970s can be seen as a response to the failure of social liberalism and the model of citizenship advanced by Marshall. Roche (1992: 39–55) identifies some commonalities between the new social movements and the New Right in their critique of social liberalism. In particular, new social movements such as feminism, the anti-racist movement and the ecological movement have developed a withering critique of the liberal welfare state and have helped to expose the elitist assumptions lying behind the post-1945 settlement (Pierson, 1991: Ch. 3). We must therefore view the insights of new social movements as an important part of our general critique of liberal citizenship.

New social movements have helped to show how the welfare state has in fact institutionalised social divisions. As we saw in Chapter 3, the welfare state is based on gendered assumptions about the desired roles of men and women in society. The welfare state is also implicitly 'racialised' because it is based on the notion of 'insiders' and 'outsiders'. As Pierson argues, 'within the welfare state, it is more typically a majority population that constitutes the "insiders" and a minority or minorities that make up the "outsiders"' (Pierson, 1991: 83).

The ecological movement has pointed to the part the welfare state plays in ever-increasing demands for economic growth to sustain public spending. In this sense the maintenance of a welfare state is part of a wider problem associated with the modernist ethos of privileging 'man's' progress at the expense of the world's resources.

Marshall's optimism about the egalitarian outcomes of the development of social rights can again be shown to be misplaced. The failure of the welfare state cannot be attributed solely to economic decline or capitalistic restructuring. Instead the problems of the welfare state need to be related back to the inherent abstract, elitist and exclusive nature of liberal theories of citizenship.

The problems highlighted by the new social movements relate to the dualistic nature of liberalism. In Chapter 2 it was argued that liberalism could be understood in terms of a series of oppositional dualisms; what feminists, anti-racists and ecologists have done is to throw a light upon some of the other dualisms inherent in liberalism. These are expressed in Table 9.1.

Table 9.1 Social movements and liberal dualisms

Social movement	Dualism
Feminist	Women subordinate to men.
Anti-racist	White 'Anglo-Saxons' privileged over other ethnic groups.
Ecological	Nature subordinate to 'man's progress'.

New social movements have increased our awareness of how liberal notions of citizenship are ideologically constructed and rest upon structured inequalities. In the case of the relationship between men and women, the work of feminists like Pateman (1988, 1989) has shown how the very category of citizens has always been gendered in liberal theory. In terms of ethnic identity, the liberal state has been defined in terms of the homogeneity of its population and such homogeneity has been taken as given by liberals like Marshall.

In the work of other social liberals like T. H. Green and Hobhouse (1964) the 'racialised' inequality of the states system, upon which the success of Britain largely rested, is ignored. Therefore the possibility that the development of citizenship rights for dominant ethnic groups was premised (or indeed made possible) by the denial of those rights to less fortunate nations is overlooked. As was argued in Chapter 6, an important element in the development of citizenship in Britain has been its imperial past.

Liberalism, as the dominant ideology of modernity, has also had at its core the ideal of economic progress and the realisation of humanity at the expense of nature and the world's resources. With the increasing problems of acid rain, nuclear proliferation, the green-house effect and increasing rates of species extinction, ecological groups have pointed to the limits of the liberal ideal of economic progress through the promotion of the unregulated market.

A fundamental problem with the social liberal conception of welfare has been its statist assumptions. In terms of the global threats raised by the ecological crisis, the nation–state is ill-equipped to guarantee the most fundamental welfare requirement: the continued existence of the planet (Twine, 1994: 47–76). The existence of the state as a national community also presents a major dilemma because any notion of nationality is, by definition, exclusive and therefore incompatible with the egalitarian logic of a common citizenship.

Liberals argue that it is the combination of the nation–state and the free market which allows for individuals to express their diversity and individuality. However, I would argue that in liberal theory the emphasis upon the success of the market as the basis for meaningful citizenship undermines diversity. By presenting the market as uncoercive and value neutral, liberals in a sense do submit to a kind of structuralism. That is, not the structures of class, gender and 'race', but of an abstracted market in which individuals rise and fall partly through their own efforts and partly by chance. The problem here, as has been demonstrated, is that the market is coercive and does not allow all individuals to compete on equal terms. In liberal societies like Britain the market, and its related state form, is structured in a way which discriminates against certain groups such as ethnic minorities, women and the working class. Also, by privileging market success over other achievements diversity is reduced. An extreme example of this was the actions of Thatcherite governments, which increasingly pathologised those who did not conform to a narrow set of market values. The argument I am making here is that because social division is built into liberal societies in an embedded structural form, the state, which has the role of attempting to maintain a stable framework for the market is, by its nature, coercive.

In its most extreme neo-liberal form this state coercion will involve increased powers of surveillance and enforcement for the police and the courts, but even in its social liberal form the state maintains its essentially coercive nature. As Hay has pointed out, the welfare state, which developed in the post-war period, can be seen to have had a coercive impact upon those who rely upon its services and benefits:

> The welfare state exercises a profound and structuring influence over many aspects of the lived experience and reality of existence of broad sections of society – particularly women . . . Welfare agencies exercise a significant surveillance role in the supervision and monitoring of particular sub-populations 'in exchange' for welfare . . . The relationship between the institutions of the welfare state and benefits claimants is very often a coercive and repressive one. (Hay, 1996: 76–7)

Because of its role of regulating the unjust outcomes of a market system and because its fortunes are bound up with the success of the market, the state can be seen to embody structured inequality. This insight helps us to understand the institutionalised nature of racism and sexism in the state apparatus. The welfare state can be said to have been a flawed project from the outset precisely because it aimed to legitimise inequality. However, because this inequality was due not to the failure of individuals but to structured inequality the welfare state was handed the impossible task of reconciling the irreconcilable.

With the growing influence of the twin processes of globalisation and localisation the question of the future of citizenship, as a status denoting membership of a state, is raised. As the nation-state becomes challenged from within by its increasingly reflexive and disaffected citizens, and outside of its boundaries by multinationals and global problems, the prospects for citizenship in Britain are unclear. Three possible strategies for the adaptation of citizenship seem to exist.

The first of these possible strategies has been the main focus of this book: the Thatcherite project of redefining the relationship between citizen and state in terms of extending market rights for some citizens and expecting universal duties from all. The approach to the processes of globalisation and localisation taken by the Thatcherites involved a clear acceptance of the development of a global economy, which was used to legitimise the cutting of public spending on welfare that was said to be no longer affordable. Paradoxically the Thatcherites argued that the best way to maintain Britain's sovereignty and economic strength was to open up Britain's economy to the new global forces such as multinationals, through policies of privatisation, deregulation and low taxation.

It was argued, by the Thatcherites, that the nation-state could still retain its central place in the world by embracing, rather than resisting, globalisation. A by-product of this may well have been some increased opportunities for some social groups (for example, women) to assert themselves in the work place via increasing part-time employment. However, the main thrust of the Thatcherite approach to processes of localisation and its associated social movements was to ignore them (for example calls for devolution) or to crush them through increased state coercion. It has been a central argument in this work that this strategy failed to deliver its promise of an enhanced citizenship. Instead for many, their citizenship was increasingly thinned out in the name of global competitiveness.

In the next section of this chapter I will examine the second possible strategy open to Britain; that is, the possibility of reinventing citizenship by reinventing (with other countries) the nation-state at a European level.

THE EUROPEAN UNION

As Giddens (1995) has remarked, the European Union can be understood 'simultaneously a response to, and an expression of, globalisation'. The European Union is an example of the process of globalisation in the sense that it aims to move beyond the limitations of the single nation-state towards a supra-national body and it is also a response to the global insecurity and economic uncertainty of the increasingly internationalised market.

Interpretations of the formation and subsequent development of the original European Community are many, but two major factors which stand out are the goals of increased security and prosperity. First, the crisis of nationalism in Europe after the second world war acted as a major initiative for the pooling of sovereignty, particularly in light of the threat of any future war in Europe being a nuclear conflict. The development of The European Union has therefore in part been a response to the irrationality of the states system and its associated nationalism. Second, economic co-operation has been increasingly seen as the only way to combat growing competition from, in particular, the countries of the Far East in the second half of the century.

An ongoing debate has existed in Europe over the best approach to take to encourage greater co-operation. At the risk of oversimplification two main schools of thought can be identified: the supra-nationalists and the intergovernmentalists. On one hand there have been those who have argued strongly for the creation of a European state which essentially aims to rescue the idea of the nation-state by reinventing it at a European level. Millward has argued that rather than seeing the shift towards European Union as a break from the tradition of the nation-state, the process should be understood as 'one more stage in the long evolution of the European state' (Millward, 1992: x). Progress towards this goal, led principally by France and Germany, has been halting but nonetheless driven by the basic goal of a Federal Europe. From the Schuman Plan in 1950 (which created a single European Coal and Steel Community) onwards a clear desire to pool sovereignty can be identified. As Schuman himself said of the creation of the Coal and Steel Community, it represented the 'first concrete foundation of a European Federation which is indispensable to the preservation of peace' (cited in Pinder, 1986: 42). The founding fathers of the European Union such as Jean Monnet, Paul Henri Spaak and Konrad Adenauer all hoped to lay the foundations for common institutions which would give a clear direction to Europe in the future, and the Treaty of Rome of 1957 was clearly federalist in its intentions with its creation of an embryonic European government in the form of the European Commission, the Council of Ministers and the European Court of Justice (Leonard, 1994: 33–69).

In the 1960s and 1970s progress to a Federal Europe was stalled by a combination of factors, including the intergovernmental approach of Gaullist France and world economic recession. However, in the 1980s and 1990s, in the spirit of people like Monnet, Helmut Kohl, Chancellor of Germany, has made the goal of extensive political and economic union in Europe his life's work. In a lecture in Oxford in 1992 Kohl made clear his ongoing fear of the nation-state, with its dark side of nationalism, exclusion and war:

> I feel carried back to an ill-fated past when I hear some people stirring up sentiment with the argument that Germany has become too large and too powerful and therefore has to be 'contained' by means of coalitions. It is a cruel irony that such talk plays into the hands of just those forces in Germany which propagate an old style nationalism. Our answer to such short sighted views is clear. The Federal Republic has made a final decision in favour of European integration. (Kohl, 1992)

In keeping with the modernist associations between nation-building and the promotion of citizenship, the European Union has attempted to engender a sense of European citizenship amongst the people of Europe

(Meehan, 1993; Rosas and Antola, 1995; Oliver and Heater, 1994: Ch. 7). Of particular importance in this regard was the Maastricht Treaty of 1992. This Treaty, which established for the first time the notion of European Union, attempted to build upon earlier efforts to encourage citizenship in Europe. These efforts included the appointment of a Committee for a People's Europe in 1984, which was given the task of promoting a sense of common identity amongst the people's of Europe. The Committee produced two reports which called for the extension of civil rights such as self-expression and assembly and a uniform system of elections to the European Parliament to enable citizens to vote in any member country in which they may be temporarily residing. The Maastricht Treaty of 1992 went beyond the rather basic and incoherent citizenship called for by the Committee. In particular the Treaty established, for the first time, the notion of European Citizenship and guaranteed basic civil and political rights. Article B of the Treaty declared that the Union should aim to 'strengthen the protection of the rights and interests of the nationals of its Member States through the introduction of a citizenship of the Union' (Clarke, 1994: 188–90). These citizenship rights included the following:

- The right to move freely throughout the member states.
- The right to vote and stand in local and European elections in any member state.
- The right to diplomatic protection in any third country via any member state's embassies.
- The right to petition the European Parliament and a European ombudsman.

The Treaty also increased the power of the European Parliament, including greater powers of amendment and veto in an attempt to further reduce the distance between the institutions of the Union and its citizens. However, perhaps the most controversial aspect of the citizenship policy of the European Union has related to the area of social rights. In 1985 the French socialist Delors became President of the European Commission and throughout his period in office, he argued for the development of a European-wide social policy to balance the move towards economic union. Significantly, though, the development of social rights in the Union has been linked by the Commission to the need for equal competition and the problem of social dumping. Social dumping is seen as a possible by-product of the single market because, it is argued, unequal levels of welfare benefits and unemployment may well have the effect of exporting poverty through the freedom of movement created by the Maastricht Treaty. Related to this is the fact that countries with high unemployment and low wages and social costs may prove more attractive to overseas investment. For these reasons the Maastricht Treaty attempted to make the European Social Charter, which had originally been signed by eleven of the twelve member countries in 1989, a central part of the Treaty. The original Social Charter was largely an aspirational, rather than legally binding, declaration of some basic rights for workers. It included protection for freedom of association, equal treatment for men and women, rights to training and social protection. It was, however, hardly a radical document for it contained no commitment to the right to work or a minimum wage (Commission of the European Communities, 1990).

Nevertheless, despite the minimal social rights of the Social Charter, increasing calls for a European citizenship have further alienated those in the European Union who have a very different view from people like Chancellor Kohl of the most desirable future for the Union. As we have seen, the British governments under Thatcher and Major sought to adopt an approach to recent social change such as processes of globalisation, which involved the deregulation of the economy, the rolling back of the welfare state and the promotion of an entrepreneurial citizenship. This vision was incompatible with European social rights, which the Conservative government saw as the return to the failed policies of social liberalism. For the Thatcherites the European Union should be almost exclusively concerned with the promotion of free trade and economic deregulation. Margaret Thatcher spelt out a vision of Europe completely at odds with that of Chancellor Kohl in an (in)famous speech in Bruges in 1988:

> My first guideline is this: willing and active co-operation between independent sovereign states is the best way to build a successful European Community. To try to suppress nationhood and concentrate power at the centre of a European conglomerate would be highly damaging and would jeopardise the objectives we seek to achieve . . . We have not successfully rolled back the frontiers of the state in Britain, only to see them reimposed at a European level, with a European super-state exercising a new dominance from Brussels. (Thatcher, 1988)

Increasingly in the late 1980s and 1990s the institutions of the European Community were criticised by the British government, and prominent figures such as Jacques Delors joined a long line of 'demonised' characters in the right-wing press and amongst many Thatcherite MPs. For the Thatcherites the Delors's vision of further European integration would, like the liberal consensus in Britain prior to 1979, weaken the active citizenship they sought to promote. Such a response to the increasing global market would have the effect of weakening Europe's ability to remain competitive. It therefore came as no surprise to find that despite the demise of Thatcher in 1990, the Conservative government under Major continued a policy of hostility to any European legislation which appeared to be threatening nation-state sovereignty. At the 1992 Maastricht Treaty Major successfully negotiated opt outs from the Social Chapter (which involved essentially the 1989 Social Charter and its implementation through the social action programme) and the move towards European Monetary Union.

The Social Chapter was perceived by the Conservative government as vague and flying in the face of economic change, which requires less, not more, social regulation. By increasing trade union power the Chapter would reduce freedom of the individual and the market; wages would be artificially high and foreign capital would therefore seek to invest in countries outside Britain. According to the Thatcherites the single market would provide a more effective regulator of the labour market than more red tape and bureaucratic control from Brussels. Also, by imposing artificial minimum standards jobs would be lost as costs to employers were increased by the provisions of the Social Chapter. Monetary union would involve the decline of the nation-state in terms of its control over economic matters such as taxation, interest rates and inflation. Again this was portrayed as a barrier to the greater flexibility required by the international economy.

The Thatcherite strategy towards the contemporary crisis of national citizenship and the state can be interpreted in two ways. First it can be seen as highly contradictory since it attacks European integration because it 'undermines sovereignty', while at the same time adopting economic policies which render British sovereignty increasingly powerless to resist the imperatives and objectives of global capital. A more cynical reading of the Thatcherite position would suggest that the Thatcherites were only concerned with limitations on sovereignty which damaged the ability of their supporters to take advantage of the opportunities of the global market at the expense of the citizenship of their fellow citizens. In this interpretation the nation can be seen to be defined in an increasingly narrow way: those who do not conform are branded as outsiders and second-class citizens. This latter interpretation is backed up by evidence of a general resistance by the Thatcherites to the protection of citizenship through its other European commitments. For example, the government came into increasing conflict with the European Court of Human Rights. By 1996 the British government had been found guilty of thirty-eight human rights violations by the court. This record was worse than other nations which had signed the European Convention on Human Rights. In keeping with their general perspective on the protection of citizenship rights in Britain, the Thatcherite response to these rulings was to attempt to restrict the influence of the court (*The Guardian*, 2 April 1996).

Given the flaws of the Thatcherite strategy towards Europe, the question arises as to whether the federalist vision of people like Delors and Kohl represents a better alternative. Certainly as recent works upon the impact of the European Union have shown, the extension of European citizenship, particularly in the social dimension, has increased the opportunities and rights of some citizens in Britain. For example, in the area of women's rights Article 119 of the Treaty of Rome has provided a basis for a series of directives which have given British women more opportunity to oppose discrimination in the work place (Meehan, 1993: Ch. 6; Leonard, 1994: 188–92). Recommendations from the European Commission have also attempted to improve the status of women in society.

Rights of workers in general have been extended in some areas through the implementation by Britain of some of the social action programmes which followed the 1989 Social Charter; these include increased rights for part-time workers such as better access to company pension schemes (*The Guardian*, 29 September 1994). In addition, Article 118a of the Single European Act has allowed for decisions on working conditions to be decided by qualified majority voting, thereby leading to a directive in 1993 restricting the working week in all member states to 48 hours for most occupations (*The Financial Times*, 5 August 1996).

However, despite some of these positive aspects, the supra-national approach to the European Union and citizenship is problematic. The Thatcherite governments tried to discredit the development of European citizenship as a socialist project and therefore inconsistent with the economic and political realities of the late twentieth century. What is clear, however, is that the supra-national approach is essentially a *social liberal* attempt to reinvent and strengthen the European nation-state by creating a new federal super-state. As such the European Union is open to similar criticisms identified in this book concerning the limits of social liberal citizenship.

The first question mark concerning European citizenship relates to the motivation for the extension of rights. It can be argued that the development of citizenship has been more about facilitating and legit-imising the creation of a single European market rather than a genuine concern on behalf of policy makers to increase inclusion and participation in the Union. The way that citizenship has developed, and the limits of the various rights which have been created, lends some weight to this criticism. In this regard similarities between the evolution of citizenship in Britain, as described by Marshall, and the path of European citizenship are striking. As Welsh argues, the civil rights contained in the Treaty of Rome and the Single European Act were 'primarily to facilitate the competition of the common market' (Welsh, 1993: 26). That is, rather like Marshall's argument that the development of capitalism in Britain in the eighteenth and nineteenth centuries required basic rights, so the plight of citizenship in the Union is bound up with the fortunes of the free market. Following the logic of this argument, the increasing development of social rights can be linked to smoothing the transition to an ever more free market, rather than serving the needs of the people of Europe.

The criticism of the evolution of citizenship in Europe also has to be linked to its limited and exclusive nature. Like the development of Marshall's category of civil rights, the Maastricht Treaty's creation of such rights is ultimately rooted in the ability of citizens to make use of those rights. Such rights as the freedom of movement are open only to those with the necessary resources to utilise the right. This is made explicit in the Treaty which qualifies the right to free movement and residence by, in certain cases, 'requiring proof that a person will not require social assistance and has adequate health insurance' (Luff, 1992: 23–4).

The notion of a European citizenship as an opportunity for genuine participation by ordinary citizens is gravely undermined by the vast democratic deficit and lack of meaningful political rights that still exists, despite the Maastricht Treaty, in the Union. The only Union body which requires a popular vote, that is the European Parliament, has little more than an advisory function in making policy. It has no right to initiate legislation and crucially its authority ultimately rests on the national sovereignty of the member nations since representatives are sent to the parliament via elections in the member states. Neither are these elections uniform in the form of electoral system used. Most decisions on legislation are still taken by the Council of Ministers, which is of course made up of government ministers elected in national elections.

The evolution of European citizenship has been shaped by the conflict between the intergovernmentalists, such as Britain, and those who argue for greater integration at the European level (Welsh, 1993). This ongoing tension has meant that the European Union has sought to embody two incompatible views, one which aims at the creation of a federation and another which seeks to maintain the sanctity of the traditional nation-state. However, resulting compromises have failed to capture the imagination of many of the citizens of Europe. Indeed, through attempts to pursue monetary union, undoubtedly a major step towards undermining national decision making, without first securing basic political rights, the Union risks the criticism that the guiding objective of the Union is in the interests of business, rather than the people. By placing monetary union at the top of Union priorities, without first ensuring democratic and accountable government, the liberal nature of the citizenship pursued by the Union is revealed. As such any citizenship that rests primarily upon economic imperatives will be, as has been argued extensively in this book, limited by the requirements of an ever-changing market. Although supporters of greater integration in Europe argue that this would not mean a monolithic super-state but a decentralised federal system, the argument is hard to sustain when monetary union is given such a high priority.

In the area of social rights the danger is that such developments are weakened because they are de-coupled from political rights. They may be seen as granted from above, rather than signifying an aspect of democratic citizenship. Also the impression that these rights have developed because of the needs of the market is a difficult one to dispel. As Wise and Gibb note, in the early days of the Union social rights were not seen as necessary because liberal capitalism would deliver prosperity for the citizens of Europe:

> In those early days there was a predominant assumption that liberalisation within a common market would lead to economies of scale and economic growth from which the greater number of Community citizens would benefit; in effect an essentially liberal economic policy would be the best social policy as well. (Wise and Gibb, 1993: 131)

The limits of the social liberal approach to social citizenship, even at the European level, were shown by the failure of the European Union to develop an effective response to the economic crisis of the 1970s. As Wise and Gibb argue, social policy up to the 1986 Single European Act was piecemeal as member states prioritised their own national responses to the crisis of capitalism. It was only the proposed creation of a single market throughout Europe that gave impetus to further social developments. However, as has already been noted, these developments have been limited and have thus far failed to solve the problems of high unemployment throughout Europe (Crompton and Brown, 1994). Indeed the emphasis upon the completion of the single market through a common currency has forced national governments to attempt public spending cuts in order to meet the necessary convergence criteria. This fact, plus the general disruption to local markets, has resulted in further social problems such as greater unemployment and social protests. This discontentment was illustrated by mass demonstrations in Germany and France in March

1997 against growing job insecurity caused by the pursuit of the convergence criteria (*The Guardian*, 12 March 1997). Moreover, Kennett (1994) argues that weak measures like the Social Chapter, even if adopted in all countries, will provide little barrier to the increasing social inequality demanded by the global restructuring of the capitalist economy.

By emphasising the needs of the single market over the creation of a genuine democratic citizenship, social rights will be bound to be limited in their impact. As Rogers argues, 'citizens have been defined in terms of their capacity to be workers' (Rogers, 1995: 4). O'Leary concludes his analysis of the social dimension of Community citizenship by arguing that paradoxically social benefits are bound up with the ability of the individual to be successfully involved in market processes:

> It is evident that the principle of equal treatment is being applied inconsistently with respect to the rights of Community citizens. Entitlement to social benefits still varies according to the role played by the claimant in the process of economic integration taking place in the Community, be it as a worker, a dependent, or an economically inactive individual. This two-speed aspect of Community citizenship leaves one wondering whether the effective enjoyment of meaningful social rights was really envisaged as part of the Community citizenship package. (O'Leary, 1995: 179)

It can be argued then that the development of citizenship rights in the European Union strongly resembles the development of social liberal citizenship in Britain. Certain civil, or market, rights developed in the early days of the Community to facilitate the common market. Limited political rights and social rights have developed largely to 'legitimise' the inequality of the market in the eyes of Europe's citizens. Even then they have developed only when economic circumstances have allowed. The European Union can be interpreted as an attempt to reinvent the social liberal alternative at a European, rather than national, level. As such the citizenship it has delivered remains abstract and elusive to many citizens of Europe.

As Welsh (1993) notes, the project of Union citizenship has not only been about the creation of rights, it has also aimed at fostering common identities among the diverse people of Europe. However, efforts to encourage a common identity through the notion of a common citizenship have focused on symbols associated with the traditional European nation-state. For example, the Union has adopted a European flag, a European anthem and passport. This artificial attempt at nation building may not only be unsuccessful but also dangerous. In terms of engendering a common identity without first securing meaningful political citizenship, the union has largely failed to secure a sense of legitimacy or common purpose amongst many citizens in the member states. Evidence for the frailty of citizens' support can be found in the narrow margins of victory in the referendums on Maastricht in France and Denmark (after a second ballot) and also in the rise in popularity of extreme right-wing groups in France and Germany. One of the dangers, then, of equating citizenship with a new 'European' nationality is that citizenship of the European nation-states may well provide an excuse for the reassertion of nationalism in some countries. The consequences of imposing federal structures upon diverse populations were dramatically exposed by events in the old Soviet Union and Yugoslavia during the 1990s, when, following the collapse of communist rule, extreme nationalistic sentiment emerged to threaten social order in these states.

The final problem with Union citizenship that I wish to discuss is also related to questions of nationality. One of the most damaging criticisms of the European Union and its related concept of citizenship is that because it is based upon the notion of a federal super-state, it is an exclusive category. There is a fear that by tying European citizenship to the concept of nationality, rather than residence, many people living and working in the European Union, but who are not citizens of one of the member states, will see their rights undermined. All too often in official European Union literature the problem of 'foreigners' is linked to the fear of crime, drugs and illegal immigration. Consequently organisations like the Commission for Racial Equality (CRE) in Britain have pointed to the dangers of a 'Fortress Europe' which excludes or harasses migrant workers. Such organisations fear that the European Union will result in discrimination and intolerance towards the many people who work in the various member states but do not qualify for citizenship. This does not represent a minor issue: the CRE estimates that there are around nine million third-country nationals resident in the European Union (CRE, 1994: 10). Since the 1980s there have been many examples of violence and discrimination against North African Muslims in France, Africans and gypsies in Italy, and Turkish 'guest workers' in Germany, but as the CRE notes, 'there has been no Community legislation against racial discrimination' (CRE, 1994: 13).

The fact that the citizenship of the Union created at Maastricht excludes all non-European Union nationals encourages an attitude of discrimination and social exclusion. Third-country nationals are prohibited from voting in European Parliament elections and rights to social benefits are restricted. The fact that European Union immigration policy is still based on decisions by national governments aggravates the CRE's fear that 'short-term considerations could lead to the most restrictive options being adopted in trade-offs between national representatives' (CRE, 1994: 28). As Horsman and Marshall note, European citizenship at the moment is very much 'an elite preserve' (Horsman and Marshall, 1995: 133).

The neo-liberal strategy of the Thatcherite governments in the UK and the social liberal approach championed by Germany are incompatible visions of Europe. As such, conflicts between the two have undoubtedly contributed to the confusion of the European Union and have perhaps restricted the development of a more meaningful concept of citizenship. However, I would argue that a third alternative needs to be considered in the search for an inclusive concept of citizenship which looks beyond the statist assumptions of liberal approaches. The debates raised by processes of globalisation and localisation have created an important opportunity to radically reconsider the relationship between citizens and the state. Debates around the future of Europe are an important part of this, but, as Giddens argues, what is required is that these debates be 'conducted in a more profound way than any of the political parties in this country have so far attempted' (Giddens, 1995). Indeed what is required is not only a rethinking of Europe but a critical reflection upon the concept of citizenship.

BEYOND MARSHALL AND MARX?

The main aim of this book has been to show the limitations of liberal citizenship in the context of modern Britain. The rapid social change which has been outlined in the course of this chapter has further illustrated the need to look beyond liberalism for an inclusive and effective concept of citizenship. Therefore in this final section of the chapter I wish to sketch out some possibilities for a citizenship beyond liberalism. It goes beyond the remit of this book to develop a comprehensive post-liberal theory of citizenship. Instead the main aim in this section is to provoke debate and encourage further research into the area of citizen – state relations in Britain.

CITIZENSHIP BEYOND THE STATE?

Central to all of the liberal theories that have been examined in this work has the been the way in which the categories of state and citizen have been abstracted from their historical, social and economic foundations. As such the theories of citizenship which they have produced have tended to treat the state in an unproblematic way. The state is seen as providing a neutral and limited framework for the market and the 'autonomous' individuals who make contracts within that market. More recent liberal theories such as the neo-liberalism of Hayek or the social liberalism of Marshall have exaggerated this problem by abandoning completely the implicit critique in the classical liberal tradition of the state as an unnatural but necessary institution. It has been shown, through an analysis of the practice of citizenship in Britain under the Thatcherite governments, that in fact the liberal state cannot operate in a neutral way but is an embodiment of class, 'race' and gender inequalities. The liberal state is therefore incapable of delivering its promises of individual freedom, autonomy and security.

However, an often uncritical acceptance of the ability of liberal societies such as Britain to provide the best foundation for universal citizenship has led many commentators to look for reasons other than the flawed nature of liberalism itself, for the continuing problems of unemployment, poverty and lack of citizen participation in British society. A recent example of this has been the easy acceptance of the idea of the existence of an underclass in Britain (see for example, Giddens, 1973, 1994: 144–9), despite the fact that this concept is imprecise and almost always defined in the most generalised way. For example, Field (1989) defines the under-class as comprising the long-term unemployed, lone parents and state-dependent pensioners. This definition can hardly be said to represent a class in any sociological sense. Evidence on the notion of welfare dependency is also virtually non-existent, as is the idea of a set of distinct underclass values or patterns of behaviour which differentiate such people from the working class (Heath, 1992; Dean and Taylor-Gooby, 1992). Also the term greatly exaggerates the sense of security felt by members of society other than the so-called underclass. With the developments of globalisation, and the related restructuring of Britain's economy, such phenomena as negative equity, house repossessions, job redundancies in previously safe professions such as banking and teaching, increased part-time and temporary work and the collapse of many small businesses have meant that few citizens can feel truly secure. Concluding an empirical analysis of the alleged existence of a British underclass, Morris contends that 'the notion of the underclass offers little by way of conceptualising social divisions . . . the idea of an underclass persists, but with little evidence of a socially cohesive group which may be so designated' (Morris, 1995: 73–4).

I would argue that such notions as the underclass are best understood as a symbol of the failure of liberalism to deliver its promises of a meaningful and universal citizenship. Because of the dualisms that lie at the heart of liberalism and particularly because of its faith in the 'uncoercive market' on the one hand and its ambivalence to democracy and politics on the other, liberal states like the Thatcherite state in the 1980s–90s have sought to explain the failures of the system in moralistic terms. The notion of an underclass is just one recent example of this process (Morris, 1994: Ch. 1), and the continual use of such concepts merely perpetuates the myth that the welfare state could ever really compensate for the structural problems and contradictions of the liberal state.

However, a wholesale rejection of the objectives of liberalism would be a mistake. Liberty of the individual, personal autonomy and security should be the basis of any post-liberal theory of citizenship. As such the challenge for political theorists and politicians is to attempt to realise the ideal of liberal citizenship, and in doing so transcend the limitations of the liberal state.

This project raises fundamental issues concerning the potential of human nature to achieve self-government and democracy. The irony of liberalism is that it is conventionally seen as the guardian of liberty and champion of the individual's potential for progress. This book has sought to show how in practice this is not the case. Liberty for the individual has applied to only a privileged elite, and even this freedom has been compromised by a narrow vision of what constitutes liberty and achievement. Freedom in liberal society has too often been about the liberty to acquire material wealth at the expense of less fortunate individuals and the environment, and as such has meant a highly impoverished and narrow vision of human potential. Autonomy and security, too, have been undermined both by the competitive individualism of liberalism and the coercive nature of the liberal state. The interdependence of individuals has meant that for all citizens, freedom is compromised by the vast inequality and associated poverty which is increasingly present in liberal societies like Britain. Theoretically partitioning off the failures of the market through concepts like the underclass will not solve the problems of liberal citizenship.

Any future theory of citizenship will need to place the individual firmly in their structural context. This book has tried to make a contribution to this by arguing for the development of citizenship in Britain to be understood as contingent upon social change. However, I would argue that a descriptive definition of citizenship is not enough: citizenship must be defined in normative terms as well.

I would suggest that citizenship is a status which necessarily demands political participation, to the best of their ability, by all individuals within society. The practice of citizenship should be based on a definition of politics which is tolerant of diversity and strictly non-violent. Violence should be seen not as 'politics by other means' but rather as the failure of politics. Whilst diversity and compromise between divergent interests would be an important element of such a society, the commonalty and interdependence of individuals must also be recognised. As Turner (1993c: 182) argues, a basis for a theory of human rights, or indeed citizenship, could be the notion that all humanity shares a common frailty in the face of universal threats such as nuclear war or environmental disaster. Underpinning this loose definition of citizenship is a view of human nature and politics that transcends the liberal perspective which is ambivalent towards the potential of all human beings to govern themselves.

By understanding people in their structural context we are better able to understand not only why some individuals are unable to acquire the resources necessary to the practice of citizenship, but how to overcome these barriers by radically altering the structures in which individuals operate. In this context the state, as a necessarily coercive and biased actor, should be seen as incompatible with a developed notion of citizenship. As Hoffman (1995) argues, the state which bases its authority ultimately on violence helps to legitimise violence throughout society and as such lowers the status of politics as a solution to conflicts of interests. Alternatively, structures of government which encourage tolerance and compromise will necessarily help to increase the standing of politics, and the potential of all citizens to govern themselves will be enhanced. This points towards a theory of citizenship which stresses the interdependence of social structures and human agency (Layder, 1994: 152–224).

The problem of how to constitute a society which transcends the limitations of the liberal state has been a key one in political theory. In the next section I will explore some efforts to envisage a society beyond liberalism.

FOR MARX, BUT AGAINST REVOLUTION

As was noted in Part I of this book, perhaps the most devastating critique of the notion in liberalism that the categories of state and citizen are neutral comes from Karl Marx, particularly in his essay 'On the Jewish Question'. Subsequent developments in Marx's thought, with its emphasis on class struggle, and the failure of historical revolutions based upon his writings have allowed many critics to portray Marx's work as wholly anti-individualist and opposed to the realisation of liberal citizenship. This analysis, however, fails to recognise how in 'On the Jewish Question' Marx powerfully shows that because the liberal state, and therefore citizenship, is not neutral but is class based and oppressive, *true* individuality is crushed. The state, like religion, is an outcome and cause of the failure of liberal society to enhance liberty and individual potential for all citizens, and therefore represents the alienation and fragmentation of the individual. Indeed the whole of Marx's work can be read as an attempt to formulate a path towards the realisation of freedom, autonomy and security for all citizens. Marx can therefore be usefully read as a champion of human freedom rather than its enemy and as such provides a platform for a post-liberal theory of citizenship.

A central insight contained in 'On the Jewish Question' is that the relationship between agency and structure is necessarily relational and efforts to privilege one over the other is a pointless exercise. The development of three-dimensional individuality, where people can begin to exercise their potential, is only possible in the context of uncoercive structures. In the essay Marx is particularly concerned with the relationship of individual agents to the liberal state. He shows that the development of the rights of the citizen in liberal society is positive but partial. With this insight Marx points to how the field of political decision making is limited in the liberal state to the public sphere. This is done in order to protect the sanctity of market inequality. In liberalism the real divisions in the private sphere between those who can afford to participate fully in the polity and those who cannot are dissolved away in an abstract sense by the concept of the state. In an important passage Marx states:

> The state abolishes distinctions of birth, rank, education and occupation in its fashion when it declares them to *non-political distinctions*, when it proclaims that every member of the community equally participates in popular sovereignty without regard to these distinctions, and when it deals with all elements of the actual life of the nation from the standpoint of the state. Nevertheless the state permits private property, education, and occupation to act and manifest their particular nature as private property, education, and occupation in their own ways. Far from overcoming these factual distinctions, the state exists only by presupposing them; it is aware of itself as a political state and makes its universality effective only in opposition to these elements. (Marx, in Turner and Hamilton, 1994: 290, emphasis added)

This analysis of the way in which the liberal state limits the legitimate areas for the operation of politics is crucial. It is a clear expression of the dualistic nature of liberalism, and therefore its inability to constitute a meaningful citizenship. Marx points the way towards many themes taken up recently by radical democrats because his theory implicitly suggests an egalitarian and democratic citizenship that goes beyond the state and which permeates the private as well as the public sphere. Marx's insights also throw light upon the ongoing debate between the latter-day theories of communitarianism and liberalism by showing that individualism and community are two sides of the same coin rather than being diametrically opposed. As such, the theoretical break between theories of late capitalism and Marxism may not be as great as some would like to believe (Hughes et al., 1995: 212–25).

However, crucial to radical political and social theory has been the question of how to transcend the limitations of the liberal state explored in this book. Critics of liberalism as diverse as Marx, Rousseau and Nietzsche have faced the problem of transforming liberal society into a more desirable form, but I would argue that the search for a 'single transforming moment' is a fruitless one. For Marx the proletariat is the 'universal class' whose suffering reflects the alienation of the whole of society. This leads him to a theory of revolution that unconvincingly privileges the identity of class over other social divisions, and in practice led to systems which ruthlessly crushed the very freedom and autonomy Marx hoped for. In actual socialist societies (such as the Soviet Union and China) that have drawn upon Marx's theories the emphasis placed by liberal theories on the individual agent, civil society and market rights was turned upside down by the communist parties in these countries, who privileged society, the state and a paternalistic social citizenship divorced from civil and political rights. Just as neo-liberalism produces an impoverished citizenship because of its emphasis on individual agency, state-imposed communism obliterates human agency with equally damaging effects for individual citizens.

Rousseau (1968), like Marx, perceives the dualistic nature of liberalism and its conception of the opposition between the individual and society. However, in trying to construct a republic of civic virtue, which is nonetheless based upon the state, Rousseau is forced to turn to the concept of a 'lawgiver' and by doing so leaves himself open to the criticism that the self-governing community he seeks would result in an externally imposed authoritarian order. Nietzsche's scathing critique of liberalism paradoxically leads him to champion the 'will to power' of the individual and therefore extends the logic of competitive individualism (Nietzsche, 1966).

In arguing for the development of a citizenship which is inclusive, democratic, non-violent and overtly political it would be a mistake to advocate the establishment of such a citizenship in a way which relies upon the actions of any one individual or one particular collective identity. A rounded concept of citizenship cannot be created by one class enacting a violent revolution, for this can only result in the antithesis of democratic consensus and compromise. Neither is the answer to be found in the superhuman powers of a patriarchal lawgiver or a nihilistic 'superman'.

What I am arguing is that citizenship, like politics itself, can never be transcended because clashes of interests between individuals and groups will be ever-present in human societies. Therefore, citizenship has to be a dynamic concept which encourages the peaceful reconciliation of conflict by being as inclusive and flexible to social change as possible. The weakness of theories which aim to turn society rapidly into a harmonious community is that they aim at human relationships which are post-political. This seems utopian and undesirable since theories which aim at absolute harmony and the transcendence of politics inevitably become distorted into cynicism and tyranny. Since conflicts of interest are inevitable, politics can be defined as the peaceful resolution of these conflicts, and is therefore an essential part of a mature and free society.

The achievements of recent theorists of radical democracy (Mouffe, 1993) and some closely related post-modern thinkers have been to point to multiple and overlapping identities and systems of domination in society. As such they have made an important contribution to debates concerning the possibility of a post-liberal citizenship. They have pointed to the need for radicals to consider the concept of individual agents, and not to be tempted to turn back towards a purely structuralist approach which views the individual as secondary to social structures and inevitable historical forces. The answer to the dualistic nature of liberal citizenship is not to assert the claims of society over the needs of the individual. Rather it is to dissolve the dualisms of liberalism though the creation of democratic structures of government. The strict demarcation of citizenship into separate kinds of rights as presented by Marshall has to be overcome, and in developing these ideas radicals can usefully build on the insights of Marx's early work. That is, citizenship rests not just on abstract civil and political rights but also the material resources to make use of those rights.

However, radical democrats must avoid the dilemmas identified by McLennan (1995). In particular the temptation to retreat into an ultra-relativist perspective which prevents any collective action to counter discernible power inequalities must be avoided. Radical democrats must engage critically with the state and the problems of capitalism in order to build structures which facilitate a political community which recognises and fosters common interests, whilst at the same time maintaining diversity and difference.

Citizenship can provide a focal point for this goal because it embodies an egalitarian and democratic logic which is implicit in classical liberal thought. Rapid movements of social change associated with globalisation and localisation are creating the space for a real challenge to the statist assumptions of liberalism, but in order to go beyond the liberal state and its associated partial citizenship, radical democrats must first play a part in reforming the state and build the foundations for real active citizenship amongst the citizens of Britain. In the final part of this book I will, therefore, briefly look at the immediate prospects for citizenship in Britain.

THE PROSPECTS FOR CITIZENSHIP IN BRITAIN

In the general election of May 1997, the Conservatives suffered a resounding defeat and New Labour was elected with a landslide majority of 179 seats. To what extent this marks the beginning of a new relationship between citizen and state is unclear. For some writers the election of a Blair government represents little more than a shift from one form of Thatcherism to another, perhaps milder version. This reflects the development of a new right-of-centre consensus, christened 'Blaijorism' by Hay (1996: 163). According to this view, the modernisation of the Labour Party after 1987 was nothing more than an expedient attempt to shift Labour away from its traditional values and to make an accommodation with Thatcherism in order to become electable (Shaw, 1996: 198).

However, the view that New Labour is intent on following the neo-liberal agenda shaped by Thatcherism has been rejected by those writers who instead detect a more profound shift occurring in British politics. For example, Perryman (1996: 2) writes of 'the potential Blair has undoubtedly unleashed for radical and momentous social change', while the former Thatcherite John Gray (1996) argues that New Labour is at the centre of a developing post-liberal consensus that seeks to move beyond the outdated social and neo-liberal models criticised throughout this book. An analysis of the strategy of Tony Blair's party lends some support to Gray's argument. For instance, one of the most articulate modernisers of the party argues that Labour must recognise the connections between radical liberalism and socialism in order to make the promises of liberalism real for *all* members of society (Wright, 1996: 26), whilst Blair himself writes of the 'need to learn from what is good in the liberal tradition, and preserve and extend it' (Blair, 1996a: 66).

The language of citizenship is at the heart of Labour's definition of a new politics. Following his election as party leader in 1994, many of Blair's speeches and articles contained extensive references to rights and duties and to the need to establish a 'change in the relationship between citizen and state' (Blair, 1996a: 51). One of the clearest statements of the values underpinning New Labour's definition of citizenship can be found in a speech Blair gave in Southwark Cathedral in 1996:

> The question for today is whether we can achieve a new relationship between individual and society, in which the individual acknowledges that, in certain key respects, it is only by working together in a community of people that the

individual's interests can be advanced. This means going beyond the traditional boundaries of left and right, breaking new ground by escaping sterile debates that have polarised our politics for too long. (Blair, 1996a: 64)

Blair's position is that New Labour needs to transcend, not only the limits of neo-liberalism, but also the dogmatic approach of the old Labour Party, with its emphasis on statism, public ownership and class politics. This shift from the language of class towards the language of citizenship was symbolised by Blair's determination to reform the central plank of Labour's constitution: the commitment to public ownership enshrined in clause four. At his first conference speech as party leader in 1994 he spoke of the need to create a 'modern constitution' that reflected Labour's values and desired ends, without tying the party to a particular set of means to achieve those ends (Jones, 1996: 139–48).

The principal values that Blair wishes to promote are community, one nationism and 'a society, strong and united and confident' (Blair, 1996a: 22). These related ideas of social inclusion have been grouped together by members and supporters of New Labour under the umbrella concept of 'stakeholding'. In some versions of this concept, the relational and egalitarian logic of citizenship is recognised (Kelly et al., 1997; Hutton, 1996, 1997).

New Labour aims to be a party of ethical rather than scientific socialism, based on 'a moral assertion that individuals are interdependent, that they owe duties to one another as well as to themselves' (Blair, 1996a: 13). At the heart of Britain's problems, Blair argues, is an 'undeveloped citizenship' and a lack of social justice 'without which citizenship will be an unrealistic goal' (Blair, 1996a: 77; The Spectator, 1 April 1995). Clause four, rewritten by the modernisers in 1995, reflected these concerns by stating that individual potential could only be fulfilled in the context of a community 'where the rights we enjoy reflect the duties we owe' (Taylor, 1997: 171).

Such an approach appears to signal a radical departure from the limited conception of citizenship embraced by the Thatcherite governments. The rhetoric of New Labour can be read as an attempt to overcome the dualisms of liberal notions of citizenship, which, as we have seen, perceive the individual to be opposed to the political community in which they reside and understand freedom as a product of market relations, rather than the outcome of political co-operation between mutually dependent citizens.

Encouragingly, Blair's acknowledgement of the failures of the Old Left and the New Right seems to point to a vision of politics where social justice and economic success are seen as complementary, rather than in conflict, and where Labour is an inclusive party that seeks to 'mobilise all people of progressive mind around a party always outward looking, seeking new supporters and members' (Blair, 1996a: 10).

This positive appraisal of New Labour is seen as naive by those who see the damage inflicted upon Britain by eighteen years of Thatcherism as more profound than Labour is prepared to recognise. Negative accounts of New Labour's approach see its rhetoric at best shallow, and at worst contradictory. For example, Eric Shaw (1996: 199) contends that much of the new clause four is 'vague and anodyne', while Taylor (1997: 190) has asserted that the clause 'provides a ragbag of different principles and ideas but without an underlying reason why they are associated and what should be regarded as their importance'.

Several commentators have identified the influence of communitarianism upon the New Labour Party (Jones, 1996: Ch. 7; Shaw, 1996: 228–9). The problem with communitarianism is its celebration of an ill-defined notion of community. As Lacy and Frazer argue, communitarianism does not offer a coherent alternative to crude individualism since 'it is difficult to discern any well delineated conception of community in the work of any communitarian' (Lacy and Frazer, 1994: 75). The apparent transcendence of neo-liberal individualism by communitarianism is, like the social liberalism of T. H. Green, illusory, since its approach to community is equally abstract. As we saw in Chapter 3, such an approach tends towards a moralistic, paternalistic and socially authoritarian approach to issues of citizenship. Because New Labour's 'sustained emphasis on the principle of community tended to obscure the abstract nature of that commitment' (Jones, 1996: 137) the fear was raised that policies to deal with concrete issues of social exclusion and passive citizenship would fail to appear, or would be misconceived. New Labour's approach to family policy, crime and individual liberties has been criticised on just these grounds (*The Guardian*, 30 March 1995). For example, when New Labour promised in their 1997 election manifesto to develop policies to strengthen the family, there was the concern that this was based on an antiquated and particularistic view of what constitutes acceptable family life.

Some critics have argued that Labour's approach to issues such as crime has illustrated its failure to set such problems in their proper structural context. Thus, 'New Labour's inability to capitalise on Tory authoritarianism has been one of the most depressing features of this opposition' (Wild, 1995). Labour's failure to oppose such draconian measures as the Criminal Justice Bill of 1994 is evidence of this authoritarian tendency.

As has been argued, an important step towards creating a truly inclusive citizenship would entail building upon the anti-statist logic of classical liberalism and moving towards the gradual dismantling of state power. However, as Taylor has asserted, the Labour Party 'uncritically embraces the British state' and still perceives the crucial issue to be 'who populates the government, not the nature of governance' (Taylor, 1997: 166). With the challenges of globalisation and new social movements outlined in this chapter this statist logic seems outmoded. New Labour emphasises strong leadership in the persona of Tony Blair, but the political realities of the late 1990s demand a more humble approach to the possibilities for radical change by any single political party. However, rather than attempting to incorporate the anti-statist challenges of new social movements into their political programme it can be argued that 'from the vantage point of Blair's ethical authoritarianism, the anti-roads movement . . . and animal rights movement are reduced to emblems of community decay' (Davey, 1996: 96).

An important element to reforming the state would be constitutional reform. Labour's 1997 manifesto did commit the party to important changes such as the adoption of a bill of rights, the removal of the right for hereditary peers to vote in the House of Lords and freedom of information legislation (Labour Party, 1997: 32–5). However, New Labour remains ambivalent towards the introduction of a fairer electoral system that would increase meaningful participation in politics and constrain the power of the state. The fact that in 1997 Blair remained unconvinced of the arguments for proportional representation raised the suspicion that Labour's conversion to constitutional reform is motivated by expediency rather than ethics (Davey, 1996).

Earlier in this chapter it was argued that the deregulated capitalism embraced by Thatcherism was incompatible with meaningful citizenship for all. However, despite New Labour's rhetoric of community and interdependence, their stance on the virtues of the 'market and the rigour of competition' (clause four, cited in Taylor, 1997: 171) has accepted much of the neo-liberal legacy: 'New Labour thinking . . . reposed a greater faith in the self-correcting mechanisms of the market and did not perceive any inherent tension between corporate profit-seeking and public welfare' (Shaw, 1996: 202).

As we have seen, a legacy of the Thatcherite years was the growing division of wealth and income between 'active' and 'passive' citizens. As Townsend (1996) comments Labour's approaches to issues of poverty 'are not encouraging': if Blair's rhetoric on social justice as a pre-condition to citizenship is to be transformed into action, Labour needs to employ more radical options than merely an acceptance of the failed neo-liberal economic agenda (Hay, 1997).

One of the key criticisms of liberalism identified in this book is the increasing separation of politics from the market. Under the Thatcherite governments, more and more decisions affecting citizens' lives were determined by the mechanisms of the market. Politics was systematically discredited as a way of organising and regulating people's lives, and this needs to be reversed if citizenship is to be extended. The market came to be seen not merely as a useful but limited tool for increasing individuals' potential, but as an end in itself. During the Thatcherite years, success was quantified in terms of a narrow set of economic figures. Measurements of economic boom or recession virtually ignored crucial issues such as citizens' insecurity, poverty, inequality and unemployment. A challenge for the Blair government is to change the criteria by which a successful and healthy society is assessed. However, Blair has consistently praised many of the actions of the Thatcherite governments and displays a lack of understanding of the insidious nature of inequality: 'perhaps the single most salient fact in contemporary British society' (Hutton, 1997: 6). Without a much more progressive and redistributive tax system than New Labour offered in the 1997 election, social division is likely to damage, directly or indirectly, the citizenship of everyone.

A truly radical government would also need to work to reduce the apparent tensions between civil, political and social rights, and between citizens' obligations and entitlements, and to reveal them as mutually dependent. However, the communitarianism of Etzioni (1995), embraced by Blair, identifies the imbalance of rights over duties as the major problem that needs tackling in Western democracies. What this book has shown, however, is that rights in Britain have been partial and selective, and have rested too often upon statist assumptions. It is not that people have been overburdened with rights, but rather that these rights have been divorced from notions of active participation by citizens. It is only by creating structures of government that are increasingly democratic and inclusive, and by providing the resources (both cultural and material) essential to democracy, that people can be expected to exercise their duties fully. In the short term, this would involve a radical rethinking of the relationship between the tax and benefit system, which the Thatcherites so skilfully polarised as symbols of active and passive citizenship: benefit being portrayed not as a right of citizenship but as a drain on the market rights of active tax payers. In the longer term, Labour must give serious consideration to creating a citizens' income (Barry, 1997; Twine, 1994: Ch. 14).

The deepening of citizenship would involve much more radical constitutional change than envisaged by Labour, with the aim of greatly decentralising and extending democracy. Also, despite Blair's insistence on the importance of education to his vision of a new society, in the 1997 election campaign he was silent about citizenship education: it is quite absurd to assert the importance of citizenship if the subject is almost completely absent from the education curriculum (Jones and Jones, 1992; Lynch, 1992).

Many of the most radical measures necessary to entrench and extend citizenship may only be practical through greater collaboration within the European Union. To this end, Labour must ensure that they neither retreat into the contradictions of neo-liberal sovereignty offered by the Thatcherites, nor succumb to the creation of an undemocratic super-state in the name of global competitiveness. The challenge for the Labour government is to campaign for a radical interpretation of the concept of subsidiarity. The question of the future of Europe creates a real opportunity to raise issues of democracy and participation that move beyond the liberal model of citizenship based upon a necessarily exclusive national identity (Meehan, 1993: Ch. 1 and 2; Roche, 1992: 218–21). Subsidiarity, with its emphasis upon decision making being located as close to the people as possible, may provide a model for Europe that looks beyond the nation-state towards more participatory regional government, and this is a project that the British government should be at the centre of.

Criticism of New Labour's approach to citizenship has to be tempered by the fact that they face the immense task of reversing many years of growing social exclusion, political apathy and poverty under the Thatcherites, without the option of returning to the discredited social liberalism of previous Labour governments. The development of a post-liberal citizenship is an enormous but necessary task and one that needs to be of central concern to the Labour government. Blair's strategy is a long-term one, aimed at securing more than one term of office, and he has already made some important conceptual shifts towards a post-liberal approach to citizenship. However, as he has recognised, 'the challenge now is to link these values both to a clear analysis of the condition of Britain today and to a compelling prescription for change' (Blair, 1996b). As this book has argued, the consequences of the failure of such a project will be an impoverished citizenship for all members of British society.

BIBLIOGRAPHY

Full references for chapters in edited works can be found under the editor(s) of the relevant collection. Square brackets [ ] indicate original date of publication.

Abercrombie, N. and Warde, A. (eds) (1994) *Contemporary British Society* (2nd edn) (Cambridge: Polity Press).
Aglietta, M. (1979) *A Theory of Capitalist Regulation* (London: New Left Books).
Anderson, B. (1983) *Imagined Communities* (London: Verso).
Appelbaum, R. (1988) *Karl Marx* (London: Verso).
Arblaster, A. (1984) *The Rise and Decline of Western Liberalism* (Oxford: Basil Blackwell).
Aristotle (1962 [c. 350 BC]) *The Politics* (London: Penguin).
Armstrong, P., Glyn, A. and Harrison, J. (1984) *Capitalism Since World War Two* (London: Fontana).
Atiyah, P. S. (1995) *Law and Society* (2nd edn) (Oxford: Oxford University Press).
Atkinson, J. (1984) 'Manpower Strategies for Flexible Organisations', *Personal Management*, vol. 16, August 1984, pp. 28–31.
Ball, T. (1995) *Reappraising Political Theory* (Oxford: Oxford University Press).
Barbalet, J. (1988) *Citizenship* (Milton Keynes: Open University).
Barker, M. (1981) *The New Racism* (London: Junction Books).
Barron, A. and Scott, C. (1992) 'The Citizen's Charter Programme', *The Modern Law Review*, vol. 55, 4 July, pp. 526–46.
Barry, B. (1997) 'The Attractions of Basic Income' in Franklin, J. (ed.) (1997) *Equality* (London: Institute for Public Policy Research).
Barry, N. (1987) *The New Right* (London: Croom Helm).
Bassett, P. (1987) *Strike Free* (London: Macmillan).
Beck, U. (1995) *Ecological Enlightenment* (New Jersey: Humanities Press).
Beer, S. (1982) *Britain Against Itself* (London: Faber).
Belchem, J. (1990) *Class, Party and the Political System in Britain 1867–1914* (Oxford: Basil Blackwell).
Bellamy, R. (1992) *Liberalism and Modern Society* (Cambridge: Polity Press).
Benn, A. (1991) *Parliamentary Debates: House of Commons*, vol. 198, 15 November (London: HMSO).

Benn, A. and Hood, A. (1993) *Common Sense: A New Constitution for Britain* (London: Hutchinson).

Benyon, J. (1987) 'Interpretations of Civil Disorder' in Benyon, J. and Solomos, J. (eds) (1987). *The Roots of Urban Unrest* (Oxford: Pergamon).

Benyon, J. and Bourn, C. (eds) (1986) *The Police: Powers, Procedures, and Proprieties* (Oxford: Pergamon).

Blair, T. (1996a) *New Britain* (abridged, *New Statesman* version) (London: Fourth Estate).

Blair, T. (1996b) 'Foreword' in Wright, T. (1996).

Booth, C. (1984 [1889]) *A Descriptive Map of London Poverty* (London: London Topographical Society).

Bosanquet, N. (1986) 'Interim Report: Public Spending and the Welfare State' in *British Social Attitudes: The 1986 Report* (Aldershot: Gower).

Bourdieu, P. and Passeron, J. (1977) *Reproduction in Education, Society and Culture* (London: Sage).

Bowles, S. and Gintis, H. (1976) *Schooling in Capitalist America* (London: Routledge).

Box, S. (1987) *Recession, Crime and Punishment* (London: Macmillan).

Boyne, G. (1993) 'Local Government: From Monopoly to Competition' in Jordon, G. and Ashford, N. (eds) (1993) *Public Policy and the Nature of the New Right* (London: Pinter).

Brazier, R. (1991) *Constitutional Reform* (Oxford: Oxford University Press).

Brittan, S. (1976) 'The Economic Contradictions of Democracy' in King, A. et al. (1976) *Why is Britain Becoming Harder to Govern?* (London: BBC).

Brubaker, R. (1992) *Citizenship and Nationhood in France and Germany* (Cambridge: Cambridge University Press).

Buchanan, J. M. and Tullock, G. (1962) *The Calculus of Consent* (Michigan: Michigan University Press).

Burke, E. (1968 [1790]) *Reflections on the Revolution in France* (London: Penguin).

Cable, V. (1996) 'Globalisation: Can the State Strike Back?', *The World Today*, May 1996, pp. 133–7.

Carnegie Trust (1993) *Life, Work and Livelihood in the Third Age* (Dunfermline, Fife: Carnegie UK Trust).

Central Statistical Office (1992) *Social Trends* (London: HMSO).

Central Statistical Office (1994a) *Social Trends* (London: HMSO).

Central Statistical Office (1994b) *Britain 1994: An Offical Guide* (London: HMSO).

Cicourel, A. (1976) *The Social Organisation of Juvenile Justice* (London: Heinemann).

Citizen's Charter Unit (1992) *The Citizen's Charter: Raising the Standard* (London: HMSO).

Claeys, G. (1989) *Thomas Paine: Social and Political Thought* (London: Unwin Hyman).

Clarke, P. (1994) *Citizenship* (London: Pluto).

Coates, D. (1980) *Labour in Power?* (London: Longman).

Coates, D. (1984) *The Context of British Politics* (London: Hutchinson).

Coates, D. (1989) *The Crisis of Labour* (London: Philip Allen).

Coates, D. (1991) *Running the Country* (London: Hodder and Stoughton).

Coates, D. (1994) *The Question of UK Decline* (Hemel Hempstead: Harvester Wheatsheaf).

Cockett, R. (1994) *Thinking the Unthinkable* (London: Harper Collins).

Colley, L. (1992) *Britons* (London: Pimlico).

Commission of the European Communities (1990) *The Community Charter of Fundamental Social Rights for Workers* (Luxembourg: Commission of the European Communities).

Commission for Racial Equality (1994) *Citizens, Minorities and Foreigners* (London: CRE).

Connolly, M., McKeown, P. and Milligan-Byrne, G. (1994) 'Making the Public Sector More Friendly? A Critical Examination of the Citizen's Charter', *Parliamentary Affairs*, vol. 47 (1), pp. 22–36.

Conservative Party (1992) *The Best Future for Britain: The Conservative Manifesto 1992* (London: Conservative Central Office).

Coole, D. (1993) *Women in Political Theory* (Hemel Hempstead: Harvester Wheatsheaf).

Cooper, D. (1993) 'The Citizen's Charter and Radical Democracy: Empowerment and Exclusion within Citizenship Discourse', *Social and Legal Studies*, vol. 2, pp. 149–71.

Cox, C. B. and Scruton, R. (1984) *Peace Studies: A Critical Survey* (London: Alliance Publishers).

Crewe, I. (1988) 'Has the Electorate Become More Thatcherite?' in Skidelski, R. (ed.) (1988) *Thatcherism* (London: Chatto and Windus).

Crewe, I. (1992) 'Why Did Labour Lose (Yet Again)?', *Politics Review*, vol. 2 (1). pp. 2–11.

Crompton, R. and Brown, P. (eds) (1994) *Economic Restructuring and Social Exclusion* (London: UCL Press).

Crouch, C. (1993) *Industrial Relations and European State Traditions* (Oxford: Clarendon Press).

Davey, K. (1996) 'The Impermanence of New Labour' in Perryman, M. (ed.) (1996).

Dean, H. and Taylor-Gooby, P. (1992) *Dependency Culture: The Explosion of a Myth* (Hemel Hempstead: Harvester Wheatsheaf).

Department for Education (1994) *Our Children's Education: The Updated Parent's Charter* (London: HMSO).

Department for Education and Employment (1997) *Meeting the Challenge of the 21st Century: A Summary of Labour Market and Skill Trends 1997/98* (Sheffield: Skills and Enterprise Network).

Dicken, P. (1986) *Global Shift* (London: Harper and Row).

Dietz, M. (1993) 'Context is All: Feminism and Theories of Citizenship' in Mouffe, C. (ed.) (1993).

Eccleshall, R. (1984a) 'Liberalism' in Eccleshall, R. et al. (1984).

Eccleshall, R. (1984b) 'Conservatism' in Eccleshall, R. et al. (1984).

Eccleshall, R., Geoghegan, V., Jay, R. and Wilford, R. (1984) *Political Ideologies* (London: Hutchinson).

Edgell, S. and Duke, V. (1991) *A Measure of Thatcherism* (London: Harper-Collins).

Elshtain, J. B. (1982) 'Feminism, Family and Community', *Dissent*, vol. 29 (4), pp. 442–9.

Etzioni, A. (1995) *The Spirit of Community* (London: Crown Publishing Group).

Etzioni-Halevy, A. (1993) *The Elite Connection* (Oxford: Polity Press).

Evans, B. and Taylor, A. (1996) *From Salisbury to Major* (Manchester: Manchester University Press).

Ewing, K. D. and Gearty, C. A. (1990) *Freedom Under Thatcher* (Oxford: Clarendon Press).

Feldman, D. (1993) *Civil Liberties and Human Rights* (Oxford: Oxford University Press).

Field, F. (1989) *Losing Out* (Oxford: Basil Blackwell).

Forsyth, M. (1988) 'Hayek's Bizarre Liberalism: A Critique', *Political Studies*, vol. 36 (2), pp. 235–50.

Frazer, E. and Lacey, N. (1993) *The Politics of Community* (Hemel Hempstead: Harvester Wheatsheaf).

Freeden, M. (1991) *Rights* (Buckingham: Open University Press).

Friedman, M. (1962) *Capitalism and Freedom* (Chicago: Chicago University Press).

Fukuyama, F. (1992) *The End of History and the Last Man* (London: Hamilton).

Fulcher, J. (1995) 'British Capitalism in the 1980s: Old Times or New Times?', *British Journal of Sociology*, vol. 46 (2), pp. 324–38.

Gamble, A. (1981) *Britain in Decline* (London: Macmillan).

Gamble, A. (1994) *The Free Economy and the Strong State* (2nd edn) (London: Macmillan).

Gamble, A. (1995) 'An Ideological Party' in Ludlam, S. and Smith, M. (eds) (1995).

Gardner, J. P. (ed.) (1994) *Hallmarks of Citizenship: A Green Paper* (London: The British Institute of International and Comparative Law).

Giddens, A. (1973) *The Class Structure of the Advanced Societies* (London: Hutchinson).

Giddens, A. (1982) *Profiles and Critiques in Social Theory* (London: Macmillan).

Giddens, A. (1985) *The Nation-State and Violence* (Cambridge: Polity Press).

Giddens, A. (1990) *The Consequences of Modernity* (Cambridge: Polity Press).

Giddens, A. (1994) *Beyond Left and Right* (Cambridge: Polity Press).

Giddens, A. (1995) 'Government's Last Gasp?', *The Observer*, 9 July 1995.

Giles, C. and Johnston, P. (1994) *Taxes Down, Taxes Up* (London: The Institute for Fiscal Affairs).

Gilmour, I. (1992) *Dancing with Dogma* (London: Simon and Schuster).

Glaser, D. (1995) 'Normative Theory' in Marsh, D. and Stoker, G. (eds) (1995).

Glasgow Media Group (1976) *Bad News* (London: Routledge).

Glasgow Media Group (1980) *More Bad News* (London: Routledge).

Gledhill, J. (1994) *Power and its Disguises* (London: Pluto Press).

Glennerster, H. (1995) *British Social Policy Since 1945* (Oxford: Basil Blackwell).

Glynn, S. (1991) *No Alternative? Unemployment in Britain* (London: Faber and Faber).

Graham, P., Jordon, A. and Lamb, B. (1990) *An Equal Chance? Or No Chance?* (London: Scope).

Gramsci, A. (1971) *Selections from the Prison Notebooks* (London: Lawrence and Wishart).

Gray, J. (1984) *Hayek on Liberty* (Oxford: Basil Blackwell).

Gray, J. (1995) *Liberalism* (2nd edn) (Buckingham: Open University Press).

Gray, J. (1996) 'What Liberalism Cannot Do', *New Statesman*. 20 September 1996.

Green, D. (1987) *The New Right: The Counter Revolution in Political, Economic and Social Thought* (Brighton: Wheatsheaf).

Green, D. (1992) 'Liberty, Poverty and the Underclass' in Smith, D. (ed.) (1992).

Green, F. and Sutcliffe, B. (1987) *The Profit System: The Economics of Capitalism* (London: Penguin).

Green, T. H. (1986 [1882]) *Lectures on the Principles of Political Obligation* (Cambridge: Cambridge University Press).

Gyford, J. (1991) *Citizens, Consumers and Councils* (London: Macmillan).

Habermas, J. (1976) *Legitimation Crisis* (London: Heinemann).

Hall, S., Critcher, C., Jefferson, T., Clarke, J. and Roberts, B. (1978) *Policing the Crisis* (London: Macmillan).

Hallsworth, S. (1994) 'Understanding New Social Movements', *Sociology Review*, vol. 4 (1), September 1994, pp. 7–10.

Halsey, A. H. (1996) 'T. H. Marshall and Ethical Socialism' in Bulmer, M. and Rees, A. (eds) (1996) *Citizenship Today* (London: UCL).

Hambleton, R. (1994) 'The Contract State and the Future of Public Management', paper presented to the Employment Research Unit Annual Conference, Cardiff Business School, 1994.

Hanmer, J. and Saunders, S. (1984) *Well Founded Fear* (London: Hutchinson).

Harvey, D. (1990) *The Condition of Post-Modernity* (Oxford: Basil Blackwell).

Hay, C. (1996) *Re-Stating Social and Political Change* (Milton Keynes: Open University).

Hay, C. (1997) 'No Left Turn? What to Expect from New Labour in Power', paper presented to the Political Studies Association Annual Conference, Belfast, April 1997.

Hayek, F. (1944) *The Road to Serfdom* (London: Routledge).

Hayek, F. (1955) *The Counter-Revolution in Science* (London: Collier Macmillan).

Hayek, F. (1960) *The Constitution of Liberty* (London: Routledge).

Hayek, F. (1976) *Law, Legislation and Liberty*, vol. II, *The Mirage of Social Justice* (London: Routledge).

Heater, D. (1990) *Citizenship* (London: Longman).

Heath, A. (1992) 'The Attitudes of the Underclass' in Smith, D. (ed.) (1992).

Heath, A., Jowell, R. and Curtice, J. (1985) *How Britain Votes* (Oxford: Pergamon).

Heineman, R. (1994) *Authority and the Liberal Tradition* (New Jersey: Transaction Publishers).

Held, D. (1987) *Models of Democracy* (Cambridge: Polity Press).

Held, D. (1995) *Democracy and the Global Order* (Cambridge: Polity Press).

Held, D. and Thompson, J. B. (1989) *Anthony Giddens and His Critics* (Cambridge: Cambridge University Press).

Henessey, P. (1992) *Never Again* (London: Cape).

Hill, D. (1994) *Citizens and Cities* (Hemel Hempstead: Harvester Wheatsheaf).

Hindess, B. (1987) *Freedom, Equality and the Market: Arguments on Social Policy* (London: Tavistock).

Hindess, B. (1993) 'Citizenship in the Modern West' in Turner, B. S. (ed.) (1993a).

Hirst, P. (1993) 'Globalisation is Fashionable but is it a Myth?', *The Guardian*, 22 March.

Hirst, P. and Thompson, G. (1996) *Globalization in Question* (Cambridge: Polity Press).

Hobbes, T. (1973 [1651]) *Leviathan* (London: Dent).

Hobhouse, L. (1964 [1911]) *Liberalism* (Oxford: Oxford University Press).

Hoffman, J. (1988) *State, Power and Democracy* (Brighton: Wheatsheaf).

Hoffman, J. (1995) *Beyond the State* (Cambridge: Polity Press).

Hogg, S. and Hill, J. (1995) *Too Close to Call: Power and Politics – John Major in No. 10* (London: Little Brown).

Holmes, R. (1982) 'Nozick on Anarchism' in Paul, J. (ed.) (1982).

Home Office (1994) *The Criminal Justice Bill and Public Order Act: An Introductory Guide* (London: HMSO).

Honderich, T. (1990) *Conservatism* (London: Hamish Hamilton).

Horsman, M. and Marshall, A. (1995) *After the Nation-State* (London: HarperCollins).

Howarth, D. (1995) 'Discourse Theory' in Marsh, D. and Stoker, G. (eds.) (1995).

Hughes, J., Martin, P. and Sharrock, W. (1995) *Understanding Classical Sociology* (London: Sage).

Hurd, D. (1989) 'Freedom will Flourish where Citizens Accept Responsibility'. *The Independent*, 13 September 1989.

Hutton, W. (1995) 'Myth that Sets the World to Right', *The Guardian*, 12 June 1995.

Hutton, W. (1996) *The State We're In* (revised edn) (London: Vintage).

Hutton, W. (1997) *The State to Come* (London: Vintage).

Hyman, R. (1989) *The Political Economy of Industrial Relations* (London: Macmillan).

Ignatieff, M. (1991) 'Citizenship and Moral Narcissim' in Andrews, G. (ed.) (1991) *Citizenship* (London: Lawrence and Wishart).

Jay, P. (1994) 'The Economy 1990–94' in Kavanagh, D. and Seldon, A. (eds) (1994).

Jessop, B., (1990) *State Theory: Putting the Capitalist State in its Place* (Cambridge: Polity Press).

Jessop, B., Bonnett, K. and Bromley, S. (1988) *Thatcherism: A Tale of Two Nations* (Cambridge: Polity Press).

Jones, G. and Wallace, C. (1992) *Youth, Family and Citizenship* (Buckingham: Open University Press).

Jones, N. and Jones, E. (eds) (1992) *Education for Citizenship* (London: Kogan Page).

Jones, T. (1993) *Britain's Ethnic Minorities* (London: Policy Studies Institute).

Jones, T. (1996) *Remaking the Labour Party* (London: Routledge).

Jordon, B. (1989) *The Common Good* (Oxford: Blackwell).

Joseph, K. and Sumption, J. (1979) *Equality* (London: John Murray).

Joseph Rowntree Foundation (1994) *A Competitive UK Economy* (London: Joseph Rowntree Foundation).

Joseph Rowntree Foundation (1995) *Inquiry into Income and Wealth*. vols 1 and 2 (York: Joseph Rowntree Foundation).

Kavanagh, D. (1994) 'A Major Agenda?' in Kavanagh and Seldon (eds) (1994).

Kavanagh, D. and Morris, P. (1989) *Consensus Politics* (Oxford: Basil Blackwell).

Kavanagh, D. and Seldon, A. (eds) (1990) *The Thatcher Effect: A Decade of Change* (Oxford: Oxford University Press).

Kavanagh, D. and Seldon, A. (eds) (1994) *The Major Effect* (London: Macmillan).

Keegan, W. (1984) *Mrs Thatcher's Economic Experiment* (London: Penguin).

Kelly, G., Kelly, D. and Gamble, A. (eds) (1997) *Stakeholder Capitalism* (London: Macmillan).

Kelly, J. (1988) *Trade Unions and Socialist Politics* (London: Verso).

Kennedy, E. and Mendus, S. (1987) *Women in Western Political Thought* (Brighton: Wheatsheaf).

Kennet, P. (1994) 'Exclusion, Post-Fordism and the New Europe' in Crompton, R. and Brown, P. (eds) (1994).

King, D. (1987) *The New Right* (London: Macmillan).

King, R. (1986) *The State in Modern Society* (London: Macmillan).

Kingdom, J. (1991) *Government and Politics in Britain* (Cambridge: Polity Press).

Kingdom, J. (1992) *No Such Thing as Society* (Milton Keynes: Open University Press).

Kinsey, R., Lea, J. and Young, J. (1986) *Losing the Fight Against Crime* (Oxford: Basil Blackwell).

Kluckhohn, C. (1951) 'The Concept of Culture' in Lerner, D. and Lasswell, H. D. (eds) (1951) *The Policy Sciences* (Stanford: Stanford University Press).

Kohl, H. (1992) *Lecture at St Anthony's College*, Oxford, 11 November 1992.

Kumar, K. (1995) *From Post-Industrial to Post-Modern Society* (Oxford: Basil Blackwell).

Labour Party (1997) *Because Britain Deserves Better* (London: The Labour Party).

Laclau, E. and Mouffe, C. (1985) *Hegemony and Socialist Strategy* (London: Verso).

Lacy, N. and Frazer, E. (1994) 'Communitarianism', *Politics*, vol. 14 (2), pp. 75–81.

Lash, S. and Urry, J. (1987) *The End of Organised Capitalism* (Cambridge: Polity Press).

Layder, D. (1994) *Understanding Social Theory* (London: Sage).

Layton Henry, Z. (1992) *The Politics of Immigration* (Oxford: Basil Blackwell).

Le Grand, J. (1982) *The Strategy of Equality* (London: Unwin and Allen).

Lea, J. and Young, J. (1984) *What is to be Done About Law and Order?* (London: Penguin).

Leonard, D. (1994) *Guide to the European Union* (4th edn) (London: Hamish Hamilton).

Letwin, S. (1992) *The Anatomy of Thatcherism* (London: Fontana).

Lewis, J. (1994) 'Community Care' in Kavanagh and Seldon (eds) (1994).

Lewis, N. (1993) 'The Citizen's Charter and Next Steps: A New Way of Governing?', *Political Quarterly*, vol. 64 (3), pp. 316–26.

Liberty (1995) *Defend Diversity, Defend Dissent* (London: National Council for Civil Liberties).

Linton, R. (ed.) (1945) *The Science of Man in World Crisis* (New York: Columbia University Press).

Lipietz, A. (1985) *The Enchanted World: Inflation, Credit and the World Crisis* (London: Verso).

Lister, R. (1990) *The Exclusive Society* (London: Child Poverty Action Group).

Lister, R. (1994) 'The Family and Women' in Kavanagh and Seldon (eds) (1994).

Locke, J. (1924 [1690]) *Two Treatises of Government* (London: Dent).

Lockwood, D. (1974) 'For T. H. Marshall', *Sociology*, vol. 8 (3), pp. 363–7.

Loney, M. (1986) *The Politics of Greed: The New Right and the Welfare State* (London: Pluto).

Lowe, R. (1993) *The Welfare State in Britain Since 1945* (London: Macmillan).

Ludlam, S. and Smith, M. (eds) (1995) *Contemporary British Conservatism* (London: Macmillan).

Luff, P. (1992) *The Simple Guide to Maastricht* (London: The European Movement).

Lukes, S. (1973) *Individualism* (Oxford: Basil Blackwell).

Lukes, S. (1974) *Power: A Radical View* (London: Macmillan).

Lynch, J. (1992) *Education for Citizenship in a Multicultural Society* (London: Cassell).

Lyon, D. (1994) *Postmodernity* (Buckingham: Open University Press).

MacInnes, J. (1987) *Thatcherism at Work* (Milton Keynes: Open University Press).

MacIntyre, A. (1981) *After Virtue* (London: Duckworth).

McLennan, G. (1995) *Pluralism* (Buckingham: Open University Press).

MacPherson, C. B. (1962) *The Political Theory of Possessive Individualism* (Oxford: Oxford University Press).

MacPherson, C. B. (1980) *Burke* (Oxford: Oxford University Press).

MacPherson, C. B. (1985) *The Rise and Fall of Economic Justice and Other Essays* (Oxford: Oxford University Press).

Maguire, J. (1972) *Marx's Paris Writings: An Analysis* (Dublin: Gill and Macmillan).

Mann, K. (1992) *The Making of an English Underclass* (Milton Keynes: Open University Press).

Mann, M. (1987) 'Ruling Class Strategies and Citizenship', *Sociology*, vol. 21 (3), pp. 339–54.

Marsh, D. (1992) *The New Politics of British Trade Unionism* (London: Macmillan).

Marsh, D. and Rhodes, R. (1992) *Policy Networks in British Government* (Oxford: Oxford University Press).

Marsh, D. and Stoker, G. (eds) (1995) *Theory and Methods in Political Science* (London: Macmillan).

Marshall, T. H. (1963) 'Citizenship and Social Class' [essay first published 1950] in his *Sociology at the Cross-roads* (London: Heinemann).

Marshall, T. H. (1981) *The Right to Welfare and Other Essays* (London: Heinemann).

Marx, K. (1994 [1843]) 'On the Jewish Question' in Marx, K. *Early Political Writings* (Cambridge: Cambridge University Press).

Marx, K. and Engels, F. (1975 [1848]) 'The Communist Manifesto' in Marx, K. and Engels, F. *Collected Works* (London: Lawrence and Wishart).

Mason, D. (1995) *Race and Ethnicity in Modern Britain* (Oxford: Oxford University Press).

Mathius, P. (1969) *The First Industrial Nation* (London: Methuen).

Mead, L. (1986) *Citizenship: Beyond Entitlement* (New York: Free Press).

Meehan, E. (1993) *Citizenship and the European Community* (London: Sage).

Merton, R. (1968) *Social Theory and Social Structure* (New York: Free Press).

Middlemas, K. (1979) *Politics in Industrial Society* (London: Andre Deutsch).

Miliband, R. (1969) *The State in Capitalist Society* (London: Weidenfeld and Nicolson).

Mill, J. S. (1872 [1861]) *Considerations on Representative Government* (London: Parker, Son and Bourn).

Mill, J. S. (1974 [1859]) *On Liberty* (London: Penguin).

Miller, D. (1989) *Market, State and Community* (Oxford: Clarendon Press).

Millward, A. (1992) *The European Rescue of the Nation-State* (London: Routledge).

Mitter, S. (1986) *Common Fate, Common Bond* (London: Pluto Press).

Morgan, K. (1990) *The People's Peace* (Oxford: Oxford University Press).

Morris, L. (1994) *Dangerous Classes* (London: Routledge).

Morris, L. (1995) *Social Divisions* (London: UCL Press).

Mosca, G. (1939) *The Ruling Class* (New York: McGraw-Hill).

Mouffe, C. (ed.) (1993) *Dimensions of Radical Democracy* (London: Verso).

Mulgan, G. (1994a) Lecture for the Institute for Citizenship Studies, London School of Economics, 8 September 1994.

Mulgan, G. (1994b) *Politics in an Anti-political Age* (Cambridge: Polity Press).

Murray, C. (1984) *Losing Ground* (New York: Basic Books).

Murray, C. (1990) *The Emerging British Underclass* (London: Institute of Economic Affairs).

Murray, N. (1986) 'Anti-Racists and Other Demons', *Race and Class*, vol. 27 (3), pp. 1–19.

Nicholson, P. (1990) *The Political Philosophy of the British Idealists* (Cambridge: Cambridge University Press).

Nietzsche, F. (1966 [1886]) *Beyond Good and Evil* (New York: Random House).

Nisbet, R. (1967) *The Sociological Tradition* (London: Heinemann).

Nisbet, R. (1986) *Conservatism* (Milton Keynes: Open University Press).

Nozick, R. (1974) *Anarchy, State and Utopia* (Oxford: Basil Blackwell).

Nyilas, J. (1982) *The World Economy and its Main Developments* (The Hague: Martinus Nijhoff).

O'Leary, S. (1995) 'The Social Dimension of Community Citizenship' in Rosas, A. and Antola, E. (eds) (1995).

O'Shea, A. (1984) 'Trusting the People: How Does Thatcherism Work?' in O'Shea, A. (ed.) (1984) *Formations of Nation and People* (London: Routledge and Kegan Paul).

Offe, C. (1985) 'New Social Movements', *Social Research*, vol. 52 (4), pp. 817–68.

Oldfield, A. (1990) *Citizenship and Community* (London: Routledge).

Oliver, D. (1991) 'Active citizenship in the 1990s', *Parliamentary Affairs*, vol. 44 (2), pp. 140–56.

Oliver, D. and Heater, D. (1994) *The Foundations of Citizenship* (Hemel Hempstead: Harvester Wheatsheaf).

Oppenheim, C. (1994) *The Welfare State: Putting the Record Straight* (London: Child Poverty Action Group).

Oppenheim, C. and Harker, L. (1996) *Poverty: The Facts* (3rd edn) (London: Child Poverty Action Group).

Overbeek, H. (1990) *Global Capitalism and National Decline* (London: Unwin Hyman).

Paine, T. (1995 [1791]) *Rights of Man, Common Sense and Other Political Writings* (Oxford: Oxford University Press).

Pateman, C. (1979) *The Problem of Political Obligation* (Oxford: Basil Blackwell).

Pateman, C. (1988) *The Sexual Contract* (Cambridge: Polity Press).

Pateman, C. (1989) *The Disorder of Women* (Cambridge: Polity Press).

Paul, J. (ed.) (1982) *Reading Nozick* (Oxford: Blackwell).

Perkin, H. (1989) *The Rise of Professional Society* (London: Routledge).

Perryman, M. (ed.) (1996) *The Blair Agenda* (London: Lawrence and Wishart).

Phillips, A. (1993) *Democracy and Difference* (Cambridge: Polity Press).

Philp, M. (1989) *Paine* (Oxford: Oxford University Press).

Pierson, C. (1991) *Beyond the Welfare State?* (Cambridge: Polity Press).

Pierson, C. (1995) 'Social Policy Under Thatcher and Major' in Ludlam, S. and Smith, M. (eds) (1995).

Pinder, J. (1986) 'European Community and Nation-State', *International Affairs*, vol. 62, pp. 410–54.

Popper, K. (1957) *The Poverty of Historicism* (London: Routledge and Kegan Paul).

Powell, D. (1992) *British Politics and the Labour Question 1868–1990* (London: Macmillan).

Purdie, B. (1990) *Politics in the Streets* (Belfast: Blackstaff Press).

Rawls, J. (1972) *A Theory of Justice* (Oxford: Oxford University Press).

Read, D. (1967) *Cobden and Bright* (London: Edward Arnold).

Rees, A. M. (1995) 'The Other T. H. Marshall', *Journal of Social Policy*, vol. 24 (3), pp. 341–62.

Rendall, J. (1987) 'Virtue and Commerce: Women in the Making of Adam Smith's Political Economy' in Kennedy, E. and Mendus, S. (eds) (1987).

Robertson, A. (1977) *Human Rights in Europe* (Manchester: Manchester University Press).

Roche, M. (1992) *Rethinking Citizenship* (Cambridge: Polity Press).

Rogers, B. (1995) *Crisis or Opportunity? Social Policy, Education and Training: Towards Social Citizenship* (Hull University: Centre for European Studies).

Rosamond, B. (1995) 'Whatever Happened to the Enemy Within? Contemporary Conservatism and Trade Unionism' in Ludlam, S. and Smith, M. (eds) (1995).

Rosas, A. and Antola, E. (eds) (1995) *A Citizens' Europe* (London: Sage).

Ross, J. (1983) *Thatcher and Friends* (London: Pluto Press).

Rousseau, J. J. (1968 [1762]) *The Social Contract* (London: Penguin).

Rowntree, B. (1901) *Poverty: A Study of Town Life* (London: Macmillan).

Ryan, A. (1986) 'Roger Scruton' in Cohen, G. et al. (1986) *The New Right* (London: Runnymede Trust).

Saggar, S. (1992) *Race and Politics in Britain* (Hemel Hempstead: Harvester Wheatsheaf).

Saville, J. (1994) *The Consolidation of the Capitalist State 1800–1850* (London: Pluto Press).

Schwarz, B. and Hall, S. (1985) 'State and Society: 1880–1930' in Langan, M. and Schwarz, B. (1985) *Crises in the British State 1880–1930* (London: Hutchinson).

Scope (1995) *Disabled in Britain: A World Apart* (London: Scope).

Scott, J. (1982) *The Upper Classes: Property and Privilege in Britain* (London: Macmillan).

Scott, J. (1990) 'Corporate Control and Corporate Rule', *British Journal of Sociology*, vol. 41 (3), pp. 351–73.

Scott, J. (1991) *Who Rules Britain?* (Cambridge: Polity Press).

Scott, J. (1994) *Poverty and Wealth* (London: Longman).

Sengenberger, W. and Wilkinson, F. (1995) 'Globalisation and Labour Standards' in Michie, J. and Smith, J. (eds.) (1995) *Managing the Global Economy* (Oxford: Oxford University Press).

Sharpe, S. (1994) *Just Like a Girl* (2nd edn) (London: Penguin).

Shaw, E. (1996) *The Labour Party Since 1945* (Oxford: Blackwell).

Shelter (1994) *Homelessness in England: The Facts* (London: Shelter).

Sinfield, A. (1981) *What Unemployment Means* (Oxford: Martin Robertson).

Skinner, Q. (1978) *Foundations of Modern Political Thought*, vol. 2 (Cambridge: Cambridge University Press).

Sklair, L. (1995) *Sociology of the Global System* (2nd edn) (Hemel Hempstead: Harvester Wheatsheaf).

Smith, A. (1976 [1776]) *Wealth of Nations* (Oxford: Clarendon Press).

Smith, A. D. (1995) *Nations and Nationalism in a Global Era* (Cambridge: Polity Press).

Smith, C. (1991) *Parliamentary Debates: House of Commons*, vol. 198, 15 November (London: HMSO).

Smith, D. (ed.) (1992) *Understanding the Underclass* (London: Policy Studies Institute).

Smith, M. (1995) 'From Thatcher to Major', *Politics Review*, vol. 5 (2), pp. 2–5.

Spastics Society (1992) *Polls Apart: Disabled People and the 1992 General Election* (London: Spastics Society).

Stewart, D. (1858) *Collected Works*, vol. 10 (Edinburgh: Edinburgh University Press).

Sullivan, M. (1992) *The Politics of Social Policy* (Hemel Hempstead: Harvester Wheatsheaf).

Taylor, G. (1997) *Labour's Renewal?* (London: Macmillan).

Taylor, R. (1994) 'Employment and Industrial Relations Policy' in Kavanagh and Seldon (eds) (1994).

Thatcher, M. (1977) *Let Our Children Grow Tall* (London: Centre for Policy Studies).

Thatcher, M. (1988) Speech at the College of Europe, Bruges, 20 September.

Thatcher, M. (1993) *The Downing Street Years* (London: HarperCollins).

Thatcher, M. (1995) *The Path to Power* (London: HarperCollins).

Thomas, G. (1992) *Government and the Economy Today* (Manchester University).

Titmus, R. (1963) *The Irresponsible Society* (London: Fabian Society).

Townsend, P. (1979) *Poverty in the United Kingdom* (London: Penguin).

Townsend, P. (1996) 'How to Beat Poverty', *New Statesman*, 4 October 1996.

Turner, B. (1986) *Citizenship and Capitalism* (London: Allen and Unwin).

Turner, B. (1990) 'Outline of a Theory of Citizenship', *Sociology*, vol. 24 (2), pp. 189–217.

Turner, B. (ed.) (1993a) *Citizenship and Social Theory* (London: Sage).

Turner, B. (1993b) 'Contemporary Problems in the Theory of Citizenship' in Turner, B. (ed.) (1993a).

Turner, B. (1993c) 'Outline of a Theory of Human Rights' in Turner, B. (ed.) (1993a).

Turner, B. and Hamilton, P. (1994) (eds) *Citizenship: Critical Concepts*, vol. 1 (London: Routledge).

Twine, F. (1994) *Citizenship and Social Rights* (London: Sage).

Walby, S. (1994) 'Is Citizenship Gendered?', *Sociology*, vol. 20 (6), pp. 379–95.

Waldron, J. (1987) *Nonsense Upon Stilts* (London: Methuen).

Waters, M. (1995) *Globalization* (London: Routledge).

Weatherby, J. (1986) *The Other World* (London: Macmillan).

Welsh, J. (1993) 'A Peoples' Europe?', *Politics*, vol. 13 (2), pp. 25–31.

White, R. (1964) *The Conservative Tradition* (London: A and C. Black).

Wild, A. (1995) 'Business as Usual in a New Suit', *The Chartist*, May–June 1995.

Willetts, D. (1992) *Modern Conservatism* (London: Penguin).

Williams, F. (1989) *Social Policy: A Critical Introduction* (Cambridge: Polity Press).

Willis, P. (1977) *Learning to Labour* (Farnborough: Saxon House).

Willman, J. (1994) 'The Civil Service' in Kavanagh and Seldon (eds) (1994).

Wilson, E. (1992) *A Very British Miracle* (London: Pluto).

Wise, M. and Gibb, R. (1993) *Single Market to Social Europe* (London: Longman).

Wolff, J. (1991) *Robert Nozick* (Cambridge: Polity Press).

Wright, T. (1996) *Socialisms* (2nd edn) (London: Routledge).

Young, H. (1991) *One of Us* (2nd edn) (London: Macmillan).

Young, H. (1994) 'The Prime Minister' in Kavanagh and Seldon (eds) (1994).

Young, I. (1990) *Justice and the Politics of Difference* (New York: Princeton University Press).

Young, K. (1994) 'Local Government' in Kavanagh and Seldon (eds) (1994).

INDEX

absolutism, 13
abstract individualism, 14, 19, 21–2, 23, 32,
  34–5, 36, 61, 86, 176
abstract liberalism, 21–3, 23–4, 25–6, 28, 32, 34
active citizenship, 127–43, 147–8, 162
Adenauer, K., 188
Aglietta, M., 98
America, 72–3, 88, 104, 110
anarchic capitalism, 101–3, 113
anti-racist movement, 184, 196
anti-slavery movement, 102
anti-social behaviour, 125, 126, 127, 129, 130,
  143, 146, 160–3
Arblaster, A., 30
Aristotle, 18, 19
Atiyah, P. S., 170
Attlee, C., 106

'back to basics' campaign 130, 165
bail restrictions 166 7, 168
Barbalet, J., 42, 144
Barron, A., 136
Barry, N., 57, 84
Bauer, B., 22
Beer, S., 77
Bell, D., 180
Bellamy, R., 32, 36
Benn, A., 139, 140–1
Bentham, J., 32
Beveridge, W., 33
Bevin, E., 106
Blair, T., 204–6, 207–9
Booth, C., 105
Bourdieu, P., 44
Bowles, S., 45
Brazil, 73
Bretton Woods Conference, 110
Bright, J., 91
Britain
  evolving social rights, 21, 32, 37–9
  liberal development, 10
  subjecthood, 3, 101
Brittan, S., 121
Brogan, C., 79

Brubaker, R., 2–3
Bruce, M., 142
Buchanan, J., 53
Burke, E., 20–2, 80, 83, 125, 128

Callaghan, J., 106, 120
capitalism
  anarchic, 101–3, 113
  beginnings, 12
  citizenship, 39–40, 52
  classical liberalism, 17, 177
  deregulated, 107–9, 112–13, 118–19, 179, 207
  labour, 35
  Labour Party, 120–1
  managed, 103–7, 109–12, 114, 120
  Marxism, 24
  State, 44, 98–103
  voting rights, 42–3
Catholics, 12, 102
centralised power, 60, 64, 65, 67
Centre for Policy Studies, 81
Chamberlain, N., 84
charity, 63, 131
Citizen's Charter, 132–43
citizenship
  active, 127–43, 147–8, 162
  capitalism, 39–40, 52
  classical liberalism, 17–30, 178–9, 180–7
  Conservative, 127, 130, 138
  international law, 2
  neo-liberalism, 66–8, 145–6, 202
  passive, 18, 102, 145–6, 147–8, 157
  social liberalism, 36–52
civil liberties, 38, 50, 161, 166
civil rights, 21, 29–30, 37, 38, 46, 51, 66, 101,
  102–3
class division, 44, 59, 70, 73, 115
class struggle, 102, 109
classical liberalism
  abstract individualism, 36, 61
  capitalism, 114–19, 177
  citizenship, 17–30, 178–9, 180–7
  conservatism 20–2
  dualism, 51, 68–9